Liberal Moments

Textual Moments in the History of Political Thought

Series Editors

J. C. Davis, Emeritus Professor of History, University of East Anglia, UK
John Morrow, Professor of Political Studies, University of Auckland,
New Zealand

Textual Moments provides accessible, short readings of key texts in selected
fields of political thought, encouraging close reading informed by cutting-
edge scholarship. The unique short essay format of the series ensures that
volumes cover a range of texts in roughly chronological order. The essays in
each volume aim to open up a reading of the text and its significance in the
political discourse in question and in the history of political thought more
widely. Key moments in the textual history of a particular genre of political
discourse are made accessible, appealing and instructive to students, scholars
and general readers.

Published

Utopian Moments: Reading Utopian Texts
Miguel Avilés and J. C. Davis

*Censorship Moments: Reading Texts in the History of
Censorship and Freedom of Expression*
Geoff Kemp

Revolutionary Moments: Reading Revolutionary Texts
Rachel Hammersley

Patriarchal Moments: Reading Patriarchal Texts
Cesare Cuttica and Gaby Mahlberg

Feminist Moments: Reading Feminist Texts
Susan Bruce and Katherine Smits

Liberal Moments

Reading Liberal Texts

Edited by Ewa Atanassow and Alan S. Kahan

Bloomsbury Academic
An imprint of Bloomsbury Publishing Plc

B L O O M S B U R Y
LONDON · OXFORD · NEW YORK · NEW DELHI · SYDNEY

Bloomsbury Academic

An imprint of Bloomsbury Publishing Plc

50 Bedford Square	1385 Broadway
London	New York
WC1B 3DP	NY 10018
UK	USA

www.bloomsbury.com

BLOOMSBURY and the Diana logo are trademarks of Bloomsbury Publishing Plc

First published 2017

© Ewa Atanassow, Alan S. Kahan and Contributors, 2017

Ewa Atanassow and Alan S. Kahan have asserted their right under the Copyright, Designs and Patents Act, 1988, to be identified as Editors of this work.

British Library Cataloguing-in-Publication Data
A catalogue record for this book is available from the British Library.

ISBN: HB: 978-1-4742-5104-4
PB: 978-1-4742-5105-1
ePDF: 978-1-4742-5106-8
eBook: 978-1-4742-5107-5

Library of Congress Cataloging-in-Publication Data
A catalog record for this book is available from the Library of Congress.

Series: Textual Moments in the History of Political Thought

Cover design by Burge Agency
Cover image © Max Krasnov/shutterstock

Typeset by Deanta Global Publishing Services, Chennai, India

To find out more about our authors and books visit www.bloomsbury.com. Here you will find extracts, author interviews, details of forthcoming events and the option to sign up for our newsletters.

Contents

List of Contributors

Ewa Atanassow is Junior Professor of Political Thought at Bard College Berlin. Her research focuses on questions of nationhood and democratic citizenship in the liberal tradition of political thought, with an emphasis on Tocqueville. She is the co-editor (with Richard Boyd) of *Tocqueville and the Frontiers of Democracy* (2013).

Roger Berkowitz is Founder and Academic Director of the Hannah Arendt Center for Politics and Humanities at Bard College and Associate Professor of Political Studies, Philosophy and Human Rights at Bard College. He is the author of *The Gift of Science: Leibniz and the Modern Legal Tradition* (2005) and the co-editor of *Thinking in Dark Times: Hannah Arendt on Ethics and Politics* (2009). He edits *HA: The Journal of the Hannah Arendt Center* and is co-editor of the forthcoming essay collection *Artifacts of Thinking: Reading Hannah Arendt's Denktagebuch*.

Reinhard Blomert is Editor-in-Chief of *Leviathan*, the Berlin social science quarterly. He has published extensively in the area of history and sociology of economics. He is the author of *John Maynard Keynes* (2007) and *Adam Smith's Reise nach Frankreich* (2012).

Nicholas Capaldi is Legendre-Soule Distinguished Chair of Business Ethics at Loyola University, New Orleans. He is the author of *Hume's Place in Moral Philosophy* (1986), *John Stuart Mill* (2005) and *Liberty and Equality in Political Economy* (2016).

Emmanuelle de Champs is Professor of British Civilisation at the University of Cergy-Pontoise and an intellectual historian. She has widely published on Bentham and classical utilitarianism. Her latest book, *Enlightenment and Utility, Bentham in France, Bentham in French*, was published in 2015 by Cambridge University Press.

Aurelian Craiutu is Professor of Political Theory at Indiana University, Bloomington. He has published extensively on modern French political thought exploring its tradition of political moderation from Montesquieu and Guizot to Tocqueville and Aron. His most recent book is *Faces of Moderation: The Art of Balance in an Age of Extremes* (2016).

George Crowder is Dean of the School of Social and Policy Studies and Professor of Political Theory, Flinders University, Adelaide, Australia. His books include *Liberalism and Value Pluralism* (2002), *Isaiah Berlin: Liberty and Pluralism* (2004) and *The One and the Many: Reading Isaiah Berlin* (co-edited with Henry Hardy, 2007).

Joshua Derman is Associate Professor of Humanities at the Hong Kong University of Science and Technology and the author of *Max Weber in Politics and Social Thought: From Charisma to Canonization* (2012).

Nouh El Harmouzi is Director of the Arab Center for Scientific Research and Humane Studies and University Professor at Ibn Toufail University, Morocco. He is the author of *Islamic Foundations of a Free Society* (2016); *The Causes of the Failure of the Arab World* (2012) in Arabic; and *The Underdevelopment in the Arab Muslim Countries* (2011) in French.

Robert Neil Harris tutors at New College and lectures in the Department of Modern Languages, University of Oxford and is a visiting scholar in philosophy at the Ludwig-Maximilian University in Munich. He specializes in nineteenth-century Russian intellectual history. His publications include 'Granovsky, Herzen and Chicherin: Hegel and the Battle for Russia's Soul', in *Hegel's Thought in Europe: Currents, Crosscurrents and Undercurrents*, ed. Lisa Herzog (2013); 'Alexander Herzen: Writings on the Man and his Thought', in *A Herzen Reader*, ed. and trans. K. Parthé (2012); 'Society and the Individual: State and Private Education in Russia during the 19th and 20th Centuries', in *Politics, Modernisation and Educational Reform in Russia from Past to Present*, ed. David Johnson (2010).

Iván Jaksić is Director of the Santiago Program of the Bing Overseas Studies Program, Stanford University. He is the author of *Academic Rebels in Chile: The Role of Philosophy in Higher Education and Politics* (1989), *Andrés Bello: Scholarship and Nation-Building in Nineteenth-Century Latin America* (2001), *The Hispanic World and American Intellectual Life, 1820-1880* (2007) and numerous edited, co-edited or co-authored books.

Jeremy Jennings is Head of the School of Politics and Economics at King's College London. He has published extensively on the history of political thought in France and is now completing a book entitled *Travels with Tocqueville*.

Edwige Kacenelenbogen has taught political science at Sciences Po (Menton and Aix-en Provence), as well as economics at La Sorbonne/Paris 1, the International University of Monaco and the University of Nice. She now works for various firms specializing in strategy and organizational consulting. She is the author of '*Le nouvel idéal politique*' (2013), which received the Raymond Aron prize.

Alan S. Kahan is Professor of British Civilization at the Université de Versailles/ St. Quentin and author of the books *Tocqueville, Democracy, and Religion: Checks and Balances for Democratic Souls; Mind vs. Money: The War Between Intellectuals and Capitalism; Alexis de Tocqueville; Liberalism in Nineteenth-Century Europe: The Political Culture of Limited Suffrage; Aristocratic Liberalism: The Social and Political Thought of Jacob Burckhardt, John Stuart Mill, and Alexis de Tocqueville.* He is the translator of Tocqueville's *The Old Regime and the Revolution* and Benjamin Constant's *Commentary on Filangieri's Work*.

James Kloppenberg is Charles Warren Professor of American History. He is the author of *Uncertain Victory: Social Democracy and Progressivism in European and American Thought*, 1870-1920 (1986); *The Virtues of Liberalism* (1998); *Reading Obama: Dreams, Hope, and the American Political Tradition* (2nd edn, 2011); *Toward Democracy: The Struggle for Self-Rule in European and American Thought* (2016); and two co-edited books, *A Companion to American Thought* (1995) and *The Worlds of American Intellectual History* (2017).

Catherine Larrère is Professor of Philosophy emerita at the University of Paris I/Panthéon Sorbonne. She is the author, among other works, of *Actualité de Montesquieu* (1999), 'Economics and Commerce' in *Montesquieu's Human Science, Essays on the Spirit of the Laws*, ed. David W Carrithers, Michael A. Mosher and Paul A. Rahe (2001) and 'Montesquieu et le "doux commerce":un paradigme du libéralisme?' *Cahiers d'Histoire, Revue d'histoire critique. Les libéralismes en question, XVIIIe-XXIe siècles*, no. 123, April–June 2014, pp. 21–38.

Michel Masłowski is Professor Emeritus at the University of Paris-Sorbonne, member of PAN (Polish Academy of Learning), Commander of the Order of Academic Palms and Knight of the Order of Polonia Restituta. He is the author of *Gestures, Symbols and Rites in Polish Romantic Theatre* (1998), in Polish;

C. Delsol, M. Masłowski and J. Nowicki, eds, *Mythes et symboles politiques en Europe centrale* (2002); Cz. Miłosz. *Traité de poésie. L'Apprenti* (translation from Polish); and *Le poète face à néant* (2013).

Reiji Matsumoto is Professor Emeritus at Waseda University, Tokyo, Japan. His recent publications include 'Tocqueville and *Democracy in Japan*', in Christine Dunn Henderson, ed., *Tocqueville's Voyages: The Evolution of His Ideas and Their Journey beyond His Time* (2014). He is the editor of Maruyama Masao, *'Seiji no Sekai' hoka Juppen* (*'The World of Politics' and 10 Other Essays*) (2014), and the translator into Japanese of Tocqueville's *De la démocratie en Amérique* (in 4 volumes, 2005–8).

John Morrow is Professor of Political Studies and Deputy Vice-Chancellor (Academic) at the University of Auckland, New Zealand. His publications include (with Paul Harris) *T. H. Green: Lectures on the Principles of Political Obligation and Other Political Writings* (1986), *Coleridge's Political Thought* (1990), (with Mark Francis) *A History of Nineteenth-Century English Political Thought* (1994), *The History of Political Thought: A Thematic Introduction* (1998) and *Thomas Carlyle* (2007).

H. Ozan Ozavci is Assistant Professor of Modern History and Research Fellow at Utrecht University, Fernand Braudel Fellow at l'Ecole des hautes etudes en sciences sociales and Associate Member at the Centre d'Études Turques, Ottomanes, Balkaniques et Centrasiatiques in Paris. His research focuses on the history of security, liberalism and the oil industry in the Middle East and Russian Caucasus in the long nineteenth and early twentieth centuries. He is the author of *Intellectual Origins of the Republic: Ahmet Agaoglu and the Geneology of Liberalism in Turkey* (2015). He is currently working on an ERC-funded book project on imperial security culture in the long nineteenth century with special reference to the 1860 Ottoman Syrian Civil War.

Diana Schaub is Professor of Political Science at Loyola University Maryland. She is the author of *Erotic Liberalism: Women and Revolution in Montesquieu's 'Persian Letters'* (1995), along with many book chapters and articles in the fields of political philosophy and American political thought. She is co-editor (with Amy and Leon Kass) of *What So Proudly We Hail: The American Soul in Story, Speech, and Song* (2011).

Chad Van Schoelandt is Assistant Professor of Philosophy at Tulane University and Affiliated Fellow with the F. A. Hayek Program for Advanced Study in Philosophy, Politics and Economics at George Mason University. His research centres on social morality, responsibility and the tradition of public reason liberalism.

Lei Yi is Professor at the Institute of Modern History of the Chinese Academy of Social Sciences (CASS). He specializes in modern Chinese intellectual history. He is the author of *A Lonely Century: Studies on Chinese Modern Intellectuals* (2015) and *Facing the Challenge of Modernity: The Reaction of the Qing Dynasty* (2012).

Michael Zuckert is the Nancy R. Dreux Professor of Political Science at the University of Notre Dame. He has written extensively in the areas of American political thought and of liberal political theory. His books include *The Natural Rights Republic* and *Launching Liberalism*. He is the founding editor of the journal *American Political Thought*.

Acknowledgements

Working on this collection has been as pleasant as it was instructive. We would like to thank the contributors, the series editors John Morrow and Colin Davis, and the editorial team at Bloomsbury Academic for their expertise, professionalism and thoughtful interventions. Special thanks are in order to Mr Yang Xiao for help on very short notice with translation from the Chinese, to Ms Julia Damphouse for help with the index and to Ms Sarah Bentley for editorial contributions.

Introduction

Ewa Atanassow and Alan S. Kahan

Liberalism today has perhaps more supporters and adversaries than any other political movement. This book traces its global ascent through chapters about twenty-four of the thinkers and actors who contributed to liberalism's rise and spread. To write about a tradition of political thought as rich as liberalism is something like trying to carry water in a leaky bucket – the bucket is never full at the end. Readers who are inspired to learn more can follow the suggestions for further reading located at the end of the book. The chapters included here are designed for readers with little or no previous background in liberal thought as much as for those seeking to fill gaps in their knowledge. They are intended to convey the wide scope, chronological, intellectual and not least geographical, of liberalism as it has developed across the globe since the French Revolution. By probing how and why liberalism found itself in today's leading position, we hope to contribute towards a better understanding of its current situation and offer readers the opportunity to develop some insight into its future prospects.

What is liberalism? Liberalism is both a constellation of ideas about the individual and society expressed in characteristic language, and a set of political practices engaged in by people in specific historical circumstances. If unobjectionable, this description is just an empty shell, and any attempt to give it some content will inevitably result in controversy. By reading the chapters that follow, readers may go some way towards creating their own definition of the conceptual ideas and language, and of the political practices at the heart of liberalism. In general, one can say that in both theory and practice, *freedom* or *liberty* has always stood at the centre of liberal concerns.[1]

As befits a movement for which freedom is central, however, there is no steel cage within which one may confine liberalism. Liberalism is a widely extended family, whose members sometimes dispute the legitimacy of one or another branch, and whether a distant cousin really deserves a place at the family table. This fuzziness mostly does not bother liberals, who tend to be confidently heterogeneous (to borrow a phrase from Kalyvas and Katznelson). Liberal thinkers, moreover, frequently celebrate heterogeneity as a prerequisite of freedom.[2] Nevertheless, this diverse body of thought and practice, however varying over time and place, is united by a shared concern with individual liberty and by the quest to understand and bring about the preconditions for its exercise.

There are some widespread features of liberal thought, characteristic of the family, even if one can always find some self-described liberal who lacks one or two of them. These include an emphasis on individual rights and interests, government that is legitimized by some form of consent, a distinction between the public and the private sphere, suspicion of concentrated authority (be it moral, political, social, economic or theological) and calls for constitutional guarantees to protect citizens from potentially harmful interference by authority. These concerns translate into a range of institutional forms, legal and cultural practices, and modes of reasoning and public discourse. Not merely abstract theories, the liberal ideas featured here were also political interventions by their authors, many of whom took an active part in shaping their own societies while contributing, often self-consciously, to a global discourse of liberty.

Liberalism, we would suggest, is the first truly global political movement. Asserting that the vocation of humanity is to be free, liberalism rapidly found champions across the planet, as the chapters in this book demonstrate. In this, as in so much else, socialism – liberalism's most ardent modern competitor – was merely an imitator and offshoot of the liberal tradition. Liberalism may be seen as a secular heir to the Abrahamic religions, Judaism, Christianity and Islam, attempting, like them, to offer salvation to all of humankind. Like the monotheistic religions and socialist thought, liberalism rests on a universal conception of humanity. Yet it is also characterized by a profound appreciation for human diversity and for the complexity and particularity of time, place and culture. Liberals have often argued whether liberalism in general, or particular liberal measures, is a suitable goal for a given society at a particular moment. This debate over whether liberalism ought to be universally practised represents a real paradox of the world's first global political movement, but paradox, after all, is often characteristic of liberalism, as the chapters demonstrate.

Liberalism's tendency to paradoxical political formulations can be seen as a strength quite as much as a weakness, however, if only because it seems faithful to some of the paradoxical qualities of human nature. More concretely, it is in the nature of liberalism, unlike many of its religious predecessors and ideological competitors, to remain open to the problem of reconciling diverse and often incommensurate interests and values, or balancing social and ethical contradictions that cannot be eliminated without violence. Liberalism has also historically been amenable to accepting the validity of many kinds of political and social solutions to the problems of creating and maintaining a free society. With the passage of time, the universality of liberalism has become less contested by liberals, as becomes evident over the course of this book. But the persistence of a wide variety of liberal solutions to the problem of freedom remains equally evident.

When and how did liberalism begin? If we look at the surface rather than the underground history of liberalism, its emergence can be dated to the moment when 'liberal' and its variants began to be widely used as descriptions of a political position. This happened (and the word 'liberalism' was invented) sometime after the beginning of the French Revolution in 1789 – precisely when is a matter of still-evolving scholarly debate.[3] From this point of departure, liberal creeds developed as critical reflections on the causes and aims of revolutionary transformation, and on the character and meaning of the modern age. By including a range of texts and thinkers that is deliberately broad, this book aims to convey the variety of liberal understandings and their creative adaptation and critical response to different historical and cultural contexts.

Although liberalism only acquired its name and crystallized as a doctrine in the aftermath of the French Revolution, its historical roots run much deeper. How deep is a subject of controversy, and there are those who would date liberalism's origins to ancient Greece, or even Mesopotamia.[4] That it only became a recognizable global movement in the modern period is beyond dispute. Yet just as it is open to question when modernity began, so too is there no consensus about liberalism's beginnings, and whether Machiavelli, Hobbes or Locke are to be numbered among its founding thinkers. This itself is testimony to liberalism's continued importance in the twenty-first century. No one cares much about the genealogy of those with no living descendants, but the genealogy of liberalism still matters. This genealogy has European roots, and many non-European branches. We make no attempt to construct a genealogy of proto-liberal thought in this book. Nevertheless, we acknowledge that liberalism was constituted from ideas and language that originated well before 1789.

To signal this philosophical lineage, the book begins with Montesquieu. A towering figure of the French and European Enlightenment, whose profound impact on the development of the liberal tradition could hardly be exaggerated, Montesquieu took a notably global perspective on the study of politics and of the conditions necessary for individual liberty. His magisterial work *The Spirit of the Laws* shaped liberal thought in numerous ways. It systematized early modern constitutionalism and the relationship between law, power and liberty, and articulated key liberal doctrines such as the separation of powers, the rule of law and the distinction and interdependence between political institutions and social practices. It also conceptualized commercial society and reflected on the interrelation between politics and economics. Perhaps first among the modern European thinkers, Montesquieu sought to understand politics and the human condition in all its actual variety and historical and global multiplicity. Thinking through the Enlightenment's universal aspirations, he theorized the critical role of mores for political life, and argued for the need to tailor political institutions to particular cultures and histories.

If Montesquieu's thought was comprehensive, its impact on ideas and events was no less so. Montesquieu's authority presided over the letter and spirit of the American founding, and guided the French Revolution in its liberal phase. He had, likewise, a formative influence on modern economics and the theorists of capitalist society. Following Montesquieu, the first set of thinkers featured here – Madison, Constant, de Staël, Tocqueville, Bentham – were greatly indebted to his work, as were many later liberals in the West and beyond. Montesquieu, in short, is a pivotal figure in setting the agenda both for modern liberalism and this book.

After Montesquieu, most of the texts and authors discussed in the collection come from the two centuries that stretched between the fall of the Bastille in 1789 and 1989, the year that saw the fall of the Soviet Union and the end of the Cold War, and seemed to mark liberalism's global triumph. But they go beyond them, just as liberalism and its challenges do. Events since 1989 have repeatedly called into question liberal triumphalism – just as they did after 1789. The chapters reflect attempts by liberals around the globe to come to grips with the meaning of both victory and defeat for liberal principles.

In addition to Western classics, the chapters in this book represent thinkers from Asia, Eastern Europe, Latin America and the Middle East. With two exceptions, occasioned by the nature of the material, the chapters are organized chronologically according to the death date of the author treated in the chapter. By using death dates rather than birth dates as an organizing principle, we take into account that an author born earlier may have outlived one born later, and thus have had the opportunity to respond to events the younger writer never saw. Chronology is one way of framing the development of liberalism. Another is suggested by the three headings under which we have organized the chapters: 'Liberal Beginnings', 'Liberalism Confronts the World' and 'Liberalism Confronts the Twentieth Century'.

Under the heading 'Liberal Beginnings', a title borrowed from the aforementioned study by Andreas Kalyvas and Ira Katznelson, we include the first generation of post-revolutionary liberals. Though vastly different in intellectual orientation and sensibilities, they were all influenced by Montesquieu's thought, and sought to re-evaluate and bring it to bear on post-revolutionary conditions. The first group, consisting of Montesquieu (d. 1755), Mme de Staël (d. 1817), Benjamin Constant (d. 1830), Jeremy Bentham (d. 1832), James Madison (d. 1836) and Alexis de Tocqueville (d. 1859), is all arguably European in outlook, although the adherents of a strong view of American exceptionalism will dispute that in Madison's case. All were, in one way or another, essential contributors to the growth of distinctively liberal ways (the plural is important) of discussing the relationship between the individual and society.

The first group of thinkers is the smallest, not in importance but in number, in order to leave room for the many branches of the liberal family tree to unfold in the rest of the book. In the second group, 'Liberalism Confronts the World', of the eight authors, only four are European or North American. This makes evident how liberalism, once formed, rapidly appealed to thinkers from Buenos Aires to Moscow to Tunis to Istanbul. The second part of the book thus explores the elaboration of the post-revolutionary liberal legacy and its adjustment to new geopolitical and historic circumstances. These include the looming constitutional crisis in the United States and the challenges of democratization in Europe, as well as modernization and nation-building outside the West and the construction of a global system of states. Abraham Lincoln (d. 1865), Alexander Herzen (d. 1870), John Stuart Mill (d. 1873), T. H. Green (d. 1882), Domingo Faustino Sarmiento, (d. 1888), Namik Kemal (d. 1888), Khayr al-Din Basha (d. 1890) and Jacob Burckhardt (d. 1897) show the reach and scope of liberal thought in one of its most dominant periods, from the 1860s to the 1890s. In this section, we depart from chronology to place the Herzen chapter, which is partly based on his response to Mill, after the chapter on Mill.

The spread of liberalism in the nineteenth century was simultaneous with the climax of European imperialism and the reaction to it. Whether liberalism played an important role in encouraging European expansionism is a controversial point. That liberalism played a role in the responses of those who encountered European hegemony is unquestionable, if often overlooked – a gap that this book helps fill by discussing thinkers from nations outside Europe and exploring their struggle to adapt and respond to European expansionism.

The last set of contributions, 'Liberalism Confronts the Twentieth Century', reflects both the global impact and the variety of liberal responses to that century's greatest trials – totalitarianism, economic crises and world wars – which were also direct challenges to liberalism's core values. Max Weber (d. 1920), John Maynard Keynes (1946), John Dewey (d. 1952), Hu Shih (d. 1962), Hannah Arendt (d. 1975), F. A. Hayek (d. 1992), Masao Maruyama (d. 1996), Isaiah Berlin (d. 1997), John Rawls (d. 2002) and Czesław Miłosz (d. 2004) are a diverse group, both geographically and ideologically. These ten thinkers represent the variety of liberal creeds, liberal left and liberal right, and testify to the diversity of thought within the liberal family. We have chosen to conclude this section – and the book – with the chapter on John Rawls, who has become a lightning rod in the contemporary debate about liberalism. By putting Rawls last, we want to emphasize the open-ended and continuing debate about the issues raised in *Liberal Moments*.

The ambition of this collection is to present in one place, for the first time, the geographic and ideological diversity of liberal thought and practice. Given liberalism's great heterogeneity and long history, the contents of this slim book necessarily had to be selective. The thinkers discussed in particular chapters have been chosen with a view to representing many, though certainly not all, strands of liberalism, and to showing its confrontation with issues as diverse as civil war, imperialism, cultural pluralism, economic depression, totalitarianism and world wars. Neither our choice of thinkers nor the issues discussed in the book are meant to be exhaustive; inevitably, much has been left out. One could construct alternative histories of liberalism and portray its global ramifications differently by including other voices. Nevertheless, this book conveys core liberal concerns and reflects key moments in the modern history of liberalism and its global outreach.

As part of the Textual Moments series, the book features the series' unique format. Each chapter opens with a critical passage from the author under consideration as a starting point for exploring the author's significance for the history of liberalism. The contributors were asked to highlight and explain the particularities of each author's liberalism in relation both to the critical passage they selected and, whenever possible, to other authors featured in the book. By facilitating a direct encounter with influential authors and texts in the liberal tradition, the book serves as an introduction both to the multiple dimensions of liberalism and to reading texts in political thought. Although not explicitly aimed to highlight specific influences or advance a particular view of the evolution of liberal thought, the textual approach allows readers to create and recreate debates and conversations, perhaps unexpected ones, across the liberal spectrum, and across time and space.

This approach also allows *Liberal Moments* to paint a richer picture of liberalism than the one that dominates contemporary academic discourse. As Kalyvas and Katznelson point out, today's academic political theory operates with a limited and stylized conception of liberalism. This conception rests on 'a series of oppositions that identify it exclusively with the primacy of the right over the good; neutral legal procedures rather than substantive values; interests, not virtues; negative instead of positive liberty; and individual persons as distinct from collectivities and the public good'.[5] By observing a larger historical vista and taking a global view, this book is intended partly to help correct this misconception. In so doing, it illustrates why liberal thought and practice should not be retrospectively reduced to sterile and abstract oppositions. In addition, it shows how national contexts were essential to the real, as opposed to anachronistically stereotyped, development of liberalism.[6]

Is, then, liberalism simply different things to different peoples? While our aim is to portray the variety of liberalism in all its many-splendored glory, it is also to show the enduring nature of certain core concerns, not to say perennial issues in the liberal tradition. Without undue simplification, the liberal thought and practice explored in this book can be understood as a response to two questions: (1) What is a supportive environment for realizing liberty in the modern world? and (2) How to bring this environment about? – questions all the more challenging as some aspects of modern life (tensions between equality and liberty on the one hand, and external conditions such as economic crises and world wars on the other) may work to undermine the possibility of liberal society.

The relationship between state and society, and the danger posed by unconstrained political authority, is fundamental, perhaps the fundamental liberal concern. What should the role of government be in a liberal state? What is the relationship between freedom and authority? What institutional arrangement best balances security, efficiency and civil freedoms? How can a stable government strong enough to carry out its essential functions be reconciled with individual liberty and a vibrant, independent social sphere? These questions have animated liberal thinkers throughout the centuries and across the liberal spectrum, and they find their most sustained treatment here in the chapters on Montesquieu, Madison, Tocqueville, Green, Kemal, Khayr al-Din, Weber, Arendt, Hayek and Berlin.

In this connection, one of the most prominent features of liberalism is the recognition and respect for the irreducible diversity of social interests and values, and the quest for institutional mechanisms and practices that would encompass this diversity in a political and constitutional process. Liberalism's distinct notion of stable and legitimate government thus rests on the aspiration, not to resolve contradictions but to mitigate them, by recognizing the permanence of conflict and making it into an engine of liberal government.

Alongside reflections on constitutional principles, delimiting the sphere of political authority and the relation between society and state, liberals in the past two centuries have sought to conceptualize the interrelation between individual and society. This collection highlights the fundamental change that was brought about by the revolutions of the eighteenth century. Nearly all post-revolutionary liberals accepted equality as a foundational principle of modern society and starting point for liberal thought. Yet, alongside the commitment to inalienable rights, to the principle of civil equality and insistence on ensuring the representation and integration of all groups and classes, nineteenth- and twentieth-century liberals also pointed out the tensions between equality and liberty, and the danger modern forms of social organization pose to individual freedom. By eroding the preconditions for free, strong individualities as the wellspring of creative energy and transformative ideas, modern society threatens to undermine liberalism. Hence the focus on individual character and on the interplay of sociopolitical and moral and psychological factors that contribute to its formation, found most notably in the chapters on Tocqueville, Herzen, Mill, Sarmiento, Burckhardt, Weber, Dewey, Maruyama and Miłosz, and more briefly in many of the rest.

Seeking to build a liberal state and a liberal society on these principles, many, if not all, of the thinkers discussed here faced questions of political reform, whether in the wholesale transformation of a political system and constitution-making or through incremental change. The reforms were often both means for attaining liberal goals and ends in themselves. Indeed, one could say that, to a large extent, the identity of ends and means is part of the liberal tradition.

That tradition is unanimous – a rare thing among liberals – about the need to limit the resort to political violence. The thinkers discussed in this book recognized that, to be liberal, social and political reform cannot be imposed or enforced from above but must be encouraged and stimulated from below.

Hence the prominence of the notion of political culture in liberal thought, its concern with developing a liberal vernacular by adapting liberal principles to religious and cultural traditions and its focus, hardly uncritical, on education as the most salient among the means to reform. This concern is present within European liberalism, but it is particularly salient in non-Western liberalisms, as the chapters in this book show. Last but not least, as the chapters in this book can testify, from Montesquieu to Rawls, liberal thinkers emphasized the necessity for a systematic study of politics and society and called on social and political science, both theoretical and empirical, to justify and offer evidence for the validity of key liberal principles and institutions.

The enduring question remains: how to embody liberal principles in concrete institutions, tailored to and grounded in existing practices and cultural traditions – an elaborately academic way of saying: What does it mean to be free? This question seems likely to occupy liberal minds for some time to come.

Part One

Liberal Beginnings

Montesquieu

Catherine Larrère

The Spirit of the Laws

Book XI, Chapter 3
What liberty is

It is true that in democracies the people seem to do what they want, but political liberty in no way consists in doing what one wants. In a state, that is, in a society where there are laws, liberty can consist only in having the power to do what one should want to do and in no way, being forced to do what one should not want to do.

One must put oneself in mind of what independence is and what liberty is. Liberty is the right to do everything the laws permit; and if one citizen could do what they forbid, he would no longer have liberty because the others would likewise have this same power.

Chapter 4
Continuation of the same subject

Democracy and aristocracy are not free states by their nature. Political liberty is found only in moderate governments. But it is not always in moderate states. It is present only when power is not abused, but it has eternally been observed that any man who has power is led to abuse it; he continues until he finds limits. Who would think it! Even virtue has need of limits.

So that one cannot abuse power, power must check power by the arrangement of things. A constitution can be such that no one will be constrained to do the things the law does not oblige him to do or be kept from doing the things the law permits him to do.[1]

From the *Persian Letters* (1721), Montesquieu's first work, to his magnum opus, *The Spirit of the Laws* (1748), Montesquieu's commitments did not change. He criticized slavery, condemned the horror and senselessness of torture and denounced religious intolerance. At the same time, he studied guaranties for freedom, whether it was a matter of the constitutional distribution of powers, or the development of commerce, whose 'natural effect … is to lead to peace' (XX: 2, 338). At the centre of this defence of human rights and civil liberties is his admiration for England, the 'one nation in the world whose constitution has political liberty for its direct purpose' (XI: 5, 156).

Montesquieu, without any doubt, was a theorist of political freedom. Does that make him a liberal? To speak of Montesquieu's liberalism is certainly an anachronism, since the term did not appear until the nineteenth century to describe many political and economic ideas unknown to Montesquieu. To what extent does Montesquieu's conception of political freedom inform what we understand today by liberalism? To respond to this question one must carefully examine Montesquieu's presentation of political liberty at the beginning of the first of the three books of *The Spirit of the Laws* (XI, XII, XIII) devoted to it.

To define political freedom, Montesquieu begins by specifying what it is not: the exercise of power. To be free is not to participate in power, it is to be protected against its excesses. This leads Montesquieu to define freedom by security: 'Political liberty is that tranquillity of spirit which comes from the opinion each one has of his security' (XI: 6, 157).

If one holds to this opposition between the exercise of power and security, Montesquieu's conception of political freedom cannot be distinguished from that presented by Benjamin Constant in his famous 1819 lecture, 'The Liberty of the Ancients Compared to That of the Moderns', where he opposed political participation, which the ancients defined as freedom, and private enjoyment which represented freedom for the moderns. Following Montesquieu, Constant judged that this change in the conception of freedom was linked to the development of commerce and the accompanying increase in the importance of satisfying individual interests.

However, Montesquieu's position cannot be reduced to the putative and purely European opposition of ancients and moderns and their forms of government. As Montesquieu understands it, political freedom does not exclude participation in power and is not based on the opposition between republic and monarchy, but on that between moderate and despotic governments, a distinction which is proper to Montesquieu and which allows him to broaden his view to a truly global perception of the political situation.

At the beginning of the first of the two chapters which he devotes to the definition of liberty, Montesquieu warns against confusing political freedom with the power of the people. This was a rejection of the ancient Greek idea that identified democracy with freedom. Montesquieu was not the first to criticize this republican definition of political freedom. Hobbes, in *Leviathan*, denounced the confusion between freedom as an individual right and political power, which is the right of the city or the state. He makes the ancients, and especially Aristotle, responsible for this mistake, which led people to believe that they would be more free in certain forms of government (republican or democratic) than in others (like monarchy), whereas the freedom which an individual enjoys should not be confused with the power of which the state disposes.[2] Montesquieu, like Hobbes, insists on making freedom an individual question. Hobbes defined the purposes of the state in relation to individuals: it is a question of shelter from foreign attack and of being capable of sustaining oneself. Montesquieu, defining freedom as security, determines it on an individual basis. It also has a subjective dimension: he characterizes it as 'tranquility of mind' and thus bases it on opinion. 'Political liberty', he insists, when he repeats the definition at the beginning of Book XII, 'consists in security or, at least, in the opinion one has of one's security' (XII: 2, 188).

But if they agree on the importance they give to the individual, Montesquieu and Hobbes divide on the relationship that they establish between freedom, as an individual right, and the law. According to Hobbes, 'Law and liberty differ as much as obligation and liberty.'[3] Since the political condition of an individual is defined by submission or obedience, civil liberties 'depend on the silence of the law' and consist in the lack of obligation established by law.[4] Montesquieu, on the contrary, links liberty and law: people are not free outside the law, or against the law. One is free with the law.

In Chapter 3, Montesquieu introduces this idea philosophically, through an opposition between power and duty: people are not free when doing what they want or what they can, but when doing what they should. Montesquieu redefines this opposition in a more political fashion as that between independence (when one is not subject to any authority) and freedom, in its relation to law: 'Liberty is the right to do everything the laws permit.' In order to establish this definition, Montesquieu shows that the proposition according to which one is free when acting against or despite the law cannot be generalized without contradiction: if everyone had the same freedom, no one would be free. This linked equality and freedom: freedom, as an individual right or power, belongs to everyone equally. It remains for the law to organize the coexistences of freedoms. Unlike Hobbes, who insists on the repressive and prescriptive character of law, Montesquieu proposes a positive conception of law, which is permissive: it makes individual action possible. Security can thus be defined as the confidence everyone possesses that he or she can perform licit activities without hostile interference. Freedom, therefore, has political conditions and requires a description of the kind of state in which it can exist, from which comes the definition of state: 'That is … a society in which there are laws.'

In declaring in Chapter 4 that 'democracy and aristocracy are not free states by their nature', Montesquieu affirms against Aristotle and the Greek tradition that freedom is not part of the essence or 'nature' of republican government, in the sense of that 'which makes it what it is' (III: 1, 21). However, he does not turn Aristotle's judgement upside down and claim that political freedom is an attribute of monarchies. He develops a different typology of governments, which contrasts moderate governments with despotic ones.

This opposition progressively emerges from the study of governments, from Book II onwards, based on the traditional classification borrowed from the Greek historians and political thinkers. Like the traditional typology, it distinguished three kinds of government, according to the number of people who shared power: the many – democracy; the few – aristocracy; and the government of an individual – monarchy. Yet Montesquieu folds democracy and aristocracy under the category of republic, and distinguishes, in government by an individual, between those where law rules – monarchies – and those where one governs without laws, solely by the whim of the person who holds power – despotisms. He then studies the three governments separately for the most part, but nevertheless makes comparisons between governments which are based on the difference between republics and monarchies, on the one hand, and between monarchy and despotism, on the other. These two kinds of comparison, at first made in parallel, later converge.

The difference between republics and monarchies is virtue, which Montesquieu defines as love of the government and of equality. Virtue is the principle (in the sense of the motive force) of republics, and especially of democracies, while it is not necessary in monarchies whose principle is honour, which is based on social distinctions, that is, on inequality. Virtue, extolled by the ancients, is in difficulty in modernity, especially because of the growing importance of commerce. Montesquieu explains the failure of the English republic after the English Civil War by referring to the opposition between virtue and commerce, which he borrows from the republican tradition: 'The political men of Greece who lived under popular government recognized no other force to sustain it than virtue. Those of today speak to us only of manufacturing, commerce, finance, wealth, and even luxury' (III: 3, 22–3). Virtue, in effect, is love of equality that presumes the sacrifice of personal interests to the common good, while commerce promotes inequality and leads people to put their own interests first.

Between monarchy and despotism, Montesquieu emphasizes the importance of recourse to law; that is where the real difference lies between the two governments. As Montesquieu's argument unfolds, the point that both are governed by a single individual is reduced to a formal characteristic which allows comparison in order to better understand their difference. Montesquieu introduces the expression 'moderate governments' in Book III to distinguish despotism from monarchy (III: 10, 29). But in the following books the expression 'moderate governments' designates not only monarchies but all governments where the law reigns, including republics. Thus, gradually, the opposition between moderate and despotic governments, through which Montesquieu will define political freedom, is put in place.

By grouping republics and monarchies in the common category of moderate governments, the number of those who exercise power ceases to be a determining criterion, and at the same time, the opposition between antiquity and modernity is erased. Despotism ends up being situated not in time but in space, in a geographical elsewhere, the Orient. It is from China, Japan and Turkey that Montesquieu takes most of his despotic examples. But if he tends to find his examples outside of Europe, he makes it clear that despotism is not limited to Asia. It threatens European governments, the absolutist governments of his time (absolutism represents the despotic deviation of the French monarchy), as much as it did those of antiquity. The introduction of despotism into his typology globalizes Montesquieu's political thought by freeing it from imprisonment in the confrontation between ancients and moderns, meaningful only in a European context.

Despotism or arbitrary rule, whose principle is fear, is the face of evil in politics. One is almost astonished that it exists: 'It seems that human nature would rise up incessantly against despotic governments.' And yet, 'Most peoples are subjected to this type of government' (V: 14, 63). If its rule is so widespread, it is because it is the default form of government, a sort of ground-level politics: 'Only passions are needed to establish it.' We thus understand that 'liberty is found only in moderate governments', but while moderate government is a necessary condition for freedom, it is not sufficient, since, as stated in Chapter

4, freedom is 'not always [found] in moderate states'. If despotism, so to speak, creates itself, moderate government is a 'masterpiece of legislation' (V: 14, 63).

Political freedom therefore has a universal antagonist: power. For 'it has eternally been observed that any man who has power is led to abuse it'. Its positive mechanism, by contrast, – the possibility of limiting the universal tendency to abuse power – can only exist in accord with circumstances proper to each country. Thus the importance of the chapter devoted to the English constitution (XI: 6). There, Montesquieu describes the political techniques of balancing power that secure the rule of law, and under which 'no one will be constrained to do the things the law does not oblige him to do or be kept from doing the things the law permits him to do' (XI: 3, 155).

For power to check power, there must be several powers. Montesquieu distinguishes three kinds, legislative, executive and judicial, a distinction which he did not invent, for it owes its distant origins to Aristotle and is also found in Locke. Montesquieu's originality lies in his thought about the mechanisms which realize this distinction. The conception he develops is more a theory of how power is distributed than of how the powers are separated from one another. The only really separate power is the judiciary, which is essentially assigned to institutions independent of the other powers (judges and juries). The two other powers (legislative and executive) are exercised by different institutions or organs (upper chamber, lower chamber, king), which are vested in distinct social groups (the nobility, the people and the king, royalty itself being simultaneously an institution and a social power). The objective is that the participation of these social powers in each of these institutions, particularly in the legislative power, prevents the monopolization of a power by one organ or class which would lead to the confusion of powers and despotism. Thus, three institutions participate in the legislative power: the people and the lower chamber propose and vote the laws, while the upper chamber and the king participate through their power to block (or their veto).

The English constitution can be understood as a technical apparatus whose function needs explanation: 'The form of these three powers should be rest or inaction. But as they are constrained to move by the necessary motion of things, they will be forced to move in concert' (XI: 6, 164). Montesquieu thus shows that the constitution functions like a machine to correct the constant imbalances represented by the attempts of the different powers to encroach on each other. No one is obliged to desire the common good, but the common good is produced as a result: it is the universality of the law, which assures freedom. Those who 'are subject only to the power of the law', Montesquieu explains, 'are really free' (XI: 6, 159).

If the characteristic of modern politics is that, unlike ancient democracies, it does not depend on virtue, defined as the love of the public good and the citizens' capacity to sacrifice their own interest to it, the political freedom made possible by the English constitution is indeed a specifically modern liberty. Nevertheless, this does not lead Montesquieu to see freedom as only a private concern for individual security, a search for personal comfort separate from the public dimension of politics. What Montesquieu defines is the freedom of the citizen, not that of the private individual, of the 'particular', as it was then called. The modern vision of freedom in no way excludes participation in power. For Montesquieu, there is no break between ancient democracy, uniting the people in a body on the public square, and modern representative government, but rather a continuity, which he expresses by the typically republican analogy between the government of one's self and that of the state: 'As, in a free state, every man, considered to have a free soul, should be governed by himself, the people as a body should have legislative power; but, as this is impossible in large states and is subject to many drawbacks in small ones, the people must have their representatives do all that they cannot themselves do' (XI: 6, 159).

There is, therefore, no reason to oppose a liberty of the ancients, republican, based on the power of the people, to a liberty of the moderns, separate from power, reduced to individual security. What Montesquieu reproaches the ancient republics with is that they were never really the power of all, and thus were more about domination than freedom: 'A popular state [democracy] means the liberty of poor and weak people and the servitude of rich and powerful people; and monarchy is the liberty of the great and the servitude of the little', he writes in a fragment on political freedom.[5] The conception of moderate government and the political liberty which the institutions of such a government make possible allow us to envisage a political freedom which is that of all citizens, not that of one part of the population to the detriment of another part. This freedom, under the shelter of the law, does not exclude some forms of participation in power. Doubtless, the fact that power is no longer derived from virtue allows everyone to satisfy their individual aspirations and, notably, to devote themselves unreservedly to commerce, which is, for Montesquieu, both an essentially private activity and a distinguishing aspect of modern society. This is one way in which Montesquieu is a liberal. But Montesquieu's chief contribution to the history of liberalism is to be sought in his conception of political freedom and in the institutions which can make it a reality.

One of Montesquieu's great originalities is his theory of despotism: he makes it into a separate form of government which, as such, ranks equally with the other forms of government in the neutral typology (its sole criterion is numeric) at the beginning of *The Spirit of the Laws*. But as the theory of governments advances, a normative opposition between moderate and despotic governments, between political freedom and public slavery, becomes clear. Political freedom is thus first defined through its opposite, the universal evil of the abuse of power. But if, in politics, evil is one, 'there are several goods' (XXVI: 2, 495). Political freedom depends on institutions – it is not the result of a spontaneous order based on practice, and its forms are multiple. England, as Montesquieu studies it, is doubtless closest to what we would today describe as a liberal regime. That Montesquieu identifies it as the locus of political freedom in his time is one of the reasons for the contemporary relevance of his political thought. But in no way does he make England a universal model. Montesquieu, whose purpose was to examine 'the infinite diversity of law and mores', did not think there were any universally valid models. His comparative method led him to judge that governments are good only in relation to the particular situation in which they find themselves. If Montesquieu belongs to the liberal tradition, his liberalism is a liberalism of plurality: of men, of institutions, of solutions; and in this respect, as in many others, Tocqueville can be considered his successor.

Translated by Alan S. Kahan.

In Praise of Liberty: Madame de Staël's *Considerations*

Aurelian Craiutu

Of all modern monarchies, France was certainly the one whose political institutions were most arbitrary and fluctuating. … Whatever may be the cause, it is an undoubted fact that there exists no law in France, not even an elementary law, which has not, at some time or other, been disputed – nothing, in short, which has not been the object of difference of opinion. … France has been governed by custom, often by caprice, and never by law. … We thus see that the history of France is replete with attempts on the part of the nation and nobles, the one to obtain rights, the other privileges; we see in it also continual efforts of most of the kings to attain arbitrary power. … The great misfortune of France, as of every country governed solely by a court, is the domineering influence of vanity. No fixed principle gains ground in the mind; all is absorbed in the pursuit of power, because power is everything in a country where the laws are nothing. … The Revolution of 1789 had then no other object than to give a regular form to the limitations which have all along existed in France.[1]

A Swiss Protestant in a predominantly Catholic country, Anne Louise Germaine, Baronne de Staël-Holstein (1766–1817) was the daughter of Jacques Necker (1732–1804), the famous Genevan banker who eventually became Louis XVI's minister of finance and was a leading actor during the initial stages of the French Revolution. Her first book, *Letters on the Works and Character of J.-J. Rousseau*, appeared on the eve of the French Revolution in 1788. She later published other works such as *On the Influence of Passions on the Happiness of Individuals and Nations* (1796), *On Literature Considered in Its Relationship with the Moral and Political State of Nations* (1800) and two novels, *Delphine* (1802) and *Corinne or Italy* (1807). At the time of her death in 1817, Madame de Staël was working on *Considerations on the Principal Events of the French Revolution,* from which the opening excerpt is taken. This became her (unfinished) political magnum opus which exercised a decisive influence on the evolution of French liberalism.[2] It is worth reminding that, during the first years of the French Revolution, she had been among those who defended constitutional monarchy; under the Directory, she advocated a conservative form of republicanism based on limited suffrage. Two decades later, her allegiance shifted back to constitutional monarchy. This explains the existence of both significant differences and affinities between the political agenda of *Considerations* and Madame de Staël's republican profession of faith in *Of the Present Circumstances Which Can End the Revolution and of the Principles Which Must Found the Republic in France,* an important yet unfinished work drafted in 1797–8 and published posthumously in the twentieth century.

Although we will never know what the final version of *Considerations* would have looked like, had it been fully revised by its author, this book offers one of the most important accounts of the nature and legacy of the French Revolution, on a par with two other famous books on this topic, Edmund Burke's *Reflections on the Revolution in France* and Joseph de Maistre's *Considerations on France.* Immediately translated into English, Madame de Staël's *Considerations* elicited a vigorous debate in Paris but subsequently fell into oblivion in France, a country which has always combined a strong passion for freedom and equality with respect for hierarchy and a marked tendency to centralization and radicalism. This eclectic book combines political and philosophical reflections, first-hand experience and personal recollections covering two tumultuous decades in French history. Written as a manifesto and a vindication of Necker's legacy, it came from the pen of an influential public intellectual who used history to make a number of important political points. Madame de Staël was hardly alone in this regard. In a conflict-ridden society like post-revolutionary France, it was common to appeal to the testimony of history and reinterpret the latter when searching for a new political compass. Within the span of fifteen years, from 1789 to 1814, the country had made the transition from one type of absolute power (the Old Regime of Louis XVI) to another (the First Empire) and back to the Bourbons (Louis XVIII), and tried several constitutions, all of which were found wanting. The spectre of the French Revolution starting over and over again worried Madame de Staël and her friends, who wondered whether the country would ever be able to overcome the dark legacy of the Terror of 1793–4 and the Jacobin dictatorship, known for its ruthless use of violence and the guillotine to punish the alleged enemies of the country.

In her *Considerations*, Madame de Staël performed a political and intellectual *tour de* force. She opposed absolute power, defended the principles of representative government (either as a constitutional monarchy or as a republic) and expressed her admiration for England's successful synthesis of order and liberty, tradition and innovation. Her interpretation of French history aimed at vindicating the legacy of her beloved father and focused on discontinuities and long-term social, cultural and political patterns. It sought to demonstrate, in the footsteps of Montesquieu, that 'in Europe, as in France, it was liberty that was ancient and despotism that was modern'.[3] Both the opening and last lines of the selected paragraph reflect Madame de Staël's liberal political agenda, which attempted to reform the obsolete institutions of the Old Regime and replace them with new representative institutions in keeping with the spirit of the age. It was an agenda that promoted liberal values such as individual freedom, civil equality, constitutionalism and the rule of law. The claim that 'of all modern monarchies, France was certainly the one whose political institutions were most arbitrary and fluctuating'[4] can be found at the outset of a seminal chapter (XI) of the first volume of *Considerations*, an unusually long chapter which addressed a highly controversial topic, namely whether France did have a genuine constitution during the Old Regime. This was a significant question that had an important theoretical side to it as well as a long history.[5] Many French thinkers and political actors, such as Abbé Sieyès in his influential pamphlet *What Is the Third Estate?* (1789), claimed that the country lacked a true constitution which was supposed to be created *ab novo* in 1789. This was a way to justify and legitimize the bold initiative of the National Assembly in mid-June 1789, when it declared itself the Constituent Assembly. The deputies took a collective oath not to separate until the constitution of the kingdom was fully established and affirmed on entirely new foundations. The controversies that ensued focused on what to us might appear as arcane and odd topics, such as the subtle differences between 'establishing', 'reestablishing', 'maintaining', 'giving', 'laying the foundations of' and 'making' an entirely new constitution. The unusual intensity of the debates on these issues revealed the weaknesses of the traditionalist position affirming the existence of an allegedly ancient constitution which should have been preserved or reformed in 1789. It also brought to the fore the difficulties encountered by those who argued that such a constitution did not exist and had to be established from scratch. If there was an old constitution, as some claimed, the National Assembly did not have the right to act as if it didn't exist. If the ancient constitution was nothing more than a figment of imagination, the door was open to all kinds of innovations, some more daring or sensible than others.

Madame de Staël's position was not devoid of an interesting ambiguity. If she followed Sieyès's call for a new constitution in France, her political moderation and unwavering admiration for the English unwritten constitution and complex government parted company with his endorsement of simple government and radical approach to political reform that had no appreciation for tradition and complexity. Like Guizot in his *History of Civilization in Europe*, Madame de Staël regarded 1789 as part of a longer historical development of the entire European civilization rather than the outcome of accidental causes limited to France, as Burke thought. In her view, both the French Revolution of 1789 and the English Glorious Revolution of 1688 belonged to the same historical trend towards the establishment of representative government. As a liberal thinker in the European (centrist) meaning of the term, she sought to defend and legitimize the movement of 1789 in the face of its conservative opponents and left-wing critics. On the right, Maistre interpreted the Revolution as a unique event in history that manifested a degree of destruction and human depravity never seen before. Against Maistre and his admirers, Madame de Staël emphasized that the French Revolution achieved many important things. She also insisted that there was no way back into the past while being aware that the task of bringing the revolution to an end was far from being completed. In her opinion, constitutionalizing the liberties gained in 1789, absorbing the shock produced by the Terror of 1793–4 and building representative institutions on the ruins of the Old Regime and the First Empire should have been the priorities of all forward-looking spirits.

Although Madame de Staël did not affirm the inevitability of the French Revolution as clearly as Tocqueville did in *The Old Regime and the Revolution* (1856), she believed that the Revolution was 'one of the great eras of social order'[6] which occurred as a response to the deep structural problems of the Old Regime. This was the liberal position that made a clear distinction between the events of 1789 and the tragedies of 1793–4. A change, Madame de Staël claimed, was necessary to introduce precisely those guarantees against the arbitrary power that had previously been missing. In her view, this made the actors of 1789 justified in their efforts to eliminate class privileges, lower the barriers between classes and establish provincial assemblies and civil liberties for all. Yet Madame de Staël was far from being an unconditional admirer of the work of the Constituent Assembly (1789–91). She was particularly critical of the Constitution of 1791, which she took to task for its immoderate distrust of executive power – a theme borrowed from Necker's works – its excessive enthusiasm for abstractions, its unlimited confidence in the legislative power and its rejection of bicameralism. Madame de Staël embraced a moderate position, one which contained, in fact, an interesting contradiction remarked by one of her most vocal critics, Bailleul. He pointed out that her position denying the existence of a true constitution conflicted with her later claim that, in France, liberty was ancient while despotism was modern.

We should remember that, like many other French liberal historians, Madame de Staël, too, offered a selective and, ultimately, subjective reading of the past. On the one hand, she claimed that nothing regulated and circumscribed in a precise and clear manner the rights of the Crown and the Third Estate in a country in which everything was possible and depended entirely on the course of circumstances and the will of the king and his courtiers. She insisted that the political influence of the *parlements* (as courts of justice) was equally limited and their authority and privileges undefined most of the time. Moreover, the Estates General were convened only eighteen times between 1302 and 1789 (and not once since 1614), which meant, in her view, that France had been governed mostly by caprice and 'never by law'.[7] On the other hand, Madame de Staël insisted that the modern history of France had been, in fact, a series of attempts on the part of the nation as a whole to obtain and secure privileges against the absolute power of the monarchs.

Under these circumstances, building a representative government on the ruins of the Old Regime proved to be a daunting task in a country which was, to paraphrase Tocqueville, one of the most brilliant and dangerous nations of Europe, destined to become an object of admiration, hatred or terror, but rarely of indifference. As Madame de Staël remarked, an excessive faith in abstract ideas fed political fanaticism and fostered immoderation and intransigence. Constitutionalism, limited power and the need for a proper balance of powers in the state were neglected, while abstract or natural rights were displaced in favour of positive rights that could be forfeited in exceptional or emergency situations. Eventually, she argued, the whole country threw itself into the hands of Napoleon, who managed to enslave the French nation by seeking to satisfy men's interests at the expense of their virtues, disregarding public opinion and giving the French nation war and conquest instead of liberty. With the benefit of hindsight, it can be argued that Napoleon's absolute power had been made possible by the previous levelling and atomization of society and the weakness of intermediary bodies during the Old Regime. The question that was in the air after his army was defeated at Waterloo was whether the French could ever become free in light of their previous political misfortunes, an issue which Madame de Staël answered in the affirmative.

She devoted the last part (VI) of her book to explaining the success of constitutional monarchy in England, Napoleon's former enemy, but her larger aim was to prove that, like the English, the French could also enjoy freedom if they showed sufficient determination, patience and strength. One finds in this part of her work dense chapters reflecting her appreciation for England's political system and culture that also shed light on her strong commitment to moderation, liberty and the principles of representative government such as balance of powers, publicity (understood as open access to information and free contestation for power), freedom of the press, decentralization and public opinion. She pointed out that in England, the government never interfered in what could be equally well done by individuals without any external support. This made the English capable of managing their own affairs, whenever possible, without the government encroaching upon local authorities. The preservation of English liberty, Madame de Staël opined, depended upon maintaining the balance of power between Crown and Parliament as well as between old and new legal and political institutions. The general respect for rights and the rule of law created a strong bond between the governed and their representatives and allowed public opinion to hold sway and reign supreme. Like her father, she believed that France could (and should) have imitated the English political model, even if importing English institutions and principles should have been done while preserving the specificity of French history, society and culture.

In spite of their nefarious legacy of centralization and despotism, Madame de Staël concluded that the French could still break free from the chains of the past if they were determined to apply their talents and skills to building free institutions. It would be a mere sophism, she argued, to require that nations possess the virtues of liberty before they obtain political freedom. In reality, a people cannot acquire these virtues until they have enjoyed a certain degree of liberty, as the effect can never precede the cause. She reminded her readers that, for a long time, the English themselves had been seen as incapable of building a regime of ordered liberty. Although they deposed, killed or overturned more kings, princes and governments than the rest of Europe together, they obtained at last 'the most noble, the most brilliant and most religious order of society that exists in the Old World'.[8] A similar perspective could be applied to the French case as well. There are in the French nation Madame de Staël opined, noble qualities, remarkable qualities such as energy, patience under misfortune, audacity in enterprise and strength, which could counteract the general inclination to frivolity and vanity. On this view, the French, too, could find their own liberty if they displayed a genuine and ardent desire to be free.[9] She ended her book on a lyrical tone in praise of liberty – 'Liberty! … All we love, all we honor is included in it'[10] – a summation of her intense life devoted to defending the freedom and moderation that had eluded France for so long.

To conclude, Madame de Staël's writings bring to light a characteristic of French liberalism – its historical and sociological approach – that makes it different from the utilitarian and analytical type predominant in the English-speaking world. French liberals had to deal with the Jacobin interpretation of equality, virtue and popular sovereignty, and their solutions and approaches to topics such as individual rights, religion, civil society and the state were often found to be unorthodox when compared with those advanced by English liberals across the Channel. French liberalism has been more political and historical than economic, and the link between political and economic liberalism has been somewhat tenuous in France compared with England or the United States. And yet, the daunting challenges faced by Madame de Staël and her peers allowed them to realize better than anyone else the fragility of freedom and the difficult apprenticeship of liberty. One finds in her writings a remarkable fidelity to a few key principles and values which define her mature political thought, at the heart of which lies the concept of political moderation. She defended the liberty of the moderns, by which she meant individual rights, respect for private property and freedom of thought and association. Two decades before Benjamin Constant's famous speech on this topic, she defined modern liberty as freedom from illegitimate encroachment by public authorities and respect for private sphere and individual rights. For these reasons alone, Madame de Staël deserves her own privileged place in the Pantheon of French liberal thought along with Montesquieu, Necker, Constant, Guizot and Tocqueville.

Benjamin Constant on the Liberty of the Ancients and the Moderns

Jeremy Jennings

Ask yourselves, Gentleman, what an Englishman, a Frenchman, and a citizen of the United States of America understands today by the word 'liberty.' For each of them it is the right to be subjected only to the laws, and to be neither arrested, detained, put to death or maltreated in any way by the arbitrary will of one or more individuals. It is the right of everyone to express their opinion, choose a profession and practice it, to dispose of property, and even to abuse it, to come and go without permission, and without having to account for their motives or undertakings. It is everyone's right to associate with other individuals, either to discuss their interests, or to profess the religion which they and their associates prefer, or even simply to occupy their days or hours in a way which is most compatible with their inclinations or whims. Finally, it is everyone's right to exercise some influence on the administration of government, either by electing all or particular officials, or through representations, petitions, demands to which particular authorities are more or less compelled to pay heed.[1]

These words were uttered by Benjamin Constant in a speech he made in Paris in 1819. In this well-known text, he not only set out a concept of modern liberty but also compared this concept to the idea of liberty he believed had been held by the ancients. By the ancients, he meant the citizens of classical Athens and Sparta as well as of the Roman republic. But this speech was no mere text of historical exposition. Its message was a deeply political one, and one intended to give guidance to the citizens of Restoration France as they sought to recover from the double trauma of the French Revolution of 1789 and the dictatorship of Napoleon Bonaparte, recently brought to an end by defeat for France at the

Battle of Waterloo. Over the course of the French Revolution, in a short span of time of just over twenty years, France had witnessed not only the descent into revolutionary terror but had also been subject to the dictates of a centralized and military regime, where many of the liberties listed by Constant had been done away with. The key question Constant sought to answer in his lecture, therefore, was how could this be explained? Why was it that liberty had not been established in France?

The short answer was that those who had led the Revolution had confused the two types of liberty he sketched out in his lecture. They had sought to give the French population a form of liberty appropriate not to the modern age but to the past. So, what was the ancient conception of liberty?

First, we should note that the description of modern liberty focuses its attention on the right of individuals to engage in a series of activities of their own choosing (practice a religion, choose a job, travel somewhere and so on) without the need to seek permission from either the government or society more generally. Individuals were to be free to spend their time and energy as they wished and to do so with whomever they wished. By contrast, according to Constant, the liberty enjoyed by the ancients was a form of 'collective freedom'. It was, above all, the right to participate in the decision-making processes of society, to decide on issues of war and peace and to vote on laws. However, this same freedom enjoyed by the ancients, as they debated in the public square, also countenanced the complete subjection of the individual to the community. As Constant said in his lecture, 'All private actions were submitted to a severe surveillance. No importance was given to individual independence, neither in relation to opinions, nor to labour, nor, above all, to religion.'[2] Indeed, for the ancients, the right to choose your own religion would have been seen as a crime. In short, the ancients had no conception of the rights of the individual.

Constant could see that this ancient conception of liberty was not without its attractions. If enslaved in his private affairs, the citizen, through public deliberation, participation in the framing of treaties with foreign powers and holding magistrates to account, participated in the exercise of sovereignty when it came to public affairs. But, Constant contended, its wholesale adoption in a modern context could only produce disastrous results. Why?

Most obviously, because the societies we now live in are fundamentally different from those familiar to the ancients. The ancient city was small in size, rarely reaching the proportions of even the smallest of modern states. The spirit of these societies was bellicose: citizens came together principally to fight wars. Finally, they were societies where most productive tasks were carried out by slaves. None of these conditions now applied. States were now much larger, thereby depriving most individuals of direct involvement in public affairs. Moral and intellectual progress had led to the abolition of slavery among European nations, with the result that free men now provided for the material needs of society. Crucially, modern societies sought to enrich themselves not through war but by engaging in commerce and trade. If, therefore, the uniform tendency of commerce was towards peace, it also inspired in men a vivid sense of their own independence. 'Commerce', Constant observed, 'supplies their needs, satisfies their desires' and it did so without any intervention on the part of government.

So, in Constant's opinion, the French Revolution had made the catastrophic mistake of offering the people an inappropriate form of liberty. It had told the people that they must behave like the citizens of classical Athens and republican Rome and when, to the surprise of their leaders, they refused to do so, the people were offered the scaffold and the guillotine as an alternative. The advent of Bonapartist dictatorship only served to continue this sorry state of affairs. Here, we should acknowledge that not only did Constant see some merit in the French Revolution but he also, albeit for a relatively short period of time, thought that Napoleon Bonaparte might have his good points. Above all, he might bring the Revolution to an end. Nevertheless, Constant quickly concluded that Napoleonic rule was something of an anachronism. This was so precisely because the regime Napoleon had created rested entirely upon a spirit of conquest. As such, it demanded only passive obedience from its population.

But there was also something remarkably new about the Napoleonic Empire. It was, as Constant wrote, a form of usurpation. This sentiment he expressed most clearly in *The Spirit of Conquest and Usurpation and their Relation to European Civilization*, first published in 1814. The regime of the usurper, Constant wrote, was a regime of corruption, treachery, illegality and violence but it was also a regime that sought to disempower all equally. It strove to reduce all of us to something akin to individual atoms on a vast level plain. And, as Constant was fully aware, uniformity reduced our existences to 'mere mechanism' and death.[3] But there was more to usurpation than this. The usurper sought to destroy the most intimate aspects of an individual's existence. It pursued that individual into the inner sanctuary of his or her soul. The result was that silence itself was a crime: the citizen had to affirm his or her support for the regime. In one brilliant insight, Constant saw the nature of modern dictatorship as it has unfolded under Hitler, Stalin, Mao Zedong and the preposterous tyrant Kim Jong-un in North Korea.

How could we free ourselves from this new, and even more threatening, version of arbitrary power? Most clearly, by recognizing that we were moderns and, therefore, by choosing modern liberty. What institutional form was this to take? The first part of the answer rested upon the argument that in 1789 the French revolutionaries had simply transferred the indivisibility of sovereign rule from the absolute monarchy of Louis XVI to the people and then on the suggestion that the unlimited sovereignty of the people was itself even more of a danger than what had preceded it. An indivisible sovereignty in the hands of the one, the many or all would remain an evil. And this was so, as Constant explained, because there is 'a part of human existence which by necessity remains individual and independent and which is, by right, outside any social competence'.[4] This was an argument that was to figure at the heart of J. S. Mill's *On Liberty*.

So, the correct strategy for anyone interested in extending the realm of human liberty was not to attack the holders of sovereignty but to redefine the concept of sovereignty itself, to recognize that no form of sovereignty – including popular sovereignty – was unlimited and that society did not have an unlimited authority over its members. In theoretical terms, this meant hostility to the ideas of Thomas Hobbes and, of course, Jean-Jacques Rousseau. Constant had an ambiguous attitude to Rousseau: like almost everyone else in his day, he could see the genius in Rousseau. But he also saw that the adoption of his ideas by the French revolutionaries had provided 'the most formidable support for all kinds of despotism'. Constant's belief that individuals were the possessors of rights independently of any social and political authority also meant that he rejected Bentham's utilitarian critique of the language of rights. The principle of utility, he believed, encouraged us to place considerations of personal advantage over those of public duty.

The task, therefore, was to set up a form of government that, in Constant's words, could not counterfeit liberty. If the key theoretical underpinnings of this project were sketched out in Constant's lecture, the institutional structure received its clearest statement in an earlier text, *Principles of Politics Applicable to all Representative Governments*, published in Paris in 1815 during the period of Napoleon's first exile. Like many French writers of a liberal persuasion, Constant drew heavily upon the example of English constitutional history for inspiration. He also reworked Montesquieu's separation of powers argument, adding the notion of the monarchy as a 'neutral' power to Montesquieu's already existing tripartite division between executive, legislative and judiciary. The only interest of a constitutional monarch, Constant believed, was the maintenance of liberty and order. He championed ministerial responsibility as well as representative government based on a restricted franchise. Leisure provided education and, therefore, a fitness to participate in politics. In political terms, he favoured landed property over industrial property, fearing that the latter might be a source of social instability.

But how was modern liberty to be protected once the all-important task of dividing up sovereignty had been accomplished? Very unusually for someone writing in post-revolutionary France, Constant endorsed the principles of federalism and of local and municipal power. 'Just as in individual life', Constant observed, 'that part which in no way threatens the social interest must remain free, similarly in the life of groups, all that does not damage the whole collectivity must enjoy the same liberty.'[5] Local self-government would not only produce better outcomes but also prevent the encroachment of the state into affairs that were none of its business. In addition, the army, with its tradition of subordination to the state, had to be reduced in size and prevented from intervening in the internal affairs of the country.

Like many a liberal both before and since, Constant defined the right to own property as one of those all-important rights that existed independently from all political authority. Nevertheless, he saw that property was a social convention and therefore that, to an extent, it did fall under the jurisdiction of society. Constant's point, however, was that, if the ownership of property should not be considered an absolute right, governments should not subject it to arbitrary power. Constant's reasoning here was that the use of arbitrary power over property would soon be followed by the use of arbitrary power over people. In short, it would prove to be contagious. States, Constant acknowledged, attacked property primarily indirectly and in two ways. The first was through such devices as the national debt, where by subterfuge the state effectively defrauded its citizens and despoiled the nation's wealth. The second was through taxation. In Constant's opinion, taxation was a 'necessary evil' but, when pushed to excess, it subverted justice, led to a deterioration of morals and, of course, reduced the capacity of the individual citizen to freely use his or her own money as he or she wished. All forms of taxation had a pernicious effect and were inevitably damaging.

Constant was equally adamant that the state should not interfere in the expression of ideas. The Athenians, Constant observed, ostracized those they disagreed with, casting them into exile. The Romans resorted to censorship. In

Constant's view, without freedom of expression, and in particular freedom of the press, all other freedoms were illusory. Without it, the state could repress at will and society would soon fall into terminal intellectual decline. For Constant, there was perhaps one form of freedom of expression that was more important than any other: the freedom to publicly profess a religion of your choice. Constant's views on religion are themselves very complex. He was raised a Protestant and devoted many years to the study of religion. He believed not only that all our lasting consolations were religious but also that religion was a vehicle to attain to human dignity. In this context, it is sufficient for us to acknowledge that Constant believed that any intervention in the domain of religion by government caused harm. He also believed that the existence of numerous competing religious opinions and sects was good for society as a whole.

All of these arguments placed the stress on the non-interference by the state in the lives of the individual citizen. Modern liberty consists of the right of people to associate with those they wish, to use their property to their advantage (or even disadvantage), to say what they want and to do so with the protection of the law and without fear of arbitrary restraint. This surely explains why Isaiah Berlin cited Constant, along with John Stuart Mill, as an exponent of the doctrine of negative liberty.

Yet we should look a little more closely at the opening quotation from Constant's lecture. There we see that Constant also says that modern liberty entails the right to influence government. This, Constant acknowledged, could not now be done in the way it had been done in the Athens of Pericles, where all male citizens could come together on a hillside, but, he believed, it could be done through the modern invention of representative government. It was through the watchfulness of the people's representatives and the openness of their debates – 'a vivid sense of political life', Constant calls it – that the constitution of the state would be preserved and our individual liberty maintained.

This last point is of considerable significance. The main weight of Constant's lecture falls upon praising the quality of modern liberty. He does not disguise his view that we need a form of liberty appropriate to modern conditions. However, in that lecture, he also tells us that modern liberty contains its own danger, and that danger is that, absorbed as we are in the enjoyment of our private independence and the pursuit of our private interests, we will all too readily and easily give up our right to participate in the discussion of those public matters that affect us all. The danger, in other words, is that we will all simply walk away from politics. And, of course, this was precisely what our masters wanted us to do – just leave it to them and all would be well.

So, Constant's conclusion was not that we should simply embrace the charms of modern liberty. Rather, we had to learn to combine the two forms of liberty. And this, as Constant explained at the end of his lecture, was because it was 'not to happiness alone' that our destiny called us but to 'self-development', and that 'political liberty is the most powerful, the most effective means of self-development that heaven has given us'.[6]

In the twelve years that remained to Constant after he had given his lecture, he spent much of the time working on his monumental study of religion (a text that is soon to appear in English). He did, however, produce one more major political statement: his *Commentary on Filangieri's Work*, published in 1824. Heavily influenced by the works of Adam Smith, Constant's emphasis fell on what governments could or should not do. It was wrong to believe, Constant argued, that governments were either more enlightened or more efficient than individuals and that governments better understood an individual's interests. Governments could do little to make people more moral and generous. The best they could do was to try to ensure that they did not harm one another. Constant argued against restraints on free trade and competition, against controls on emigration and against attempts by the state to limit population growth. Summarizing his position, Constant wrote: the 'idea is that the functions of government are negative: it should repress evil and let the good take care of itself'.[7] Here were ideas that were to become central to the European liberal tradition in the nineteenth century. Here too were ideas that allowed Isaiah Berlin to describe Constant as 'the most eloquent of all defenders of freedom and privacy'.[8] Yet it must not be forgotten that Constant also believed that if we did not participate in the public decision-making processes of our society, if we turned our backs completely upon the ancient liberty of the Greeks and the Romans, then the private liberties we all enjoyed as moderns would all too easily be crushed by a state eager to take them away from us.

4

Jeremy Bentham

Emmanuelle de Champs

Nature has placed mankind under the governance of two sovereign masters, pain and pleasure. It is for them alone to point out what we ought to do, as well as to determine what we shall do. On the one hand the standard of right and wrong, on the other the chain of causes and effects, are fastened to their throne. They govern us in all we do, in all we say, in all we think: every effort we can make to throw off our subjection, will serve but to demonstrate and confirm it. In words a man may pretend to abjure their empire: but in reality he will remain subject to it all the while. The principle of utility recognises this subjection, and assumes it for the foundation of that system, the object of which is to rear the fabric of felicity by the hands of reason and of law. Systems which attempt to question it, deal in sounds instead of sense, in caprice instead of reason, in darkness instead of light.

But enough of metaphor and declamation: it is not by such means that moral science is to be improved.

The principle of utility is the foundation of the present work: it will be proper therefore at the outset to give an explicit and determinate account of what is meant by it. By the principle of utility is meant that principle which approves or disapproves of every action whatsoever, according to the tendency which it appears to have to augment or diminish the happiness of the party whose interest is in question: or, what is the same thing in other words, to promote or to oppose that happiness. I say of every action whatsoever; and therefore not only of every action of a private individual, but of every measure of government.[1]

In the opening lines of *An Introduction to the Principles of Morals and Legislation*, written in 1780 and published in London nine years later, Jeremy Bentham (1748–1832) stated the fundamental principles of a new philosophical system based on a simple and incontrovertible principle, that of 'utility'. These principles were the cornerstones of the legal, political and ethical philosophy he later called 'utilitarianism'.

The principle of utility is asserted at the outset in the form of a scientific rule: human beings are ruled by 'two sovereign masters – *pain* and *pleasure*'. In other words, all behaviour is guided by attempts to avoid pain to oneself, on the one hand, and to increase one's pleasure, on the other. By equating pleasure with 'happiness' and, in turn, with 'interest' and 'utility', Bentham drew on a multifaceted tradition in Enlightenment Europe. At the beginning of the eighteenth century, Bernard Mandeville's provocative *Fable of the Bees* (1714) unveiled the self-interested motives at work behind so-called 'virtuous' behaviour and showed that, paradoxically, 'public virtue' could follow from 'private vices'. Though his ideas were discussed at the time, few were prepared to go as far as Claude-Adrien Helvétius, who refused to equate self-interest with vice. Instead, he argued, interest should be recognized as the only source of virtue (*On Mind*, 1758). In this extract, Bentham follows in the footsteps of the Frenchman when he claims that not only do the quest for pleasure and the avoidance of pain exclusively explain our actions, but that they also legitimate them. For Bentham, an action is ethically good when it increases the quantum of pleasure and wrong when it diminishes it. In other words, utility is the sole 'standard of right and wrong', a normative principle (stating what *ought to be*) as well as a descriptive one (stating what *is*). Logically and ethically, such a proposition is fraught with difficulties: Are we being advised to do what we are already doing?

Leaving these difficulties unresolved in this paragraph, Bentham added that the principle of utility must serve as a guide not only for 'every action of a private individual' but also for 'every measure of government'. Again, despite its apparent simplicity, this statement is open to objections: we can all think of actions that promote our individual interest at the expense of someone else's and of society as a whole. This difficulty is compounded by Bentham's definition of 'public interest' in the pages immediately following this extract. 'The interest of the community', he claimed, is 'the sum of the interests of the several members who compose it' (*Introduction*, 12). Does the extreme pleasure of the master make up for the misery of the slave? On a larger scale, is it legitimate to sacrifice the happiness of one person to the well-being of a greater number? Believing, as Bentham did, that the happiness of the community can be calculated by aggregating individual happiness seems to open the door to all sorts of abuse. Moreover, there seems to be an internal contradiction between this aggregative view of collective interest and the statement that 'the fabric of felicity' must be 'reared by the hands of reason and of law': What can the role of the legislator or of the philosopher be if private interests add up naturally to make up the public interest?

Bentham's rhetorical confidence, his cursory dismissal of alternative approaches that 'deal in sounds instead of sense', should not blind us to the provocative aspects of these opening lines, nor should they obscure the philosophical difficulties that underlie the presentation of the principle of utility as the key to philosophical, ethical and political questions. Bentham's extensive writings can be read as attempts to explore the fields opened by these questions. What is a utilitarian political system? What issues does this raise for the Liberal tradition?

Having identified interest as the root of all human actions, Bentham set out to explore the psychological implications of this statement. In *An Introduction to the Principles of Morals and Legislation*, he took into account the varying sensibilities of different people to pleasures and pains and listed the four sources from which such sensations can flow: the operation of the physical laws of nature, the laws of political society, the actions and opinions of other people or the infinite pleasures and pains meted out by God. Bentham acknowledged the social dimension of pleasure and pain, examining, for instance, the pleasure created by benevolence or good repute or the pain caused by a fine or a prison sentence. Confronted with the variety of pleasures and sensibilities, Bentham insisted that each individual was the best judge of his or her own interest and that no kind of pleasure was in itself more valuable than another (*Introduction*, ch. III–V). Though he does not demonstrate it, he believed that individuals always weigh prospective pleasures and pains, consciously or not, accurately or not, before taking action: 'Passion calculates, more or less, in every man' (*Introduction*, ch. XIV). Utilitarianism, as a philosophy, thus rests on explicit psychological foundations. But whereas we can assume that everyone is guided by self-interest, we cannot claim to penetrate their motives or their intentions. It follows that, from the point of view of civil and political society, the morality or the legality of an act should be assessed only from its consequences on all individuals affected by it, not according to the alleged intentions of its author (*Introduction*, ch. VII–X).

This method was in line with that of contemporary European reformers in the field of penal law. Like the Milanese Cesare Beccaria (*On Crimes and Punishments*

[1764]), Bentham used arguments drawn from utility to argue in favour of clearly expressed rules of law punishing crimes according to their tendency to detract from the greatest happiness of the greatest number. In *An Introduction to the Principles of Morals and Legislation* and *Of the Limits of the Penal Branch of Jurisprudence* (written 1781–2 but only published in the twentieth century) he laid the foundations for a utilitarian analysis of legal systems: laws should issue from a recognized sovereign, be stated in clear everyday language and be accompanied by punishment proportional to the harm caused, not to the alleged intentions of the criminal, legal tradition or the supposed will of God. Only when the legal consequences of their actions are predictable can people use the law as a guide to shape their private behaviour. The English common law system, in which judges derive rules from precedent cases and use an array of technical words and phrases, was thus directly opposed to utility. Beyond penal law, Bentham also called for the codification of civil and constitutional law according to utilitarian standards. Though the idea of codification did not gain much ground in Britain, his ideas were widely influential in the gradual reform of English law that took place in the nineteenth century. Though they remained unpublished until the 1970s, his arguments in favour of decriminalizing homosexual acts are a persuasive illustration of the principle that the law should not punish actions that exclusively cause harm – if indeed any harm is caused – to those who commit them.

In *A Fragment on Government,* published in 1776, Bentham conducted a simultaneous attack on two pillars of the British Establishment: English common law and the British Constitution. He used the principle of utility to expose the fictions, the incoherence and the contradictions of the legal political doctrine presented by William Blackstone in *Commentaries on the Laws of England* (1765–9). He argued that the happiness of the people, and not conformity to a mythical contract, is the only test of good government, and that present obedience is based solely on present interest (in which past habit plays a part), and not on a fictitious original contract, an analysis for which he drew on David Hume's *Treatise of Human Nature* (1739–40). Bentham also criticized Blackstone's argument that the British Constitution combined the qualities of the three classical forms of government (monarchy, aristocracy and democracy) and harmoniously organized executive, legislative and judiciary functions. Though Bentham's main object in this work was to criticize and not to construct a new theory of government, he did however hint at the desirable features of 'a free government' conformable to utility: the source of authority should be clearly stated, power should be established on a secure basis ensuring obedience and people should partake of the power of government by 'frequent and easy *changes* of condition between govern*ors* and govern*ed*'. Crucially, the press should be free to ensure the accountability of rulers.[2] Bentham then actively sought to secure freedom for individuals: freedom from arbitrary power and oppression, freedom to actively participate in government, freedom of the press and of public discussion. These tenets, to which he adhered throughout his life, win him a place in the Liberal tradition.

By calling for open institutions ruling according to, and in favour of, the happiness of the greatest number in 1776, Bentham contributed to the transatlantic debate opened by the Declaration of Independence. However, though he was critical of British institutions, he also explicitly rejected calls for independence. Indeed, the greatest happiness of the greatest number requires stability, and citizens should obey as long as 'the probable mischiefs of obedience are less than the probable mischiefs of resistance'.[3]

A Fragment on Government is not a call to armed insurrection. This early pamphlet exemplifies the specific place occupied by Bentham's political thought: unlike many of his contemporaries, he refused to vindicate the British political system inherited from the Glorious Revolution of 1689, while also refusing to support the American colonists who wished to break with it. Indeed, for him, both sides shared a belief in limited government (the ideas of an original contract and of the separation of powers) that was incompatible with the strongly centralized power, which Bentham considered necessary to utilitarian government, and with the idea that the state had some responsibility in engineering individual happiness. For these reasons, critics have pointed out the illiberal aspects of his system.

The foundations of Bentham's political thought outlined in *A Fragment on Government* help us understand how it evolved in the following decades, in an age of political and institutional experimentation in Europe and in America. Never abandoning his campaign to reform English law at home, Bentham saw more opportunities for political reform abroad. Under the patronage of Lord Lansdowne, former British prime minister and an active supporter of the French Revolution in its early stages, Bentham submitted ideas and pamphlets, in French, across the Channel. Plans for the reform of the judiciary found their way to France alongside those of a circular prison, the Panopticon, in which offenders would be placed under constant surveillance from a central tower, the management of the prison being in turn watched by the general public (see *Panopticon Letters*, 1788). Privately, Bentham also drafted a manuscript, 'Plan for a Constitutional Code for France', in which he explained under what conditions a democratic system of election could ensure the best representation of interests. But, like the British, the French system rested on fictitious theories and principles opposed to the greatest happiness of the greatest number. Among those theories, and in line with his earlier rejection of the fiction of an original contract, Bentham singled out the doctrine of the universal and imprescriptible rights of man. This position followed logically from his theory of law: a law was valid only if it issued from a recognized sovereign and was backed by effective sanctions. Like the American Declaration of Independence (*Introduction*, 310n), the French Declaration of the Rights of Man and of the Citizen failed to meet this test: it proclaimed universal rights without providing the state with the means to implement them. Moreover, by making those rights imprescriptible, the Declaration of Rights tied the hands of future legislators and precluded later adjustments for the greatest happiness of the greatest number. According to Bentham, such declarations could only foster unhappiness and drive citizens to violence when the state proved unable to defend their rights.

In the later years of his life, Bentham's attention turned towards constitutional reform at home and abroad. The *Constitutional Code*, which was begun in 1822 and published in part in 1830 with the subtitle 'For the use of any nation professing liberal opinions', laid out the institutions of a representative democracy geared towards the maximization of happiness. 'One man, one vote' annual elections would ensure that each citizen would be given a chance to select the candidate closest to his own interest (Bentham privately justified opening the vote to women, though he refrained from it in his public proposals), and forums such as political assemblies and a free press would serve as debating grounds in which interests could be weighed and debated publicly. The assembly of the people's elected representatives would be the strongest organ of government, controlling the executive and the judiciary. In order to ensure that, once in power, representatives and functionaries did not favour their own interests over those of the community, Bentham devised a strict system of transparency and accountability. Through popular education schemes and unfettered debates, the political education of the people would prepare them to stand for office to ensure that power changed hands regularly. Bentham's constitutional architecture was thus devised in order to organize and channel the expression of personal interests and translate them into effective policy and legislation, the people keeping a watchful eye on their representatives throughout. If political institutions were set up as a mechanism for the aggregation of interests, they also acted on the way individual interests were expressed and transformed their contents. This, Bentham believed, provided true security against a possible tyranny of the majority.

After the Congress of Vienna in 1815, Bentham offered direct support to liberal groups in Spain, Portugal and Greece campaigning for constitutional reform and the establishment of a free press. He also supported independence movements in South America and voiced arguments against colonial rule. In Britain in the 1820s, his commitment to democratic politics aligned him with radical campaigners. In economics, he remained committed to safeguarding individual property and opposed all but the most gradual redistributive schemes (*Radicalism Not Dangerous* [1819]). A close friend of David Ricardo and James Mill, he also contributed to the spread of classical political economy. In these respects, utilitarianism was part and parcel of the liberalism that developed in Europe in the early nineteenth century and was picked up on by early Liberal movements in Spain and Latin America.

But utilitarianism also posed a challenge to early liberalism. Indeed, as we have seen, Bentham strongly opposed doctrines such as the separation of powers and the rights of man, two mainstays of nineteenth-century political liberalism. Benjamin Constant, who had read Bentham's writings in French translation, was openly critical of a theory that placed self-interest at the centre of political and moral action. For him, without the safeguards of virtue and rights, the rule of interests would lead to oppression and violence. Tocqueville's position was more ambiguous: while he acknowledged the force of the doctrine of self-interest and its relevance to democratic societies, he also pointed out the dangers of unfettered individualism and of withdrawal from public life as the result of citizens focusing on their private happiness.

In the twentieth century, influential liberal thinkers also tended to be critical of utilitarianism. Friedrich Hayek believed that Bentham's system relied too much on the state to affect the junction of interests (*Individualism and Economic Order*, 1948), while John Rawls expressed strong doubts about the liberal credentials of a philosophical tradition that refused to recognize the intrinsic value of human life and the plurality of persons (*A Theory of Justice*, 1971). Though twentieth-century liberals did not recognize Bentham as one of their own, critics did not hesitate to see utilitarianism as representative of the dangers and contradictions of liberalism. From a Marxist perspective, C. B. Macpherson pointed out the fallacies of the kind of methodological individualism adopted by Bentham (*The Political Theory of Possessive Individualism: Hobbes to Locke*, 1962). Postmodern critics such as Michel Foucault believed Bentham's Panopticon prison was emblematic of the covert guidance of individual conduct in contemporary societies, despite their stated commitment to individual freedom and liberal values (*Discipline and Punish*, 1979). Today, these debates continue to shape perceptions of classical utilitarianism in general, and of Bentham's thought in particular.

Bentham's liberalism amounts to more than the preference for a society encouraging the pursuit of private interests with the protection of the state. Indeed, for him, the state is an active force shaping individual interests while also being shaped by them. Without attempting to assess the conformity of his ideas to a predefined 'liberal' ideal, reading Bentham helps us understand how, at a key historical moment in the formation of Western liberalism, utilitarianism shaped debate on its foundational values and brought to light the choices, and perhaps the contradictions, on which it rests.

James Madison

Michael P. Zuckert

We may define a republic to be ... a government which derives all its powers directly or indirectly from the great body of the people; and it is administered by persons holding their offices during pleasure, for a limited period, or during good behavior. It is essential to such a government, that it be derived from the great body of the society, not from an inconsiderable proportion, or a favored class of it. ... It is sufficient for such a government that the persons administering it be appointed, either directly or indirectly, by the people; and that they hold their appointments by either of the tenures just specified. (Federalist #39)

Among the difficulties encountered by the convention, a very important one must have lain, in combining the requisite stability and energy in government, with the inviolable attention due to liberty and to the republican form. ... On comparing, however, these valuable ingredients with the vital principles of liberty, we must perceive at once, the difficulty of mingling them together in their due proportions. (Federalist #37)[1]

James Madison (1751–1836), often described as the 'father of the American Constitution', made important contributions to the development of liberalism as a political orientation. Most significantly, he pondered deeply the problem of how to reconcile what we would call liberal politics, that is, politics aiming to secure rights and liberty, with republican or (as we would now call it) democratic government. Madison's chief contributions to the analysis and solution of this problem occurred in *The Federalist*, a series of newspaper essays later collected into a book aimed at explaining and defending the constitution he helped draft during the summer of 1787. After a disappointing decade or so under the previous constitution, called the Articles of Confederation, some of the leading politicians of the American states concluded that a major reform of the Articles was needed and they prevailed on Congress under the Articles and the various state legislatures to back the idea of a new convention. A convention was called to meet in Philadelphia in May of 1787 and was attended by many of the leading lights of the age, including Hamilton and Madison. The new constitution produced by the convention was deeply controversial, especially in New York, the home state of Hamilton and John Jay. These two, together with Madison, agreed to write a series of articles for the newspapers explaining and defending the new constitution, which became *The Federalist* when the articles were collected as a book. Alexander Hamilton, Madison's collaborator in *The Federalist*, put the problem Madison was addressing very pointedly when he asserted that the 'enlightened friends of liberty'; that is, what we would call the partisans of liberalism, would have to abandon the republican form of government if better models of republicanism were not discovered.[2] Madison's chief contribution to liberal political thought consists of the development of those 'better models'.

Scattered through *The Federalist* is the recognition of a large number of flaws and failings revealed in the historical record of republics that seemed to make that form of governance ill-suited to establishing and maintaining a free or liberal society. One flaw had been well recognized long before Madison embarked on his efforts. The great French political philosopher Montesquieu had argued in his *The Spirit of the Laws* (1748) that whatever virtues republics had, they were at a disadvantage in the international arena because it was in the nature of republics to be small and thus to be vulnerable to larger monarchic or despotic neighbours. Montesquieu's suggested solution to this difficulty was that republics confederate and, in union, acquire the strength to resist larger neighbours. The American colonies followed Montesquieu's advice immediately upon declaring independence in 1776 when they drafted the Articles of Confederation. Unfortunately for the Americans, the nation did not thrive under the Articles; the failures of the Articles prompted the calling of the Constitutional Convention in 1787. Madison's first great contribution to liberal theory was to develop an analysis of why the Articles and other similar confederacies did not succeed in producing the effective and harmonious union Montesquieu had projected. In place of the Articles, Madison proposed a new kind of federal system with a much greater promise of achieving the goals Montesquieu had set out. But, important as was Madison's development of a new kind of federalism, this was not his most important contribution to liberal theory and practice.

His more important contributions are captured in his analysis of three other potential failings of republicanism or democracy as a mode of liberal governance. First, and probably most famously, he diagnosed the problem of majority tyranny and devised a solution to that problem. Second, he laid out the qualities any liberty-respecting and fostering government must have and revealed the difficulties republics can have in meeting these needs. Third, in response, he laid out a plan by which a republic may meet these needs. Perhaps the best way to summarize Madison's contributions to liberalism is that he showed how a liberal regime can be established in a wholly republican manner. Before Madison, the best minds who had turned to that question – Locke and Montesquieu in particular – had maintained that this was not possible: according to them, a liberal regime is possible only on the basis of governmental structures Madison and the Americans deemed non-republican.

Despite seeing himself to be among 'the enlightened friends of liberty' and sharing doubts about the compatibility of liberty and republicanism, Madison, like most of the Americans of his day, was committed to 'that honorable determination which animates every votary of freedom, to rest all our political experiments on the capacity of mankind for self-government' (*The Federalist*, #39). Despite the possible incompatibility between liberalism and republicanism, there was also a deep convergence between them, for, says Madison, 'no other form [than a republic] would be reconcilable ... with the fundamental principles of the revolution'. As Madison understood it, those principles were expressed in the Declaration of Independence, issued in July of 1776. According to those principles, the American Revolution was a thoroughly liberal affair for it was based on 'the unalienable rights' of all human beings and posited the end of government as the security of rights, prominent among which was liberty. So, Madison saw the Americans (and the friends of liberty more generally) to face a dilemma: liberal principles imply republicanism, but republicanism may be incompatible in practice with liberal regimes. A great difficulty indeed.

Madison's definition of a republic in the first extract is central to his efforts to resolve that dilemma. The definition is important for two main reasons: it brings out the principled elements in liberal theory that establish the sole legitimacy of republican government, and at the same time points towards forms of republicanism that can resolve the dilemma Madison faced.

We should note that, in his definition, Madison identifies two sets of criteria: what is 'essential' for a republic to be a republic and what is 'sufficient' for a regime to be a republic. *Essential* is that the government draw all its power directly or indirectly from the great body of the people, and that office holders serve under terms of tenure that makes them, in principle, removable. Being derived from the great body of the people means that no particular class of persons has a claim on power merely by virtue of being who they are. This aspect of the definition rules out many regimes that had called themselves republics and had been called such by political thinkers of the past. So, Rome, to take an important example, had a body, the senate, as part of its constitution that drew its members exclusively from the patrician class. Likewise, the British constitution, considered by Montesquieu to be a republic, had a king who came exclusively from the royal family and a House of Lords drawn from the hereditary aristocracy. No regime with a hereditary element or an official-class-assigned governmental body can meet Madison's definition of a republic. This criterion rules out most of the regimes called republican throughout known history. Only a wholly popular or democratic regime can count as a republic.

Madison believes that this kind of popular republic is mandated by the liberal principles of the American Revolution. He, along with most of his fellow Americans of the age, considered the Declaration of Independence to be *the* authoritative statement of the principles of the revolution. The declaration presents a theory of the origin and purposes of legitimate government, and that theory points towards a republic as defined by Madison to be legitimate. The beginning point of thinking about government, according to the declaration, is human equality. 'All men are created equal' in the sense that nobody has a right, by virtue of what they are or of any qualities they possess, to rule any other person. Thus, nobody has a 'divine right' or a hereditary right to rule. Nor does a right to rule result to any person by virtue of some outstanding quality, such as intelligence, beauty or wealth. Government, that is to say, legitimate rule by some over others, derives from 'the consent of the governed', as the people in principle consent to the existence of ruling authorities for the sake of remedying the ill situation that arises when there is no rule. Under conditions of pure equality, rights are greatly insecure due to the use of illegitimate force by some against others. Government, that is, organized and legitimate coercive authority, is constituted by the people to protect their rights.

Since all legitimate authority arises as described above, it follows that legitimate government is government that recognizes and reflects that origin in rejecting all hereditary and self-selecting power holders. The republic, as defined in its essential character by Madison, is the governmental form that corresponds to the underlying principle of a liberal regime. That essential criterion of legitimate government can be met by a variety of forms of popular government. One might meet the requirement that political power be drawn from 'the great body of the people' by instituting a direct democracy, where the people rule in an unmediated fashion. Madison's good friend Thomas Jefferson, who also was the drafter of the declaration, proposed, for example, a rather different definition of republic from Madison's: 'Were I to assign this term [republicanism] a precise and definite idea, I would say; purely and simply, it means a government by its citizens in mass, acting directly and personally.'[3] The standard of republicanism for Jefferson is what we would now call direct democracy. Madison would agree that the government thus defined by Jefferson would count as a republic, but he would not accept the idea that this was the *only* kind of republic.

If we turn to the conditions Madison identified as 'sufficient' to define a republic, we will see that he is contemplating a form of government much less directly democratic than Jefferson's. It suffices that all office holders be drawn from the great body of the people, directly or indirectly. Madison differs from Jefferson in two important respects. First, he accepts representative democracy as quite sufficient to qualify a government as a republic. Second, he accepts indirect appointment as well. He does not require that all authorities be appointed by the people themselves, but only that they be appointed indirectly by the people. To give a concrete example of what he means: he thinks it perfectly fine that the justices of the Supreme Court be appointed by the indirectly elected president, with the advice and consent of the indirectly elected senate. The judges are thus quite removed from the people in their appointments, in that both senate and president in the original constitution are two steps removed from the people, making the judges three steps removed. By contrast, Jefferson would have judges be elected by the people and thus only one step removed.[4] A more distant relation between people and government is, in Madison's view, acceptably republican. His definition satisfies the principled reason requiring a republic, and his 'sufficient' condition allows the construction of a republic that can work in practice to reconcile republicanism and liberty.

In the second extract, Madison calls attention to a serious difficulty those drafting the American Constitution faced. Since governments exist to achieve certain concrete and objective goals, they need to have certain qualities that enable them to meet those goals. In this context, Madison mentions three qualities in particular: energy, stability and liberty, all within the republican form. His thought here is very complex. As opposed to many of the anti-federalists, who opposed the constitution, and to many contemporary democratic theorists, who believe that the ability to effectuate popular preferences is the one thing necessary to properly constructed government, Madison emphasizes that the needful governmental qualities are multiple. Among these requirements is 'energy', a trait 'essential to' the securing of rights against internal and external threats that is the main business of government (*The Federalist*, #37). Madison understands 'energy' to be the ability to act forcefully and quickly.

Governments must also provide stability, a quality that conduces to one of 'the chief blessings of civil society' (*The Federalist*, #37). By stability, he means a regime marked by regular and infrequently changing laws. Stability in government complements energy by giving the people an environment in which they can act with 'repose and confidence', based on their confidence that the legal environment will be much the same tomorrow as it is today. Where energy activates government, stability activates the people in the sphere of life we have come to call 'civil society', that is, the sub-political sphere of individual and associational activity. Liberty, the ability of the people to act on their own without fear or insecurity, partly results from energy and stability but is a separate requirement as well, because liberty also includes what one may call safety, the guarantee of the non-oppressiveness of government, a quality not automatically supplied by energy and stability.

The plurality of requisite governmental qualities demonstrates that the task of constitutional construction is complex: it is not enough to maximize one desired quality. But the problem of constitutional design is even more complex for there is a great 'difficulty [in] mingling [the desired qualities] together in their due proportions' (ibid.). The difficulty derives from two facts. The first is that the kinds of political structures that tend to produce one quality are antithetical to those that produce the others. As Madison briefly puts it, 'Energy ... requires not only a certain duration of power, but the execution of it by a single hand', while stability 'requires, that the hands in which power is lodged, should continue for a length of time the same', since 'frequent change of men will result from a frequent return of elections, and frequent change of measures, from a frequent change of men' (*The Federalist*, #37 [181–2]). Deeply at odds with both are the apparent structural requirements of 'republican liberty', which 'seems to demand on one side, ... that those entrusted with [power] should be kept in dependence on the people, by a short duration of their appointments; and that, even during this short period, the trust should be placed not in a few, but in a number of hands' (*The Federalist*, #37).

Combining the different qualities seems very difficult indeed, but the task is rendered even more difficult in the American context, for the Americans are committed to doing this strictly within the bounds of 'the republican form'. The definition of republic discussed previously complicates the achievement of the mixture of governmental qualities Madison is calling for. The typical solution to achieving that mixture in past theory and practice was the mixed regime. That regime, as described, for example, by Montesquieu, involved the mixing of different estates or classes in government, with only one part satisfying the Madisonian definition of republicanism. As Madison says of England, which had been Montesquieu's model for such a mixed regime, it 'has one republican branch only, combined with [an unacceptable] hereditary aristocracy and monarchy'. It is therefore not a genuine republic (*The Federalist*, #39, 194). In a proper republic, all parts of the government must be drawn from the people and thus it is even more difficult to achieve the various qualities needed for good governance since the qualities a monarch and a House of Lords might bring, energy and stability, respectively, are unavailable.

Madison's great discovery, which he and Hamilton draw out at length in the pages of *The Federalist*, is that intelligently structured, wholly republican institutions can mimic the operation of the mixed regime and supply the different qualities needed by all good governments. Thus, to simplify considerably, they demonstrate how the unitary presidency can supply energy, the senate stability and the House of Representatives republican liberty. The separated powers, it turns out, are only partly for the sake of the checks and balances with which they are normally identified. More fundamentally, the separated powers, that is, the separate institutions, are for the sake of providing the mixture of necessary governmental qualities.

The point of Madison's less popular, less stringent definition of the republic compared with Jefferson's becomes clear in the context of the discussion of the way cleverly constructed institutions can mimic the non-republican institutions of the mixed regime. Constructing the kind of institutions Madison sought requires a major shift in the way institutional design was conceived prior to him. The older idea, encapsulated in the mixed regime analysis of Montesquieu and others, was that office holders would be recruited from specific parts of society and would bring the needed qualities with them when they entered government. This is especially true of the monarch and the aristocrats, whose family connections, wealth and hereditary status would arm them with personal and psychic qualities that would allow them to bring to government what was needed from them.

Things were very different for Madison. Here, it was not the persons who would make the institutions but the institutions that would make the persons.

The institutions had to be designed in such a way that they would elicit certain qualities in their holders and allow these qualities to be expressed. In all cases, this depended on representation rather than direct democratic governance, and, in many cases, it required the sort of indirect selection, responsibility and dependence that Madison insisted were sufficient to make a republic. The details of Madison's approach to institutional design are impossible to present in the brief space available here, but a careful reading of *The Federalist* will repay the student with myriad insights into how institutions can shape behaviour.

In this short statement, I have omitted Madison's best-known contribution to liberal theory – his notion of the tyranny of the majority and the large (as opposed to the small) republic as the solution to this problem. A close reading of Madison's *The Federalist* (#10) will satisfy the curious about Madison's ideas on this topic. Likewise, I have failed to discuss two other of Madison's major contributions – his doctrine of religious liberty, as expressed in 'Memorial and Remonstrance', and his authorship of the Bill of Rights. These are perhaps Madison's better-known contributions but they are, for all that, not more important than his contribution to the solution of the problem of reconciling liberalism and republicanism or democracy.

6

Tocqueville's New Liberalism

Ewa Atanassow

I know only two manners of making equality reign in the political world: rights must be given to each citizen or to no one. ... One must not dissimulate the fact that the social state I have just described lends itself almost as readily to the one as to the other of its two consequences.[1]

One will never encounter, whatever one does, genuine power among men except in the free concurrence of wills. Now, there is nothing in the world but patriotism or religion that can make the universality of citizens advance for long toward the same goal ...

What I admire most in America are not the administrative effects of decentralization, but its political effects. In the United States the native country makes itself felt everywhere. It is an object of solicitude from the village to the entire Union. The inhabitant applies himself to each of the interests of his country as to his very own. ... He has for his native country a sentiment analogous to the one that he feels for his family, and it is still by a sort of selfishness that he takes an interest in the state.

Thus he has conceived an often exaggerated but almost always salutary opinion of himself. He trusts fearlessly in his own forces, which appear to him to suffice for everything. A particular person conceives the thought of some undertaking; should this undertaking have a direct relation to the well-being of society, the idea of addressing himself to the public authority to obtain its concurrence does not occur to him. He makes known his plan, offers to execute it, calls individual forces to the assistance of his, and struggles hand to hand against all obstacles. Often, doubtless, he succeeds less well than if the state were in his place; but in the long term the general result of all the individual undertakings far exceeds what the government could do.[2]

Alexis de Tocqueville (1805–59) was a liberal, yet, as he insisted, 'a liberal of a new kind'.[3] First among the novel facets of his liberalism was his understanding of the character of modern society and the unprecedented dilemmas it faced. Many of Tocqueville's liberal predecessors, notably Montesquieu and Constant, considered commerce and the social reorganization it involved as that which made society modern. Against this socio-economic thesis, Tocqueville proposed an ethical–political one: not capitalism, but democracy and its core value – equality – is the defining feature of the modern age. Born into an old aristocratic family decimated in the French Revolution (his parents barely escaped the guillotine), Tocqueville was preoccupied all his life with the meaning and causes of this world-historical upheaval. Viewing the Revolution as part of a centuries-long development, he pointed to the soon-to-be-global rise of democracy as the motor behind it.

Modern democracy, for Tocqueville, is premised on the notion of the moral equality of all human beings, and the idea that no one has by virtue of origin or other qualities a precedence over any other person. Not primarily a set of political institutions, democracy is a 'social state', or a condition of society where status is not fixed at birth but must be acquired. Equality, in short, means social mobility: the possibility of rising – and falling – on the social ladder. It also entails a peculiar mindset characterized by the 'ardent, insatiable, eternal, invincible' love of equality itself.[4] Tocqueville credited this egalitarian passion with ceaselessly revolutionizing all aspects of life: economic and political relations as well as the conceptual and moral horizon within which we moderns live. Rather than a static arrangement, democracy so understood is an ongoing process of equalization.[5]

As early as 1835, Tocqueville proclaimed the rise of a comprehensively egalitarian form of life as the distinctive feature of modernity. He believed that, once brought into broad daylight by the eighteenth-century revolutions, the principle of social equality and its counterpart – popular sovereignty – had left no politically viable or morally respectable alternatives. From then on, the primary political question was not whether but how to embody the democratic principle in political practice. Tocqueville expected this question to reach and upturn every corner of the world. From its opening pages, *Democracy in America* announced the impending global democratic revolution and called for 'a new political science' to illuminate and guide it.[6]

Yet if Tocqueville considered democratization 'irresistible', he did not view it as following a fixed path.[7] As the first passage signals, equality is compatible with, and may lead to, two radically different political scenarios: one that postulates universal rights and equal freedoms, and another predicated on an omnipotent centralized state that pursues universal equality by demanding the equal powerlessness of all. Not only does democracy not necessitate a liberal outcome, the drive towards ever-greater equalization makes liberty's prospects ever less certain. Tocqueville's account of the egalitarian dynamic of modernity anticipates the rise of a specifically democratic form of despotism.

To warn against this new despotism, and strengthen democracy's liberal safeguards, was the overarching purpose of Tocqueville's life and work. Wary of theoretical abstractions – another signature of his new liberalism – Tocqueville set out to explicate the promises and dangers of modern democracy by describing what he saw as its paradigmatic liberal manifestation: the American Union, then half-a-century old. Rather than defend liberty in theory, he studied it in American practice, seeking to draw portable lessons from this particular democratic experience.[8] Published in two volumes (in 1835 and 1840), *Democracy in America* gives a comprehensive account of the American polity: its beginnings, constitution and intellectual and moral underpinnings. It also elaborates a diagnosis of democratic ills, for which Tocqueville prescribed liberal remedies.

While the first passage above gives, in a nutshell, Tocqueville's view of the nature and problem of modern society, the second offers a glimpse into his proposed solutions.[9] If the main danger Tocqueville foresaw was the rise of an all-powerful, ever-expanding state, prefigured in the centralizing tendencies of post-revolutionary France, the set of remedies he proposed was modelled on the vibrant associational life he witnessed on his 1831–2 journey to America. Generalizing the American experience, Tocqueville argued passionately for the crucial importance of civil society for liberal democracy. He went so far as to dub the art of associating the 'mother science' on which hangs not only democratic freedom but modern civilization itself.[10]

Among the institutional means of encouraging association, Tocqueville highlights a decentralized system of administration. Our second passage begins with his meeting the most serious objection against such a system: that it would weaken government. In the pages preceding this passage, Tocqueville engages the partisans of centralization on their own turf by revisiting the claim that concentrated decision making is indispensable for an efficient and powerful state. Tocqueville does not deny the need for strong central power: indeed, he expressly affirms it. Yet, questioning what makes a state strong, he contends that 'genuine power' rests not in the ability to compel, but in the capacity to inspire and sustain voluntary obedience. Tocqueville, in short, accepts the professed goal of centralization: an 'active and powerful' government.[11] However, while the advocates of centralization call for consolidating all decision-making capacity, Tocqueville insists on distinguishing between the state's 'administrative' and 'governmental' competencies and (as in the second paragraph of our passage) between centralization's 'political' and 'administrative' effects.

In explaining, at the outset of the section from which our passage is taken, the distinction between governmental and administrative centralization, Tocqueville readily grants that modern society cannot exist without centralized government. Pointing to the medieval principalities and contemporary German states (before their 1871 unification) as examples of a baneful lack of centralization, he maintains that strong central authority is key to a functioning economy, effective foreign policy and the rule of law. And he criticizes, later in the book, the constraints on governmental centralization embedded in the American Constitution (prior to the Civil War amendments) for preventing the Union from governing effectively and from protecting racial minorities against white majority tyranny. In this respect, though admiring the US Constitution, Tocqueville was an insightful critic of American Federalism.[12]

While conceding the need for centralized government to address issues of concern to all, Tocqueville strongly opposed what he called 'administrative centralization' – the idea that the central authority should decide all issues, no matter how local or minute – on the grounds that it was bound to weaken, not augment, state power. For, returning to our passage, real power rests in 'the free concurrence of wills' and there are only two ways to produce this concurrence. Love of country and love of God, Tocqueville claimed, are the two mainsprings of civic dedication that alone can make the 'universality of citizens advance for long toward the same goal'.

Before seeing how a decentralized system helps encourage civic engagement and 'genuine power', we should pause to reflect: In what sense is Tocqueville's advocacy of religion and patriotism liberal? Are not liberals supposed to defend individual freedom against social interference, individualism against collectivism, however justified? This is an occasion to signal another novelty of Tocqueville's liberalism: his pioneering critique of democratic individualism.[13]

Like Constant before him, Tocqueville considered individual independence the quintessential modern liberty. In his view, the desire to shape and direct one's life underpins the struggle for equality and drives it forward. Yet, a central feature of modern society, the drive for individual independence is also its foremost danger. Encouraging an exclusive fixation on private interests and goals, thus blinding citizens to their interdependence and civic duties, it can lead to political disengagement that poses an inherent threat to freedom. Left to itself, individualism can weaken solidarity and the capacity for self-organization by making citizens forget the art of associating and of attaining common ends in common, which, for Tocqueville, is the essence of free democratic governance. At the same time, when each fends only for himself, the need for government to step in and take care of public business is bound to grow. Paradoxically, Tocqueville argued, if taken to extremes, the obsession with individual independence is likely to enlarge the government's power and tip public opinion in favour of expanding central authority. It prepares, from afar, the rise of a paternalist state that dehumanizes less by oppressing than by relieving citizens of their civic and personal responsibility.[14]

So how do decentralized institutions guard against individualism, big government and a self-absorbed citizenry? Decentralized administration means that local problems are addressed locally. Instead of being centred in the capital and wielded by professional bureaucrats, administrative power is scattered and responsibility diffused so as to 'interest more people in public things' (64). Distinguishing between the 'political' and 'administrative effects' of this arrangement, Tocqueville recognizes that the distinction is not clear-cut; he also concedes that there is a trade-off involved. This reflects another characteristic feature of his liberalism: for the most part, one cannot have the cake and eat it too but must choose between competing, often incommensurable goods. Tocqueville readily admits that decentralized administration may not lead to orderly procedures or well-executed public works.[15] Yet, in his view, administrative imperfections are more than offset by decentralization's influence on citizens' mentality. Here, and elsewhere, Tocqueville highlights the effect 'on the very souls' of the citizens, both as an important aspect of institutional analysis and key criterion for political choice.[16]

In light of our second passage, the main advantage of decentralization consists in its fostering participation and, therewith, a sense of ownership and belonging. As the citizens play an active part in public affairs, they come to identify with their community much in the way they do with their family. Seeing themselves reflected in the political order, they regard it as their work and feel its successes and needs as their own. As Tocqueville claims in the next paragraph, by merging the public and private, patriotic identification enlarges the citizens' self-image and encourages trust in their own strength. Though 'often exaggerated', the resulting self-confidence propels them into civic action. Seeing their country's interests as their own motivates individuals to work for the common good. Trusting their own capacity to produce desired change, they voluntarily exert themselves for the 'well-being of society'. The public support required for the success of individual ventures brings home the need to cooperate and promotes a spirit of solidarity. In this way, the civic pride of the Americans energizes their voluntarism and the ensuing social effort 'far exceeds what the government could do'.[17]

In Tocqueville's account, by stimulating patriotic attachment, decentralized institutions activate a virtuous circle: love of country elevates the citizens' self-esteem, which facilitates effective civic action. This, in turn, helps sustain the people's commitment to the democratic order and their self-understanding as being in charge. So, what Tocqueville 'admire[s] most in America' is decentralization's double impact: on the one hand, it strengthens society by diffusing energy and activity throughout the body politic; on the other, it enhances individual agency and cultivates able and confident citizens, eager to take their destiny into their own hands.

Tocqueville, as already noted, stresses the pivotal role of decentralized institutions and active citizenry for liberal democracy. Yet, while praising the 'political effects' of decentralization – increased civic participation and psychological commitment to politics – Tocqueville also points to their downside. His analysis of the psychology of civic spirit signals its problematic cognitive and moral status. Not only is the self-perception fostered by civic pride 'often exaggerated', hence irrational. Because it is premised, like a family feeling, on 'a sort of selfishness', patriotism is morally ambivalent and may, under certain conditions, turn positively menacing. Later parts of *Democracy in America* spell out the nature of this menace: sectionalism and racial pride posed existential threats to the integrity and future of the American Union.[18] Thus, while insisting that decentralized institutions 'are to freedom what primary schools are to science', Tocqueville shows that they are a 'dangerous freedom' which, to be salutary, requires institutional and moral checks, as well as favourable circumstances.[19]

Among those checks, Tocqueville held religion to be especially important. His penetrating discussion of religion's role in modern society is one more outstanding feature of his new liberalism. As our second passage suggests, religion is another way to inspire and sustain civic spirit and 'make the universality of citizens advance for long toward the same goal'. For Tocqueville, in short, religion has an important political function. It is not simply an alternative to civic dedication but a necessary complement to it: by establishing a shared moral horizon, religious commitment helps orient individual and collective choice and poses generally recognized limits on political action. Along with balancing political liberty and guarding against its abuses, religion also helps to strengthen and perfect freedom. Moving 'the object of human action' beyond the immediate and the material, religion calls attention to a larger horizon and a fuller notion of humanity that elevate the citizens' self-understanding and enlighten their interests. By providing, as Alan S. Kahan has argued, indispensable 'checks and balances for democratic souls', religion, for Tocqueville, plays a crucial role in sustaining political liberty and individual flourishing.[20]

Democracy in America offers a case study for the mutually supportive relationship of religion and democracy. Yet it also cautions against extrapolating too mechanically from the American experience. Tocqueville celebrated American society for its religious pluralism, and expressly endorsed the separation of church and state as indispensable means for preserving the power and benefits of religion. At the same time, he made clear that the happy combination of faith and freedom in America was the product of a particular historical development attained in centuries-long religious and political conflicts. While pointing to the separation of religion and politics as a universal good and crucial prerequisite for liberal democracy, Tocqueville made clear that such a separation might not be easily replicated in another political and cultural context, be that of Catholic France or of Muslim Algeria or of Hindu society, which he also studied closely.[21]

Tocqueville elaborated a new liberalism to address what he saw as democracy's unprecedented challenges to liberty.[22] Chief among the challenges he diagnosed is the twin danger of individualism and despotism: the dialectic of withdrawn, feeble citizens and an ever-expanding state. The remedies Tocqueville prescribed were all aimed at encouraging a vigorous civil society and self-reliant democratic citizenry, an example of which he encountered in America. Such a citizenry, he understood well, is a hard-won and inherently fragile achievement that requires delicate political balancing tailored to specific cultural conditions. In highlighting this achievement and describing in detail its institutional and moral mechanisms, Tocqueville's work exemplified the careful attention to 'time and place ... circumstances and men' he demanded in his call for a new political science.[23] He also developed a sophisticated moral psychology of liberalism: a new understanding not only of the social and political, but also of the ethical and psychological preconditions of democratic freedom.[24]

Part Two

Liberalism Confronts the World

Abraham Lincoln's Commentary on the 'Plain Unmistakable Language' of the Declaration of Independence

Diana J. Schaub

Chief Justice Taney, in his opinion in the Dred Scott case, admits that the language of the Declaration [of Independence] is broad enough to include the whole human family, but he and Judge Douglas argue that the authors of that instrument did not intend to include negroes, by the fact, that they did not at once, actually place them on an equality with the whites. Now this grave argument comes to just nothing at all, by the other fact, that they did not at once, or ever afterwards, actually place all white people on an equality with one or another. And this is the staple argument of both the Chief Justice and the Senator, for doing this obvious violence to the plain unmistakable language of the Declaration. I think the authors of that notable instrument intended to include all men, *but they did not intend to declare all men equal* in all respects. *They did not mean to say all were equal in color, size, intellect, moral developments, or social capacity. They defined with tolerable distinctness, in what respects they did consider all men created equal – equal in 'certain inalienable rights, among which are life, liberty, and the pursuit of happiness'. This they said, and this meant. They did not mean to assert the obvious untruth, that all were then actually enjoying that equality, nor yet, that they were about to confer it immediately upon them. In fact they had no power to confer such a boon. They meant simply to declare the* right, *so that the* enforcement *of it might follow as fast as circumstances should permit. They meant to set up a standard maxim for free society, which should be familiar to all, and revered by all; constantly looked to, constantly labored for, and even though never perfectly attained, constantly approximated, and thereby constantly spreading and deepening its influence, and augmenting the happiness and value of life to all people of all colors everywhere.*[1]

Abraham Lincoln is best known as the sixteenth, and arguably the greatest, president of the United States – the statesman who freed the slaves, saved the Union from dismemberment and, in the immortal phrases of his Gettysburg Address and Second Inaugural, explained the meaning of the war and the nature of republican self-government. Lincoln's performance of these consequential deeds was prepared for during the tumultuous decade that preceded the American Civil War. In his antebellum speeches and debates, Lincoln often invoked the Declaration of Independence. By reminding citizens of 'the principles of Jefferson', he tried to rescue 'the definitions and axioms of free society' from the oblivion into which they were falling.[2] In the excerpted passage, written in response to the Supreme Court's 1857 ruling in the *Dred Scott* case (which, among other outrages, decided that blacks had no rights which whites were obliged to respect), Lincoln offered a commentary on the foundational clause of the nation's founding charter.

What does it mean to declare that 'all men are created equal'? What does politics based on such a declaration look like? In answering these questions, Lincoln aimed to correct a dangerous misreading of the declaration put forth by his political opponents. Lincoln's generation, no less than our own, struggled to make sense of the stark contrast between the declaration's ringing endorsement of mankind's natural equality and the existence and persistence of the institution of chattel slavery. Some, like Roger B. Taney (chief justice of the Supreme Court and author of the *Dred Scott* ruling) and Stephen A. Douglas (leading Democrat and long-time Lincoln rival), sought to free the Founders from the charge of hypocrisy by simply reading blacks out of the declaration. They narrowed the application of the declaration's 'all men' to 'all white men'. Lincoln rejected that exclusionary reading as nonsensical. He reiterated the original, expansive and inclusive reading of the declaration. Instead of denying the gap between theoretical principles and political practice, Lincoln honestly acknowledged the gap and the obstacles to closing it. He emphatically reminded his audience that democratic statesmen – constrained as they always are by tradition and public opinion – are not free to 'place' folks, whether black or white, instantly on a footing of full equality. Nonetheless, the words of the declaration are not empty platitudes. Properly understood, they vitalize and guide political life. Lincoln's refutation of his opponents highlights the role that logic and common sense can play in resolving disputed questions. Not all interpretations of the declaration are created equal.

Lincoln begins his explication with a certain narrowing of his own. Human beings are equal, but they aren't equal every which way.[3] They are equal only in a highly specific way. Before specifying that way, however, Lincoln first details some of the manifold ways in which humans are unlike one another. The list he constructs is intriguing. It begins with two visible natural differences: colour and size. If we think about how contemporary liberal society approaches human difference, the first two categories that spring to mind are probably 'race and gender'. Lincoln's categories may have some connection to those, but they are definitely not identical to them.

Let's take colour first. Given that Lincoln's dispute with Taney and Douglas concerned the Founding era's view of black people, it isn't surprising that Lincoln begins by acknowledging a difference that presents itself to all eyes. Human beings don't look the same; they come in different colours. Lincoln, however, does not endorse the essentialism of 'race' as a category permanently fixed (or nearly so) by either nature or history. Instead, Lincoln presents the difference between blacks and whites as a purely superficial difference of skin tone. Moreover, in other writings, he points out that skin tone is not binary (black and white) but a matter of degree (lighter and darker). Thus, he warns slaveholders that if they regard whiteness as a title to mastery, they can't escape the logical conclusion that they themselves should be enslaved to the first person who comes along with paler skin than their own.[4] By speaking of colour rather than race, Lincoln suggests the existence of a spectrum of infinite gradations. Although he highlights the visible difference of colour among human beings, he hints at its individual rather than class character. He bridges the racial divide with a rainbow, such that by the end of this passage he is able to envision 'all people of all colors everywhere' enjoying the inestimable benefits of 'free society'.

What about size? Whereas an individual's 'colour' remains constant, 'size' changes dramatically over the lifecycle. Each of us starts as an extraordinarily tiny, indeed embryonic, being, only gradually attaining our mature form. Even in adulthood, weight (unlike height) is subject to fluctuation. Differences in size are not purely individual since they can be correlated with certain category differences. For instance, adults are generally larger than children; males, on average, are larger and stronger than females. However, mostly what we see is an array of individual differences from short to tall and light to heavy. Size, like colour, is spread along a continuum. Compounded from these two properties, the visible spectacle of humanity is astonishingly varied. What we experience is not sameness, but diversity.

The next (and central) item on Lincoln's list is 'intellect'. He has moved from external to internal differences among human beings. He has also moved from qualities that are given by nature to a quality that is perhaps more complex and ambiguous inasmuch as intellect has long been thought to have both natural and acquired components. Differences with respect to intellect can also be a very significant driver of economic and social inequality. We know that Lincoln's overall aim in this passage is to define and defend the self-evident truth of equality. What we note is that equality, in the sense intended by the declaration, can be upheld while at the same time acknowledging the range of intellect among human beings, a range that presumably entails differences in degree of intellect (from dumb to brilliant) as well as differences in type of intellect (as, for instance, verbal as compared to spatial abilities).

The fourth item on the list is 'moral developments'. The phrase is interesting since it suggests that good morals must be instilled and promoted. Even if there is such a thing as a conscience or an inborn moral compass, it requires support and development. Lincoln perhaps agrees with Aristotle who, quite sensibly, attributed ethical excellence to the combined operation of nature, habit and reason.[5] Because of the effects of early habituation on our moral formation, institutions like the family, the church and the political order itself can profoundly influence, if not determine, the degree of one's moral development. Unfortunately, those institutional influences can be deleterious as well as salutary. Thus, the long-continued existence of an unjust practice like slaveholding (a pertinent example for both the Founders and Lincoln) might compromise one's moral development. Slaveholding had the power to corrupt family life, religious faith and fidelity to the principles of republican self-government. Certainly, Thomas Jefferson worried about the effects of slavery on the moral character of both masters and slaves. In his *Notes on the State of Virginia*, he noted ruefully that 'the man must be a prodigy who can retain his manners and morals undepraved' when faced with the daily temptation to behave as a tyrant.[6] Meanwhile, for slaves, the institution had effects reaching well beyond the immediate loss of liberty and danger to life. Slavery could be expected to lessen the attachment of its victims to the rule of law, private property and patriotism, since those good things had been long misaligned on the side of oppression. By his mention of 'moral developments', Lincoln indicates his acute awareness that human differences are not simply individual in nature, manifesting a range of virtue and vice; rather, those differences can assume intractable social and political shapes which can imperil the achievement of a liberal order.

The final item on Lincoln's list is 'social capacity'. What, one wonders, is this? Lincoln seems to be saying that human beings differ in their ability or power or fitness for social interaction. We know, of course, that there are introverts and extroverts. Extremely shy individuals might find it hard to participate in social activities, while extremely overbearing individuals might find themselves less than welcome at social gatherings. We also know that some forms of social disability are so extreme as to be considered 'antisocial' pathologies. Whatever the range of individual possibilities, we might also wonder whether the notion of 'social capacity' implies that human beings are, by nature, social creatures. Aristotle famously argued that we are not only social, or gregarious, by nature, but political as well, by which he meant that we are justice-seeking beings who must live in political community in order to achieve our highest flourishing.[7] Of course, other political theorists, especially those we term 'modern', have argued, contrarily, that human beings are originally asocial or apolitical, overwhelmingly, or maybe exclusively, concerned with individual self-preservation. Atomized individuals might be driven into political association out of desperation, but they are not drawn there. Lincoln's suggestive phrase does not tell us how he viewed this matter, other than that he thought human beings manifested some degree of difference with respect to social capacity, whether as a result of natural gifts or acquired sensibilities, whether as individuals or political collectives (which might be the beneficiaries of civilizational inheritance). We note also that the previous category of 'moral developments' might have some bearing on this ultimate quality of 'social capacity'. So, for instance, a people with a long history of living under the rule of law – and with the moral developments to match – might be more ready for the rigorous demands of self-government as compared to a people who have suffered under generations of tyrannical rule or a people who have grown used to ruling over others tyrannically. Neither mastery nor slavery prepares one for the peculiar self-restraint at the moral heart of 'government of the people, by the people, for the people'.[8]

A little reflection on Lincoln's list shows how carefully constructed it is – ascending from simpler, physical differences to more complex, multidimensional differences – and how it aims to be comprehensive, capturing the tremendous variety of humanity: in appearance, in faculties and in character. The list also hints at a difficult question: What account, if any, must be taken of these inequalities in a just political system?

Having acknowledged the scope of differences among men, Lincoln returns to the matter of our essential similarity. What is the precise respect in which all human beings are alike? Lincoln quotes directly from the declaration: we possess 'inalienable rights', which is to say, rights that belong to us by virtue of the kind of creature we are. According to Lincoln, there should be no confusion about the meaning of equality. Equality isn't some vague generality. Quite the contrary, the declaration offers a definition of its central concept. Equality means equality with respect to natural rights. Thus, Lincoln binds together the first two self-evident truths of the declaration. He understands the first ('created equal') in light of the second ('endowed … with … rights').

None of the significant differences among human beings, which Lincoln went to the trouble of listing, invalidates the equal entitlement to 'life, liberty, and the pursuit of happiness'. Lincoln's verdict echoes that of the declaration's main author. In a letter to the French abolitionist Henri Grégoire, Thomas Jefferson insisted on the irrelevance of intellectual differences to the truth of equal rights: 'Because Sir Isaac Newton was superior to others in understanding, he was not therefore lord of the person or property of others'.[9] Rights are not contingent on anything but membership in what Lincoln calls the 'human family'. Another of Jefferson's letters, written just days before his death, makes a similar point through a memorable image. The declaration, Jefferson explains, was premised on 'the palpable truth, that the mass of mankind has not been born with saddles on their backs, nor a favored few booted and spurred, ready to ride them legitimately, by the grace of God'.[10] There are no natural rulers – no queen bees or alpha wolves – among human beings. Each is a king onto himself. His 'life' and 'liberty' are his own, to be employed in the 'pursuit of happiness'. The declaration does not claim that its listing of rights is exhaustive; the three mentioned are said to be 'among' our inalienable rights. But like Lincoln's list of differences, the declaration's list of likenesses does aim to be both concise and reasonably comprehensive ('pursuit of happiness', after all, covers a lot of ground).

Lincoln's next step in his explication of the declaration is crucial to his moral vindication of the Revolutionary generation. He considers again what the authors did not intend to say. While they were deadly serious about the truth of human equality (after all, they were staking the justice of their cause on it), they knew full well that not all were, as Lincoln puts it, 'actually enjoying that equality'. Indeed, by their assessment – see the declaration's lengthy list of accusations against King George – they themselves were not enjoying equal rights. To be enjoyed, rights must be secured. The Creator who endowed us with rights did not, apparently, guarantee their actualization or protection. Human beings must perform their own act of creation: bringing into being governments founded on the consent of the governed (which just happens to be the third of the declaration's self-evident truths). In the original liberal understanding, security of rights is the aim of legitimate government.

By focusing on what the Founders did not mean to say, Lincoln reminds his audience of how insecure rights are and how often they are violated. It's not going too far to say that most people in most times and most places have not enjoyed the equality to which they are entitled. What did the authors of the declaration propose to do about this nearly universal disrespect for the rights of man? According to Lincoln, 'they had no power' to set the world (or even their own small portion of it) 'immediately' to rights. Remember, at the time, it was pretty unclear whether the colonists would have sufficient power to reclaim their usurped rights, much less anyone else's. It would take eight years of war against the British Empire to achieve 'the separate and equal Station to which the Laws of Nature and of Nature's God entitle them'.[11]

Having tempered utopian hopes with a sobering observation, Lincoln concludes with two ringing sentences stating what the Founders did mean. They declared 'the *right*', and by doing so generated the expectation that 'the *enforcement*' would follow as soon as possible. Whereas the declaration of right is universal and absolute, enforcement is dependent on circumstances. To take the case of black slavery: by the premises of the declaration, it is undeniable that black persons possessed a natural right to liberty that was being wrongfully denied by the laws and practices of the colonists. The rectification of that injustice would prove no easy or quick matter. As it turned out, it required a civil war, followed by the 13th, 14th and 15th Amendments to the Constitution, and a long, torturous process of societal reconstruction stretching over the next century and into our own. Of course, President Lincoln's issuance of the Emancipation Proclamation in 1863 was a decisive moment in this stride towards equal freedom. But what must be stressed is Lincoln's own conviction that the declaration of right in 1776 was itself epoch-making. It established a lodestar – or what Lincoln calls a 'standard maxim' – guiding incremental improvement, or at least shining the torch of reason on oppression. Without that clearly articulated standard, there would be no inherent pressure for reform. This is a truly new thing: a government that has within it a principle of self-correction. Fidelity to the origins – indeed, fidelity to the point of reverence – becomes the engine of perpetual progress.[12] According to Lincoln, this asymptotic approach to a politically instantiated equality of rights is not limited to the United States. The Declaration of Independence is global in its reach, not because the United States will impose regime change by force, but because awareness of the foundations of free society moves men longingly towards it. Knowledge of the truth ('familiar to all') produces attachment to the truth ('revered by all') which in turn produces action on behalf of the truth ('constantly labored for').

At the same time that the standard maxim catalyses liberal transformation, it also inspires a certain kind of conservatism, since the declaration posits a definition of equality that sets limits to the egalitarian impulse. Equality understood as equality of natural rights is proof against a results-based, homogenizing understanding of equality that aims to eradicate all significant differences among human beings. This is the democratic levelling of which Alexis de Tocqueville warned in *Democracy in America*, gloomily prophesying 'the spectacle of this universal uniformity'.[13] According to Lincoln, holding to the self-evident truths of the declaration is our best resource against the tendency of democracy to degenerate into tyranny of one stripe or another, whether the majoritarian white supremacy of his day or the equal-every-which-way administrative despotism of our own.

Of course, even the 'plain unmistakable language' of the declaration does not settle all disputes. Indeed, the language could be said to prompt partisan struggle over the policy implications and precise boundaries of equality. However, that partisan contention is also moderated when it is structured around a shared vocabulary and an underlying agreement about the linkages between equality, rights and consent. Lincoln helps students of politics understand the partisan dynamic that animates liberalism. Just as important, by returning his audience, both then and now, to the text and its meaning, Lincoln does what he can to perpetuate the declaration's unique contribution to 'the happiness and value of life to all people of all colors everywhere'.

Abraham Lincoln was a statesman, not a political theorist; he spoke of liberty, not 'liberalism'; of equality, not 'egalitarianism'. But Lincoln was as philosophic a statesman as the world is likely to see – deeply thoughtful and truth-loving, and whose contributions to liberalism are significant. In the years of terrible crisis, Lincoln did what was necessary to ensure that democratic government 'shall not perish from the earth'.[14] He also left us clarifying words as great as his deeds. Because liberal political orders depend on the sound understanding of ordinary citizens, Lincoln's speeches remain a permanent resource for liberalism, inviting renewed commitment to our political creed.

John Stuart Mill

Nicholas Capaldi

*The appropriate region of human liberty ... comprises, first, the inward
domain of consciousness ... liberty of thought and feeling; absolute freedom
of opinion and sentiment on all subjects. ... The liberty of expressing and
publishing opinions.... . Secondly ... liberty of ... framing the plan of our life
to suit our own character ... so long as what we do does not harm [others].
... Thirdly ... the liberty within the same limits, of combination among
individuals; freedom to unite. ... The only freedom which deserves the name, is
that of pursuing our own good in our own way, so long as we do not attempt to
deprive others of theirs, or impede their efforts to obtain it. ...*[1]

*The sole end for which mankind are warranted, individually or collectively, in
interfering with the liberty of action of any of their number, is self-protection
... to prevent harm to others. ... There are good reasons for remonstrating with
him, or reasoning with him, or persuading him, or entreating him, but not for
compelling him, or visiting him with any evil. ... Over himself, over his own
body and mind, the individual is sovereign.*[2]

Different versions of liberalism and all modern alternatives to (including
rejections of) liberalism depend on how one understands the relation of the
individual to the community. As a first rough approximation to differentiating
Mill's position from many of the other versions of 'liberalism', we might say that,
for Mill, the autonomous individual is supreme and all social endeavours are
to be judged in terms of the extent to which they serve that autonomy. On the
other hand, there are versions of liberalism that acknowledge the fundamental
and *equal* importance of 'all' individuals (as opposed to 'the' individual) and seek
social contexts within which all individuals can be fulfilled. These egalitarian
liberals do not necessarily advocate a substantive communal good, but they

do advocate a communal responsibility to help liberate all individuals. From Mill's perspective, the egalitarians misunderstand what it means to liberate an individual and they suffer from envy. From a Rousseauean and later Marxist/ Socialist perspective, the espousers of autonomy are at best insensitive or patronizing and at worst exploiters.

This brings us to why Mill wrote *On Liberty*, from which the excerpts above are taken. There are two reasons. First, and foremost, Mill wanted to restate the case for individual autonomy. It needed to be restated, in his estimation, because previous versions, from the seventeenth-century English philosopher John Locke to Jeremy Bentham (a philosophical radical, social reformer, founder of utilitarianism and Mill's godfather) had failed to make a good case. There is no doubt that Mill is writing within the English tradition of civil, political and legal liberties; there is no doubt that he is attuned to the English emphasis on individualism. More important, the restatement also reflects what Mill had learned from the continental German philosopher Immanuel Kant. Mill first discovered Kant through his relationship with the English romantic poet Samuel Coleridge. In his *Autobiography*, and in his essays on *Bentham* and on *Coleridge*, Mill makes abundantly clear that the previous English understanding of 'liberty' needs a better defence, philosophically.[3] In short, Mill believes that he is bringing together in a new synthesis the best insights of the British and German philosophical traditions.

Second, Mill thought that liberty, defined as individual autonomy, was under a new threat, a threat that Mill understood as a too-egalitarian version of liberalism. That threat had been previously identified by the French liberal writer Alexis de Tocqueville. In his enormously influential book *Democracy in America*, that Mill reviewed, Tocqueville identified this threat as the 'tyranny of the majority'.[4] Mill noted in Chapter One of *On Liberty* that liberals in the seventeenth and eighteenth centuries had rightly sought to place limits on government. But, in the nineteenth century with the advent of democracy, other liberals saw in democracy a different way (what we would now call democratic socialism) in which the community through politics and increased governmental power on the one hand, and through the ever more effective power of public opinion on the other, could liberate every individual to achieve fulfilment. The new or different way entailed an increasingly powerful government that could potentially silence dissent. It assumed that human beings lacked freedom of will and reduced all social problems to issues of resource allocation and the panacea of redistribution. In Mill's estimation, this enormous misunderstanding of individual freedom reinforced the importance of restating the case for liberty in a way that reflected what Mill thought was essential to being an individual human being.

Like John Locke who, in the *Second Treatise on Government* (1689), had argued that our right to property was based on the labour we put into developing it, and like the economist Adam Smith who had emphasized the benefits of the division of labour and specialization in his book on the *Wealth of Nations* (1776), Mill understood that human labour and ingenuity were the key both to economic growth and to personal fulfilment. Unlike his predecessors, he did not want to rest the case for individual autonomy on a quasi-religious foundation – either natural rights derived from God as in Locke, or in Smith's 'invisible hand' argument about a natural social harmony. You cannot get universal agreement on these theological or philosophical foundations. Moreover, as much as Mill applauded economic growth, he insisted not only that other forms of human endeavour besides business were worthy expressions of human fulfilment but also that growth was not merely a means to consumption but also to achievement. It is precisely because growth is a means and not an end in itself that his endorsement of a market economy is a qualified one. Moreover, government and law should function to liberate individual development and not serve the bidding of a particular interest group, even if that interest group is the majority. In short, none of the major institutions of modernity or the post-feudal world can be understood apart from a social context which promotes individual autonomy. Therefore, liberalism for Mill is not ultimately about technology, or markets, or 'representative' government, or the rule of law. It is about individual autonomy.

So, how are we to understand autonomy? In the first place, it has no objective end goal or *telos*, as had been argued by the ancients or even by many modern thinkers. Empirical observation belies this ancient claim. Worse yet, those who dismiss the variety of ways in which individuals pursue happiness and insist upon an underlying *telos* inevitably opt for an oppressive social and political structure designed to 'force' them to be free, that is, achieve the requisite end, as Rousseau had urged.

Nor does Mill believe that human beings are totally a product of their environment. Autonomy, for Mill, requires that human decisions must sometimes be undetermined by anything except the choice of the individual will, that is, free will. Any form of determinism would undermine Mill's entire world view. While some adherents of determinism opt for benign philanthropy, others are seduced into Benthamite reductivism about human beings, or worse yet, the totalitarianism as expressed by the French sociologist August Comte. In any case, a coherent and consistent determinism eliminates any notion that one way of life is objectively better than any other or that oppression is inherently evil. Throughout his life, from the time of his nervous breakdown as a young man to his later works, Mill was troubled by the idea that he might not have free will, and wrestled with the relationship of cause and effect with regard to human beings.

By the time of his last major work, *An Examination of the Philosophy of Sir William Hamilton*, Mill was able to articulate a clear statement of the philosophical foundation of human freedom. Mill believed himself to have joined a conversation that was defined by Kant. 'Kant ... holds so essential a place in the development of philosophic thought, that until somebody had done what Kant did, metaphysics according to our present conception of it could not have been continued ... he has become one of the turning points in the history of philosophy.'[5] What Kant had done was reorient our thinking. The ultimate source of intelligibility is neither the physical world nor a supersensible conceptual world, but the practical, everyday pre-theoretical world constituted by the interaction of human beings with their environment and with each other. Any attempt to give a scientific account of how human beings interact with the world and attempt to manipulate the world for practical purposes would itself be an interaction with the world. Any meta-theoretical explanation of the theoretical explanation of practical knowledge would itself be another interaction, ad infinitum.

The human mind, then, is not a mirror of nature but something that interprets and interacts with nature. That interpretation, moreover, presupposes a self that is spontaneously free. Philosophy cannot prove the existence of either a self or of freedom. Individual freedom is a presupposition of daily, common-sense morality. Self-understanding precedes our understanding of everything else. Each individual discovers these things for himself/herself through self-reflection. One of the things we discover is that we can control ourselves, and even change our character by an act of will. It is worth noting that in Chapter Two of *On Liberty*, Mill focuses on freedom of thought and discussion. The most important point he makes in presenting arguments against censorship is that doctrines have no meaning unless the individual thinks it through on his or her own. Character transformation takes place when one thinks for oneself, even if one's thoughts are not original.

In further elaboration of his moral psychology, Mill noted that the will becomes independent of desire. 'Will, the active phenomenon, is a different thing from desire, the state of passive sensibility, and though originally an offshoot from it, may in time take root and detach itself from the parent stock; so much so, that in the case of a habitual purpose, instead of willing the thing because we desire it, we often desire it only because we will it.'[6] This is a point of which Mill will make further use in his later address at St Andrews – the importance of free will for virtue. The problem with the middle class is that they pursued virtue as a duty and not as an end in itself. What Mill urged divinity students to recognize was their capacity to let virtue become an end in itself.

What Mill had presented in his genetic (i.e. historical) account of the development of our moral conscience has the advantage of being inductive or proceeding from individual experiences, of denying the validity of the claim that the sense of virtue is innate or intuitive, of showing how we come in time to discover the importance of autonomy. It is not a matter of association or conditioning, it is a matter of self-discovery, of irreversible emancipatory knowledge, of character formation. Nor can we appeal to social context. There are no hidden rigid substructures to social practice, such that one can predict future permutations of that practice (there are no rules for the application of rules) and no structures that would show the 'hidden' logic of a practice. The application of an understanding of a practice to a *novel* set of circumstances requires imagination. Since no culture dictates its own future, human beings are free to accept, reject or redeploy specific features of their inheritance. Note that this also means that we can never start *de novo* behind what the late twentieth-century philosopher John Rawls called a 'veil of ignorance'.[7]

One of the most important consequences of Mill's conception of human beings as fundamentally free is that no one can constrain another (sane, rational) adult for the alleged best interest of that adult. By definition, nothing can be in the best interest of someone of this sort unless that person has chosen it for herself or himself. Liberty is necessarily understood as negative – restraining others. Liberty cannot be understood positively as obligating anyone to provide resources for others to fulfil themselves. Given this inner freedom, we need to distinguish between 'freedom' and 'liberty'. Liberty, as understood in the British philosophical tradition of Thomas Hobbes/John Locke/David Hume/Adam Smith, is the absence of arbitrary external constraints. When are those constraints arbitrary? They are arbitrary if they violate the inner domain of freedom. Freedom is never licence, but living a life of self-imposed rules. Mill's life was marked by an enormous amount of self-denial and self-discipline. For example, his long affair with his future wife Harriet Taylor did not involve sexual gratification until after they were married.[8] Freedom, for Mill, is a matter of self-discipline in the service of some ideal of the self-chosen meaning of one's life, hence the opening reference in *On Liberty* to German philosopher Wilhelm von Humboldt.[9] It can never involve imposing on others, for to do so is to define oneself in terms of others.

When is the constraint on liberty justifiable? Mill insists that liberty is often granted where it should be withheld, and often withheld when it should be granted. Constraint is justifiable if there is physical harm (violating someone's 'body'). Yet no one should prevent others from exercising their mind in an independent fashion (freedom of the press, education, censorship, etc.). Nor should anyone deliberately undermine anyone's capacity for economic advancement (more on this follows). But the worst form of harm is undermining the autonomy of another person. As Mill stated in *Utilitarianism*, 'the moral rules which forbid mankind to hurt one another (in which one must never forget to include wrongful interference with each other's freedom) are more vital to human well-being than any maxims. … Thus the moralities which protect every individual from being harmed by others, either directly or by being hindered in his freedom of pursuing his own good, are at once those which he himself has most at heart, and those which he has the strongest interest in publishing and enforcing by word and deed.'[10]

As a philosopher, Mill is aware of the objection that the class of free acts might be empty. That is, what happens if everything we do impacts the well-being of others? He answers this objection in the latter part of *On Liberty*. Even if it is the case that everything one does impacts others, the application of constraint is justifiable only if (a) we prove that the harm is real, not merely alleged, and (b) the consequences of the restraining acts are not more harmful than the original alleged harm. In short, the onus is on the constrainer. This principle harkens back to the ancient Anglo-Saxon and British legal tradition in which one is innocent until proven guilty.[11] This deeply ingrained principle is not found in the traditions and current practice of other legal systems, including, and most especially, the civilian tradition represented, among other places, in France. This legal difference is significant even among societies that otherwise all claim to be liberal.

Let us briefly return to the economic issue. When Mill wrote the *Principles of Political Economy* (1848), he announced his support for free markets but insisted that economic freedom rests on different grounds than the points he would later make in *On Liberty*.[12] Why is that? In economic competition (we are not discussing fraud and force) there will be temporary winners and temporary losers. Hence, some will be harmed. However, the advantages of competition far outweigh the disadvantages, in Mill's estimation. Hence, restricting the liberty of commerce does more harm than the harm done to temporary economic losers. 'Even in those portions of conduct which do affect the interest of others, the onus of making out a case always lies on the defenders of legal prohibition.'[13] If we review the major institutions of liberal societies, namely an industrial and technological world view, a market economy, limited government and the rule of law, we can see that all of these so-called liberal institutions are dependent for their meaning on a particular cultural preconception, namely one that espouses individual autonomy. For Mill that is the key to liberalism.

What are we then to make of the question of how the individual relates to the community? In discussing the conditions of permanent political society, Mill noted (in his essay on *Coleridge* from 1840) the need for a feeling of allegiance or loyalty, that is, a feeling for the common good. He claims that the only shape in which the feeling is likely to exist hereafter is in attachment to the principles of individual freedom and political and social equality, as realized in institutions which as yet exist nowhere, or exist only in a rudimentary state. Given Mill's personal emphasis on the supreme value of individual autonomy, and given the rise of nationalism in the nineteenth century, it is important to raise the question of Mill's attitude towards nationalism. 'Nationalism' is here understood both as (a) the recognition of the historical and social context out of which we have emerged or within which we function and (b) an identification with something larger than ourselves. For Mill, this is not as problematic as it may seem. To begin with, he objected to xenophobic forms of nationalism. As he expressed it in a letter to Maurice Wakeman, 'No one disapproves more … strongly than I do of the narrow, exclusive patriotism of former ages which made the good of the whole human race a subordinate consideration to the good, or worse still, to the mere power and external importance, of the country of one's birth. I believe that the good of no country can be obtained by any means but such as tend to that of all countries, nor ought to be sought otherwise, even if obtainable.'[14] Second, individuals who are autonomous seek greater fulfilment and achievement by forming voluntary attachments to other autonomous individuals. That is why, among other things, he focused on the importance of the relationship between men and women. Third, Mill endorsed a form of patriotism that he thought was conducive to a cosmopolitan commitment to helping humanity at large become autonomous. That is why, despite his many criticisms of Britain, he was proud of the role that he thought Britain played internationally in its foreign policy of promoting freedom.[15]

Alexander Herzen

Robert Neil Harris

*We need Europe as an ideal, as a reproach, as a good example; if she were not
so, it would be necessary to invent her. A lie for salvation may be a good thing,
but not all are capable of it. One month ago [John Stuart Mill] published a
strange book in defence of freedom of thought, speech, and the individual; I say
'strange,' for indeed is it not strange that in the country where two centuries ago
Milton wrote on the same theme, it again appears necessary to lift one's voice
'on Liberty.' He decided to speak because evil was growing worse. Milton had
defended freedom of speech against the aggression of authority, against violence.
Mill has an entirely different foe: he defends liberty not against an educated
government, but against society, against custom, against the numbing force of
indifference, against small-minded intolerance, against 'mediocrity.' The constant
depreciation of personalities, taste, and manner, the hollowness of interests, the
absence of dynamism, appalled him; he looks intently and sees clearly, how all
is degenerating, becoming commonplace, ordinary, effaced – more 'respectable,'
perhaps, but more banal. He sees in England ... that generic, herd-like types
are being produced. Shaking his head in earnest, he says to his contemporaries:
'Look – your soul is dwindling away.' The truly important question, which
Mill has not touched upon, is this: are there shoots of new strength which can
reinvigorate the old blood? This question will be answered by events, not by
theory. If the people is crushed, a new China and new Persia are inevitable.
The transition will occur imperceptibly. No right will be abrogated, no freedom
eroded. The sole loss will be the ability to utilise those rights and this freedom!* [1]

During the late 1850s, at the very time that progressive Russian thinkers were
looking to Europe for models of good governance and social amelioration,
Alexander Herzen (1812–70), to the dismay of his close compatriots, unsparingly

attacked Western political, economic and cultural paradigms in the name of his bold and eclectic liberal synthesis of socialist, anarchist and Slavophile thought. The scion of a wealthy Muscovite nobleman, Herzen had left his homeland in 1847, spending his remaining decades in Western Europe. His mature doctrine speaks both to the catholic, transnational appeal of liberal values and to the cultural specificity of his idiosyncratic variant, which is imbued with Russian terms, perceptions and realities.

More a publicist and polemicist than theoretician, Herzen is largely a reactive writer who tends to set his ideas against those of others. Though he rarely engages in the sustained analysis of concepts in their own right, his writings were profoundly influential on following generations of ideologues and activists – from the Populists to Lenin – who fleshed out Herzen's broad outlines according to their own conceptual bent and political inclinations. Among his most striking statements on liberalism and the conditions he considers necessary for its unfettered advance is his 1859 review of John Stuart Mill's *On Liberty*.

A distinct and dissenting voice in the midst of Moscow's emerging intelligentsia, Herzen ardently disputes the supposition that European models will lead to a society in which individual freedom is bound to flourish. Like many of his peers, he had once been 'enthralled' by the West. However, his experience in France, during which he witnessed class division, public unrest and the 1848 revolts, persuaded him that the Continent was 'typhic', an 'ailing organism' in the last throes of death.[2] In his missives from Paris, he highlights the chronic antagonisms, inequalities and social divides which, more than a half-century after the Revolution, continued to impede meaningful progress.[3]

In 1852, Herzen arrived in London, ensconcing himself in a leafy suburb. However, the comfort of England and the fact that he could write without fear of censorship or reprisal was not enough to remove his unsettled thoughts. His warnings – relayed back to his native countrymen – that the West was destined for a 'terrible' future from which Russia must shield itself,[4] were met with accusations of 'contempt for democracy, for the masses, for Europe'.[5] He suggests that his sombre message was scoffed at because these were *his* opinions. Who was he to speak against the lofty ideals of the civilized world and shatter the hopes of his liberal comrades?[6] Herzen sought to expose the West, with its veneer of freedom, as a false idol, but believers refused to listen to such heresy from a fellow Russian – *non est propheta sine honore nisi in patria sua*.

It was, therefore, with a great sense of vindication that Herzen found corroboration for his thesis from an unlikely individual – not an activist or revolutionary, but an eminent logician and former high-ranking civil servant, John Stuart Mill, who exposed flaws that ran deep, not only in contemporary political theory, but in the sclerotized arteries of Western society itself. Mill's essay confirmed, with the authoritative imprimatur of the leading liberal thinker of the age, what Herzen had been suggesting for over a decade. Yet Herzen's essay is less a considered review of Mill's treatise than a springboard to launch his own, more stringent critique of Western liberalism. He is bothered neither by the consistency of Mill's position nor by the problems of the main argument itself. Maintaining that abstract doctrines are unable to provide adequate answers to complex existential questions, Herzen had little interest in the hair-splitting distinctions in which some critics indulged. What so excited him about Mill's essay was its remarkable span and overview, combined with its incisive analysis of the bovine behaviour of the contented masses, the sameness and predictability that was increasingly characteristic of modern society.

Using Mill as a foil, Herzen questions why, if liberal teachings have proven so successful in the West, Mill perceives the need to return to the very theme that Milton long ago had dealt with so admirably?[7] Certainly, in England, where there was an electoral process, a parliament with opposition parties, a robust adversarial press and the right to assemble – civil liberties that Russian reformers could but dream of – was freedom not a fact?

Indeed, in London Herzen had witnessed town hall meetings and lively political debate; he mingled among journalists and activists, and established his own Russian-language press that printed landmark dissident books, journals and pamphlets. Yet he did not conclude that such benefits were enough to justify emulation of Britain, which, he asserts, had failed to create a truly free society. Despite the nation's impressive political achievements and its prodigious economic, military and technological prowess, these advances had not significantly enhanced – and in some respects had actually degraded – the sphere of personal autonomy.

In one of Herzen's most intriguing insights, he observes a disturbing paradox: as the external structures of the liberal nation state expand, providing electoral representation and legal rights, the *inner liberty* of the person appears to decrease, leading to 'moral servitude'. The intolerant throng instinctively steps into the role of the previous enforcers of thought and behaviour, subjecting the nonconforming citizen to the 'torture chamber' of public opinion, which is amplified by the tabloid press. 'The Englishman's liberty is more in his institutions than in himself or in his conscience. His freedom is in the "common law" … not in his morals, nor his way of thinking.'[8] Conversely, in countries where people are 'politically enslaved' and 'powerless before authority,' they are 'morally freer,' with more 'ideas and doubts.' Herzen's object lesson, his most powerful cautionary tale, is Holland, the envy of nations, whose denizens could boast of their ample lifestyle. Of this perfect paradise, Herzen rhetorically asks: 'And so what – what does one gain from such a life? What comes from it?' Having reached the pinnacle of success, the Dutch have become eminently comfortable, yet lacklustre and grey, a nation of businessmen and functionaries chained to the wheel of commerce. Rather than the expected images of happy citizens, Herzen presents the reader with a young man strapped to his desk, a hamster on a career treadmill, working without pause until his departure in a 'posh, varnished coffin.'[9]

'The liberty of the individual is paramount; it is on this and *on this alone* that the true will of the people can develop.'[10] This personal freedom is expressed through distinctiveness, originality and creativity. Representative government has contributed to the fight against oppressive regimes, but it does little for the growth of the individual. 'Democracy is not able to create anything. … It will be a nonsense after the death of its last enemy.'[11] Moreover, it can result in what Adams and Tocqueville referred to as 'the tyranny of the majority'. More insidious than any repressive ruler or censor is the invisible presence of public sentiment, what one might refer to as 'groupthink'. The stifling silence and inertia of foregone conclusions can be as pernicious as any authoritarian government. Modern society needs protection against this 'tyranny' of opinion, ideas, custom and practice.

The values that Herzen champions centre on what Russians refer to as *dukhovnyi*, in the wide-ranging sense of the German *geistig*; that which relates to the non-material elements of the human experience. At the very centre of his doctrine is the Russian notion of *lichnost'*, a vibrance, independence and essential dignity of personality. The mere presence of liberal institutions does not facilitate these inner processes. Moreover, as Herzen well knew from outstanding individuals such as Pushkin, even under despotic rule one may still manage to cultivate one's intellect, character, artistry and humanity to a remarkable degree. The greatest threats to the fashioning of *lichnost'* are not political or legal restrictions but far more intangible dangers. These include blind adherence to custom, a reluctance to stand out from the dull, undifferentiated pack and an uninspiring public sphere. The resulting apathy and passivity continually pull one into the centre and down to the average. This 'mediocrity' – the term, both in Russian translation (*posredstvennost'*) and in the original English, occurs six times in Herzen's review of Mill – is the antithesis of everything Herzen stands for. He extols most of all the productive potential that emerges from breaking custom and routine, from disruption and disorder. Variety, experimentation and chance enable eccentricity of personality, the spice of life, allowing each individual and each generation to make a unique and meaningful contribution to humanity.

The emphasis on *Innerlichkeit* – the ethereal world of the mind and the spirit – is pronounced in Herzen's writings, but this does not mean that he considers concrete factors irrelevant to these internal processes. Impressed by early socialists, including Saint Simon, Owen, Fourier, Proudhon and Blanc, Herzen argues that the economic framework of modern industrialized nations is particularly detrimental to personal development. Although capitalism is often associated with individualism, Herzen regards it as an irrepressible levelling and homogenizing force. Thriving on efficiencies of scale, it dictates standardization and replication, generating not only a uniform material environment but a bland mass culture. A reservoir of independent spirit remains in those who are less affected by the corrosive effects of capitalism and its bourgeois values. Europe's proletariat still display vibrant folk traditions, which Herzen contrasts with the drab lifestyle of the property owner, broker and banker. America, despite its much-vaunted liberty, is much the same as Europe; it is the old world on new soil, 'old buildings from new brick'.[12] With its unabashed market-driven commercialism, it dissipates its creative energy, funnelling it into a single mind-numbing aim: business.

The liberal ethos in Herzen's writings is not expressed as a bald, abstract ideal but within a concrete, historically determined context, for the universality of freedom can only be realized within the consciousness of a specific individual who belongs to a particular era and civilization. The 'true sensitivity of soul' of Parisian workers is 'the product of the life of whole generations, of a long series or organic, psychic, and social influences'; it is a culmination of a received cultural inheritance and the labour of self-development, 'internal work' and 'cerebral activity'.[13] Herzen revels in his encounters with the common folk of Italy, who are marvellously indifferent to the state and to politics. Recoiling from the monotony of bourgeois discipline, their saving grace has been precisely their 'elusive lack of order'. They exude a 'respect for oneself, for personality' and have internalized these values in their daily life.[14]

Yet, these bright flickers of Europe's folk are regarded as the dying embers of a civilization rather than hopeful sparks of rejuvenation. Influenced by the notion of progressive historical stages, Herzen declares that Europe has entered its 'final form ... its coming of age, its maturity'. With the malignant spread of bourgeois aspirations, ensconced in the 'calm, sandy haven of liberalism', all significant growth has come to a halt.[15] The lower classes are 'sad and deserving of compassion' but, bereft of self-understanding, these 'semiconscious masses' will not likely be able to save Europe from its downward trajectory.[16] Grand public gestures, such as extending the franchise to a 'crowd of ignoramuses', will not lead to the formation of a liberal society: 'And what result *could* emerge from *suffrage universal*? Whom could the peasants – voting for the first time, without preparation, without education, under the influence of the clergy, wealthy landowners, and urban bourgeoisie – elect?'[17]

The question of Europe's future, claims Herzen, is glaringly absent from Mill's discussion. If the proletariat is 'crushed' – not by despotism, deprivation, injustice or censorship, but by assimilation into the middle class and the mindless acceptance of vox populi – then Mill's essay will prove to be a eulogy for liberalism in Europe, which will follow the path of other spent civilizations.[18] By contrast, Russia is a virgin land of opportunity. Precisely because of its isolation from world history and the antipathy of its people to the contrived social arrangements of more developed nations, it has escaped the ills of the West.

What, then, is Herzen's vision for a healthy society in Russia? He provides few details. A liberal existence cannot be reduced to a universal formula, and even were this possible, it cannot be dictated to or foisted upon a people. Herzen insists upon the absolute inviolability of the person, who should not be sacrificed or subordinated to any political, social or religious system. In this regard, as one astute commentator has noted, Herzen's liberalism 'is not so much a political doctrine as a mode of resistance against doctrines – an assertion of human freedom against all political projects, including those that claim to serve the cause of freedom'.[19] The pursuit of liberty must be worked out freely by individuals who are conscious, to as great a degree as possible, of their potential to develop the sole elements which are truly theirs – mind, spirit and personality – within an environment that is supportive of this aim. To facilitate this process in Russia, Herzen refuses to endorse any all-embracing programme or ideology, but rather petitions for the right of free speech[20] and the elimination of serfdom and corporal punishment.[21] Even with these major concessions, could Russia succeed where the West had failed? Herzen admits that, in Russia, liberalism as a doctrine remains 'quite alien to the national character',[22] while socialist theory has hardly made inroads beyond a few literate individuals. He suggests, however, that the embryonic seed of a model society already exists in the form of the *mir*,[23] the peasant village commune.

How could a premodern, paternalistic, agricultural society embody Herzen's notions of liberal socialism? By conceiving liberalism as an open-ended process of personal actualization and self-expression, Herzen essentially requires a community that does not exert undue pressure, whether material or psychological, on its members.[24] His idealized image of a harmonious, self-governing *mir*, derived from the Romantic accounts of Haxthausen and the utopian conservative writings of the Slavophiles, was informed by Rousseau's vision of the freedom and equality of pristine man and Proudhon's communitarian anarchism. Precisely because of its remarkably primitive construction and relative lack of controlling administration, bureaucracy or hierarchy, the peasant commune provides a flexible platform, *Spielraum*, in which the distinct *lichnost'* of each associate can achieve true liberty.

However, this is not quite enough to instantiate freedom in Russia. The *mir* represents potential; it does not yet constitute realization. For the latter, the peasants must comprehend their essential nature and seize the opportunity to participate in the historical process of the actualization of liberty – not a simple task for those who are entirely unaware of such constructs and conceptions. Here, Herzen effectively writes himself and a few close associates into this epic historical process. In some eras, there were as few as 'five or six intellects that understood the general contours of the social process and that nudged the masses to the fulfilment of their destiny'.[25] Those with the most highly developed level of consciousness must guide the transformation of society, crafting enlightening essays and socially engaged literature for those who could read[26] and, for those who could not, venturing into the countryside, going 'to the people'.[27] Thus, it will be on Russian soil and with the Russian people – following a Russian *Sonderweg* – that the next important phase of the global iteration of liberalism and socialism will unfold.

Ever the iconoclast, Herzen resisted attempts by his readers to pigeonhole and assign labels to his thought.[28] Notwithstanding his acute criticism of Western liberalism, he incorporates key tenets of European liberal thinkers into his socialist doctrine, which, he conceded, would eventually encounter its own challenges. Herzen believed in no structural or ideological panacea, as national, historical, and cultural factors, along with the vagaries of human behaviour, play a significant role in determining the ultimate efficacy and benefit of any political or social system.

T. H. Green

John Morrow

We shall probably all agree that freedom, rightly understood, is the greatest blessing; that its attainment is the true end of all our effort as citizens. But when we thus speak of freedom, we should consider carefully what we mean by it. We do not mean merely freedom to do as we like irrespectively of what it is that we like. We do not mean a freedom that can be enjoyed by one men or one set of men at the cost of a loss of freedom to others. When we speak of freedom as something to be highly prized, we mean a positive power or capacity of doing or enjoying something worth doing or enjoying, and that, too, something that we do or enjoy in common with others. We mean by it a power which each man exercises through all the help and security given him by his fellow-men, and which he in turn helps to secure for them. When we measure the progress of a society by its growth in freedom, we measure it by the increasing development and exercise on the whole *of those powers of contributing to social good with which we believe the members of the society to be endowed; in short, by the greater power on the part of the citizens as a body to make the most and best of themselves. Thus, though of course there can be no freedom amongst men who act not willingly but under compulsion, yet on the other hand the mere removal of compulsion, the mere enabling a man to do as he likes, is in itself no contribution to true freedom.*

The passage that heads this chapter comes from T. H. Green's 'Liberal Legislation and Freedom of Contract'. This lecture, delivered on 18 January 1881, was doubly credentialed with a liberal pedigree by being given under the auspices of the Leicester Liberal Association in the city's Temperance Hall.[1] Green, Whyte's professor of Moral Philosophy at the University of Oxford and a fellow of Balliol College, was active in local liberal politics. No other work in political theory was published during his lifetime but his teaching and personal example profoundly influenced a range of later writers. Green's moral and political ideas enjoyed a wide circulation after his death in 1882, with his *Lectures on the Principles of Political Obligation* and *Prolegomena to Ethics* being reprinted until the middle of the twentieth century. They played a significant role in the 'new liberalism' which emerged at the turn of the century.

The general philosophical position of Green and his immediate followers (often referred to as the 'British' or 'Oxford' Idealists) was marked by an overt antipathy to the empiricist cast of prevailing British philosophy as represented in the writings of Locke, Hume and the nineteenth-century Utilitarians. It was sympathetic towards, but by no means uncritical of, aspects of Kant's, Fichte's and Hegel's moral and political philosophy. Green identified Kant and Hegel with the idea that the reality of freedom depended on the quality of the objects to which the will was directed.[2] His writings promoted a conception of free action in relation to the fulfilment of human potentiality (or 'self-realisation') that stressed the socially embedded character of individuality. They presented a conception of individual interaction with its locus in the state that evoked aspects of the political philosophy of Fichte and Hegel.

These ideas underpinned the liberal moment represented in 'Liberal Legislation and Freedom of Contract', but that lecture was firmly grounded in the history of practical liberal politics in Great Britain and contemporary debates among liberals in that country. It looked back to liberal objections to aristocratic privilege and class government that were prominent in early nineteenth-century political argument, and forward to the state-sponsored promotion of labour protection, public health and popular education and the questioning of prevailing conceptions of private property rights that characterized 'new liberal' policy at the turn of the century. It advanced a conception of freedom and its political implications that challenged both conservatives and 'classical liberals'. Green's liberal moment is a riposte 'not only on those interested in keeping things as they are, but ... [to] others to whom freedom is dear for its own sake, and who do not sufficiently consider the conditions of its maintenance in such a society as ours'.[3]

Green shared J. S. Mill's commitment to a moral ideal that made liberty a necessary condition of human development, or 'self-realisation'. But his understanding of this requirement was set within a theological framework in which an ideal of human perfection was already embodied in the 'eternal consciousness' or God. He rejected Mill's lingering attachment to hedonistic utilitarianism on the grounds that it substituted a natural object for a moral one, stressing, in a manner reminiscent of Kant, the primacy of a good, and hence rational, will which had the moral goal of self-realization as its object. 'The determination of will by reason ... which constitutes moral freedom or autonomy, must mean its determination by an object which a person willing, in virtue of his reason, presents to himself – that object consisting in the realisation of an idea of perfection in and by himself.'[4] Green used the term 'freedom' to refer to autonomous human agency, that is, the 'freedom of the will', and to 'juristic' freedom: the social and legal recognition of free agency in laws and practices or 'juristic' freedom.[5] He insisted, however, that these forms of freedom were only morally significant when they were integrated with and sustained 'real' freedom, that is, free agency that optimized self-realization. Green's idea of real freedom took positive account of the moral qualities of actions and the motives that impelled them, rather than focusing exclusively and negatively on actors' immunity from compulsion by others. Isaiah Berlin claimed that Green's position involved the dangerous Rousseauean idea that individuals could be forced to be free, but this criticism rests on a misreading. Real freedom consists in doing what is right because one thinks it is right and necessarily involves freedom of the will.[6]

Although Green thought that it made no sense to talk of human improvement 'except as relative to some greater worth of persons', he insisted that the acts through which individuals realized their moral perfection could only be understood in relation to the pursuit of a 'common good'. This object derived from the reliance of individual moral personality on the recognition of other such personalities, and its integration with the eternal consciousness.[7] Shorn of its theological presuppositions, Green's idea of the basis of the common good reflects an embedded notion of individuality similar to that espoused by modern 'communitarian' thinkers.[8] While there were avenues for self-realization – through art or religious experiences, for example – that were primarily individual, Green's idea of the common good drew attention to its collective dimensions and to the social institutions (political forms, law, customs, mores) which helped to secure it. These institutions were expressions of a historically conditioned moral consciousness; they embodied particular understandings of the requirements of self-realization and they harmonized individual efforts to pursue the common good. Contrary to Berlin's characterization, he saw the self-realization of individuals taking place through their *freely* determined pursuit of the common good, whether in the restricted confines of personal relations, through wider community engagement, through the active membership of a political community committed to its advancement or through the genuine recognition of the claims of humanity. Green's 'advanced' liberalism involved the promotion of democracy within political societies and a commitment to liberal internationalism beyond their boundaries.[9]

Liberalism was seen by Green as the underlying creed of all 'genuine political reformers'; it was the most recent fruit of what he termed a timeless 'passion for improving mankind'.[10] While he regarded personal freedom as a necessary condition of human improvement, he argued that the political implications of this requirement varied with time and place. Earlier liberals had focused on relieving individuals from the legal burdens imposed by an oligarchic state presided over by an aristocratic caste. As a result, many layers of aristocratic privilege and corrupt practice had been stripped away, and the parliamentary Reform Act of 1832 and radical changes to local government that followed had begun to democratize British government. Nevertheless, the pursuit of human perfection in contemporary British society continued to be hamstrung by legacies of its feudal past that inhibited the efficient use of resources and the redistributive tendencies of free markets, turned large sections of the urban working class into a self-perpetuating proletariat and reduced the Irish peasantry to a condition of utter degradation. In these circumstances, it was a mistake to restrict reform to freeing individuals from legal constraints. In contemporary debate, this view of liberalism was expressed in terms of resistance to any attempts by government to undermine 'freedom of contract' and the related ideas that individuals were the best judges of their interests, with an absolute right to 'do what they liked with their own'.

Green argued that these claims rested in part on conventional liberals' misunderstanding of the significance of the history of liberal reform in early nineteenth-century Britain. In traditional European societies, where political power was monopolized by aristocratic elites and used to further their interests at the expense of the common good, the liberal cause could be served initially by attacking class privilege in the name of individual freedom. Once this goal had been achieved, however, the impediments to human development arising from the economic and sociocultural legacies of feudalism still remained. Liberals who advanced 'freedom of contract' as a dogmatic axiom of their reforming faith laboured under a fundamental philosophical misunderstanding about the relationship between morality and freedom and the role of rights in giving positive effect to it. When analysing rights, it was useful to consider them in relation to 'a claim of the individual arising out of his rational nature, to the free exercise of some faculty' on the one side and 'a power given to the individual of putting the claim in force by society' on the other, but Green cautioned against seeing these two sides as having any separate existence. The recognition of the claim by others reflected their appreciation of the moral status of the liberty in question as an expression of *rational* will, not merely an expression of will.[11] Free action and the recognition of particular rights in relation to it were not ends in themselves: as the passage above states, 'though ... there can be no freedom among men who act not willingly but under compulsion, the mere enabling a man to do as he likes, is in itself no contribution to true freedom'.

Although Green never offered an explicit critique of 'On Liberty', it is clear that he did not share Mill's distrust of state action as such. In a political environment in which both liberals and conservatives strenuously resisted 'government interference' in the name of individual liberty, the prospect that the state might overawe society must have seemed very distant. More significantly, Green rejected John Austin's Hobbesian and Benthamite idea that sovereign power derived ultimately from the fear of those subject to it. To the contrary, he argued that rulers were obeyed because subjects understood the role that states and law played in furthering the common good.[12] Green thought that this argument explained the moral ground of political obligation and provided the basis for evaluating state action in particular cases. That is, legal enactments had to be considered in relation to their capacity to promote the common good, and could not be condemned out of hand because they infringed on the liberty of subjects or shifted the balance of power and responsibility between government and the governed. In some cases, individuals might 'obey' the law for reasons that had nothing to do with its coercive capabilities, following its requirements out of an appreciation of the role it played in facilitating what was, for all practical and moral purposes, the self-directed pursuit of the common good. Green thus suggested that legally enforced school attendance did not impinge on the liberty of those parents who would, in any case, ensure that their children's educational needs are met.[13] Even where particular interventions relied on the force of law, however, no general principled objections could be made to them if they were necessary to promote the conditions under which individuals could contribute freely to the advancement of the common good. The test here was whether the curtailment of individual autonomy in given cases seemed likely to enhance the general capacity for true freedom in the future.

Green applied this test to proposed measures giving local residents the right to decide whether licensed liquor outlets should be allowed in their neighbourhoods, and if so, their number and location. He argued that the restrictions adopted would reflect the views of those most directly concerned and would not impinge on the freedom of the sober; they would support the resolution of those who were well disposed towards sobriety but open to temptation and reduce the sociocultural impact of public houses on the communities in which they were permitted. These measures clearly impeded free action and in radically different circumstances that might be a matter of regret. Green argued, however, that the extent and intractability of the threat posed to the advancement of the common good by alcohol abuse, and the relative insignificance of the moral potentiality that was being interfered with, justified restricting access to liquor by those whose abuse of it contributed to a culture of crime, domestic violence, the neglect of parental responsibilities and the degradation of the quality of life in working-class neighbourhoods. Since it was not the good of the drunkard that was at stake here, the Millite objection to paternalism did not apply.

Green regarded rights to private property as an instance of the 'powers' that societies recognized as being particularly significant in relation to individuals' capacity to contribute freely to the common good.[14] He considered, but rejected, the idea that private property, economic competition and the other features of capitalist economies were responsible for the existence of a self-perpetuating proletariat. He saw commercial and industrial wealth as virtually unlimited and argued that, provided that the principle of freedom of trade was upheld, the acquisition of property by some did not necessarily preclude acquisition by others. Once the barriers imposed by ignorance, drunkenness and morally debilitating living and working conditions disappeared, all members of the population would have opportunities to acquire morally significant amounts of property – that is, sufficient property to allow them to frame and pursue ways of living that advanced self-realization – without state interference in the accumulation and distribution of commercial and industrial wealth.[15]

These assumptions did not, however, apply to landed property. Land was a finite resource and private property rights in it always carried some risk of monopoly. These rights were open to abuses that restricted the circulation of land, inhibited access to it and reduced the stimulus to effective exploitation of these key resources. In addition, the implications of current patterns of landholding were affected directly by economic, social and moral distortions arising from the feudal origins of modern British society. Industrialization and urbanization swept up a rural population that was already demoralized by poverty and dependence. Moreover, the aristocracy and gentry had used their power and status to maintain practices that were incompatible with the rationale of rights. Thus, while landlords' retention of hunting rights over agricultural land might appear to be justified by reference to property owners right to do what they liked with their own, it ignored the unequal bargaining power of landlords and tenants and compromised efficient production. Devices that ensured the ongoing consolidation of large landed estates by bequeathing them to single heirs and tying their hands as to their future transmission interfered with property-holders rights to dispose of their property in morally appropriate ways, and left agricultural land in the hands of those who often lacked the capital and will to exploit it efficiently. In a predominately rural society such as Ireland, the prevailing pattern of property rights deprived the bulk of the population of access to the primary means of subsistence on terms that were consistent with their moral status and potentialities. Green argued that the ongoing damage arising from these feudal vestiges outweighed any moral or social advantages of allowing landholders to continue to do what they liked with their own, and justified the 'social control of land'.[16] Since such control was necessary to remove barriers to the pursuit of the common good, it was entirely consistent with real freedom and with the rationale of rights. Rights were claims recognized as conducive to the common good, and if some features of prevailing private property rights in land were incompatible with that good, there could be no principled objection to their modification, or indeed, their abolition.

Green's conception of liberalism was based on presuppositions arising from his moral–political economy and involved an understanding of individual liberty that was premised on a socially embedded notion of individuality focused on the common good. This conception of human well-being made the recognition of particular rights conditional on their role in promoting a common good to which the moral good of all individuals was necessarily integral. Green believed that the movement towards democracy in 'advanced' societies opened up new opportunities for ordinary citizens to freely contribute to identifying and furthering the common good within their community and enhancing their scope for self-realization. When he applied these ideas to shaping liberal political programmes, Green focused on issues – the ongoing impact of aristocratic power and values on modern society, popular education, temperance reform, the wider distribution of electoral rights – that were characteristic of mid-century Victorian middle-class liberalism, and continued to accept assumptions about the operation of free-market capitalism that were central to it. These assumptions shaped the policy prescriptions that Green drew from them but they were incidental to the underlying character of his liberalism. As a result, when some late-nineteenth-century liberal thinkers (who were more sophisticated political economists than Green) questioned these assumptions, they were able to utilize his political and moral theory to develop a form of democratic liberalism that regarded extensive intervention in the market, and significant levels of welfare provision, as being necessary to sustain a society which integrated moral (rather than merely legal) autonomy with the pursuit of the common good and maintained material and social conditions where Green's ideal of active citizenship might be realized.[17]

Sarmiento: Liberalism between Civilization and Barbarism

Iván Jaksić[1]

The Argentine Republic at that time [1825] presented a lively and interesting picture. All interests, all ideas, all passions met together to agitate and argue for their cause. Here, a caudillo who wanted nothing to do with the rest of the Republic; there, a people that asked only to emerge from isolation farther away, a government that brought Europe to America; elsewhere, another one that hated even the name of civilization; in some places, the Inquisition was reinstated; in others, freedom of religion was declared the first right of man; some shouted 'federation', and others 'central government'; each of these diverse positions had strong interests and passions, invincible in their support. I need to clear this chaos a bit, to show the role that [Juan Facundo] Quiroga was called upon to play and the great work he should have achieved. To portray the campaign commander who takes power over the city and finally annihilates it, I have had to describe the Argentine land, the customs it engenders, the characters it develops. ... Life in the Argentine countryside ... is not just any accident. It is the order of things, a system of association that is characteristic, normal, in my view unique in the world, and it alone suffices to explain our revolution. In the Argentine Republic before 1810, there were two distinct, rival, and incompatible societies, two diverse civilizations: one Spanish, European, cultured, and the other barbarous, American, almost indigenous. The revolution in the cities would serve only as a cause, as a driving force, whereby these two distinct ways of being in one people would be brought together, would collide, and after long years of struggle, one would absorb the other. I have indicated the normal association of the countryside, the lack of association a thousand times worse than that of a nomad tribe. ... This phenomenon of social organization existed in 1810, and it still exists, modified on many points, modifying slowly on others, and on many still intact.[2]

Domingo Faustino Sarmiento (1811–88) published these words in 1845 while in exile in Chile from the dictatorship of Juan Manuel de Rosas. It was in the freer environment of Chile that Sarmiento wrote the masterpiece that made him famous and became a classic in Spanish-American letters, *Facundo: Civilization and Barbarism* (1845). Sarmiento's political target was not Juan Facundo Quiroga, a regional warlord who was assassinated in 1835, but Rosas, the current dictator of the Argentine Confederation who governed the country with an iron hand and without a constitution from 1829 to 1852. Coming from a provincial background in Western Argentina, Sarmiento was only vaguely aware of the liberal reforms that had taken place in the Atlantic port of Buenos Aires that eventually led to Rosas's takeover in 1829. Sarmiento's views developed not so much from this early liberalism, which he considered abstract to the point of naivety, as from his experience under dictatorship in the 1830s and exile in Chile in the 1840s. It was in the latter nation that he developed a long-term vision for the future of his country.

As the passage quoted above suggests, Sarmiento identified both circumstantial and structural factors in his analysis of the recent history of the Río de la Plata region: among the former, he emphasized the ideological struggles that characterized post-independence Argentina (as in much of Latin America) concerning the establishment of republics after three centuries of centralized monarchical rule. As he recognized in the passage quoted earlier, revolutionary ideas had developed in cities like Buenos Aires, in close contact with European ideas, while the hinterland followed its own pragmatic dynamics in response to regional sources of power. The latter constituted the deeper, more structural elements that gave rise to the dictatorship. In Sarmiento's view, the countryside had prevailed over the civilized cities, led by figures like Facundo Quiroga and Rosas, due to social, cultural and economic conditions that were more influential than imported revolutionary ideas. Among the most important was the lack of a spirit of association, 'a thousand times worse than that of a nomad tribe', characteristic of the Argentine plains that prevented the development of civil society. Sarmiento's views in this respect came directly from Alexis de Tocqueville, whose *Democracy in America* he read for the first time in the 1840s in Chile, and whom he invoked as a model in the introduction of his *Facundo*. Not only did he follow the book's format (beginning with a detailed review of geographic conditions), but some central ideas as well, to the extent that liberty and progress depended on the strength of voluntary private associations. He did not follow Tocqueville entirely, as evidenced by his enthusiasm for centralized political rule and his contempt for indigenous peoples, areas in which the French thinker was, respectively, more sceptical and more sympathetic. Sarmiento's fundamental agenda, as reflected in the passage, became the transformation of the countryside in order to introduce a vibrant civil society based on immigration, the widespread distribution of land for agricultural purposes and free public education.

As stated above, Sarmiento's main target was the dictatorship of Juan Manuel de Rosas. Free from any strong ideological convictions, Rosas governed on behalf of a class of powerful landowners who had opposed the centralizing efforts of the early generation of liberals, the so-called Unitarios, whose centralist constitution of 1826 had offended provincial sensitivities by making governors appointees of the national government. Promulgated in a context of war against Brazil, the constitution alienated provincial interests in other ways as well, due to the demands of the war effort. Rosas's alternative to the form of constitutional government advocated by Río de la Plata liberals in the 1820s was a loose federal structure based on informal alliances that placed the province and port of Buenos Aires directly under his control. Ironically, Rosas did more to unite the country than his liberal predecessors ever accomplished, although at the cost of heavy and often cruel persecution of dissidents. He had established the principle of supreme authority that liberals reluctantly but increasingly recognized as the cornerstone of any viable government. As Sarmiento put it in *Facundo*, thanks to Rosas, 'the Unitarists's idea has been carried out; only the tyrant is unneeded. The day that a good government is established, it will find local resistance conquered and everything in place for the union'.[3] From the safety of Chile (home to many other Argentine exiles), Sarmiento agitated against Rosas, denouncing his abuses of authority while, at the same time, proposing a scenario for liberal development after a putative victory against the dictator.

The vehicle for Sarmiento's twofold strategy was *Facundo*, a book that was part essay, part political pamphlet, part history and part fiction, drawing from the popular technique of *folletines*, or stories delivered in instalments in the thriving Santiago press of the period. Finding inspiration in the writings of Edward Gibbon and the historians of the French romantic school, Sarmiento's main focus was the barbarism that he saw as deeply rooted in the land. Such barbarism was not simply a consequence of the instinctive cruelty that drove Sarmiento's Juan Facundo Quiroga, but rather the product of a land so uninhabited as to lack the fundamental conditions for minimal human association. In that terrain, the absence of settled agriculture, commerce and ultimately civilization, the heartland of Argentina could only produce the gauchos (cowboys of the plains) who lived off cattle and led a fiercely independent life in defiance of any semblance of political order. These plainsmen, according to Sarmiento, would always flock to charismatic leaders like Facundo, perpetuating the lack of any form of civil society. Beyond Facundo, he had in mind other warlords such as José Félix Aldao (1775–1845) and a multiplicity of other minor figures. And yet, his main purpose was to describe the obstacles for the emergence of a national state, and the near impossibility of bringing one about without a deliberate effort to eliminate both the gauchos, along with their leaders, and the conditions that made them possible.[4]

What is most significant about Sarmiento's *Facundo*, as a powerful political tract, is the argumentative dynamics that he skilfully established: if the land produced Juan Facundo Quiroga, and he had been vanquished by someone even more clever and ruthless, then the real and final obstacle for national development was the man who allegedly had him assassinated: Rosas. Sarmiento deployed all his powers as a writer to point an accusing finger against the dictator, whom he made responsible for the ills of Argentina and whose removal was nothing short of an epic struggle between civilization and barbarism.

Sarmiento underscored the authoritarianism of Rosas, but his platform for a successful movement against the regime was a more realistic and determined liberal approach to nation-building than that attempted by the Unitarios of the 1820s. He called upon the younger generation to embrace the ideas of political, economic and cultural development emerging from Europe in general, though especially from France since the Revolution of 1830. On practical grounds, he proposed a policy of European immigration to populate the land that would also be echoed by other members of his generation, like Juan Bautista Alberdi (1810–84), with whom he nevertheless had strong disagreements on matters of national organization. The point was to not only stimulate rural production in the vast expanses of the Argentine territory, but also to introduce the working values that had been squandered by the lifestyle of the gauchos. He concurrently advocated the free navigation of the rivers, especially those tributaries to the La Plata River, to provide more opportunities for agricultural production. Sarmiento added a number of standard policies for national development, including a standing army, a network of transportation and communication, a public education system, civil liberties and freedom of the press. It was a powerful package, one that did not fall on deaf ears, but it would take two decades before Sarmiento could implement some of these cherished policies, when he became president of the nation from 1868 to 1874.

Of all the policies he promoted in *Facundo*, education was perhaps the most central aspect of his overall programme for national development. In Chile, he designed textbooks to facilitate literacy and, with Andrés Bello, advanced an orthographical reform of the Spanish language for the same purpose. In Chile, he observed and contributed to the foundation of the public educational system, which he saw as fundamental for republican citizenship. Visiting the United States in 1847, he was inspired by his discussions with Horace Mann, the founder of the public educational system in the state of Massachusetts, one of the largest in the union. Later, he published a book based on Mann's life and writings, maintained contact with his widow, Mary Peabody Mann (who in 1868 published the first English translation of Sarmiento's *Facundo*) and, as president, invited sixty-five schoolteachers from New England to teach elementary school in the provinces of Argentina.

Sarmiento's emphasis on education as a pillar of the construction of citizenship deserves particular attention because it is more firmly attached to republican than to liberal theory. The republic, in Sarmiento's conception, was not only based on virtue but also involved the central duty of inculcating virtue in its members through education. While he praised and promoted the freedom of citizens to pursue their own interests, Sarmiento placed a higher value on a concept of republic that required civic duties, electoral participation and defence of the homeland, including armed defence, by its citizens. Sarmiento made no distinction in this regard between the native-born and the immigrant, and expected the same allegiance to the republic from both. Immigrants were particularly important, for they could drive the creation of new towns and villages in the countryside. The government would play the role of facilitator for the creation of municipalities, the implementation of free education and the promotion of agriculture in small landholdings. But the entire project rested on a republic of virtuous citizens, educated for that purpose.

Such emphasis on education for republican citizenship may seem at odds with other aspects of Sarmiento's agenda. As president of Argentina, he showed a marked tendency to build the state from above, providing it with the means to crush provincial autonomy should it interfere with the aims of the central government. This emphasis must be seen in the context of a larger liberal concern in nineteenth-century Latin America. What was required in the post-independence context, liberals of the second generation believed, was not so much limiting the power of the state as building it in the first place. Much of the chaos that followed independence had been blamed precisely on the weakness, if not absence, of the state, thus allowing the persistence of corporate groups and enclaves of regional power dominated by figures like Facundo. After the defeat of Rosas, Sarmiento and many liberals of his generation took a decided turn towards strengthening the powers of the central government to confront tumultuous regions and any other challenges from competing interest groups.

After his return to Chile in the late 1840s, Sarmiento developed a clear admiration for the political system of the United States. Sarmiento thus tended to support the autonomy of the provinces under a federal framework, as opposed to the more centralist tendencies of the 1853 Constitution. This was the charter promulgated by the government of Justo José Urquiza after the defeat of Juan Manuel de Rosas, under the inspiration of Juan Bautista Alberdi, which still failed to unite the entire country (this did not happen until Buenos Aires agreed to join the union in 1859, an arrangement sanctioned by the constitutional reform of 1860). At this stage, Sarmiento took a favourable view of the United States. In contrast to the small republics of antiquity, the Renaissance or even Chile, the United States was a large country that in many ways resembled Argentina: vast amounts of available land, a shortage of labour that led to increasing immigration and an enormous potential as a vibrant democratic society where both markets and the institutions of civil society kept gaining strength.

The experience of exile and travel through foreign lands, moreover, helped cement Sarmiento's views with regard to strong government. The Chilean Constitution of 1833, which he saw at work, eliminated the provincial assemblies and replaced the elected governors of the previous 1828 charter with appointed ones. The executive also had the power to suspend the constitution in cases of internal turmoil. Both he and Alberdi agreed that this was one of the fundamental factors that explained Chilean stability for most of the nineteenth century. Sarmiento also had a chance to observe the effect of Abraham Lincoln's decree suppressing habeas corpus in the secessionist states while he was Argentine ambassador to the United States (1865–8). These two concrete examples informed his own policies as president when dealing with internal unrest. There, he found the political and juridical basis for imposing order in the republic.

As Natalio R. Botana has shown, three tendencies coexisted in Sarmiento's notion of republic: 'A forward-looking liberal tradition; a strong republic capable of concentrating power in the State (and combating the still-existing characters portrayed in *Facundo*); and the old idea of a republic inspired by the civic virtue of the citizen dedicated to the public good.'[5] Much of this multilayered approach to nation-building can be explained as a result of the transition from republicanism to liberalism, which took place in Latin America from the early period of independence in the 1810s and 1820s, through the consolidation of liberal institutions (although neither in every place nor at the same time) from the 1850s through the 1880s.[6] Republicanism had been adopted in Latin America as an ideological weapon against the principles of monarchical rule, and as a way to rally the citizenry behind the notions of popular sovereignty, constitutionalism and the division of powers. What is consistent about Sarmiento, who embraced the second, post-1820s version of liberalism, is his lingering commitment to virtue as the fundamental basis for republicanism. In this respect, he was not unique, as even Rosas promoted republican virtue, a facet of his rule that Sarmiento chose to ignore.[7]

Lastly, the question remains as to the particular moment, or insight, that led Sarmiento to develop his political ideas, granting that such ideas usually take time to mature and develop, as they clearly did in his case. Going back to the quote that opens this chapter, one cannot escape Sarmiento's reference to 'the interests' and 'the passions'. In his view, they were both represented in the Argentina of the 1820s. Both had equal status and neither could be subordinated to the other for the larger sake of the public good in either a Hamiltonian or Madisonian sense. They clashed, as tectonic plates, wreaking havoc on the country. Such a situation was inherent in the land, the product of the clash between Europe and America, or civilization versus barbarism, making it nearly impossible to form a viable political society. Writing in 1845, Sarmiento argued that the struggle continued in order to mobilize opinion against the regime of Rosas. Defeating the dictator but using his accomplishments (especially in terms of uniting the region) provided the basis for a new liberal era of national institutions, international commerce and republican virtue. It was an era unlike the exuberant 1820s, perhaps more realistic and effective, but remarkably indebted to the dictatorship it left behind.

Sarmiento's eclectic combination of nation-building elements such as a strong state, education for citizenship and a more pragmatic approach to the necessary equilibrium between national, state and local institutions stands as the most significant rethinking of republican ideas, from a liberal standpoint, in nineteenth-century Spanish-American political history. His views developed, not as an exercise in theory, but as a product of reflecting on unsuccessful earlier nation-building experiences, a concrete engagement with the implementation of national institutions and a drive to adapt liberal philosophy to local conditions.

Namik Kemal's Constitutional Liberalism: Sovereignty, Justice and the Critique of the *Tanzimat*

H. Ozan Ozavci

The truth is in our [country] we [the people] are the sovereign, we all have the right to participate in government. But we delivered to the [Ottoman dynasty] the right to govern with a legitimate bi'at, ... we [only] demand legitimate governance. ... I believe that the Ottoman community [Islamic community] ... want freedom, but if they forget that this quintessence is a divine favour and seek favour elsewhere, they would derogate their glory and undermine their interests. Since I was born free, why would I agree to abstain [from my rights], why would I silently permit, by accepting their legitimacy, the recurrence of deeds that enslave me?[1]

General freedom is safeguarded within society because society can provide a preponderant force to secure the individual from aggression on the part of another individual. ... Correspondingly, the service rendered by society to the world consists of the invention of such a preponderant force, which is absolutely indispensable for the protection of freedom that the maintenance of humanity is dependent upon. ... Just as all individuals have the natural right to exercise their own power, so too aggregate powers naturally belong to all individuals as a whole, and therefore in every community the right to sovereignty belongs to the public.[2]

[Can] the origins of laws [be found in a principle] which we seek in the universe? Or is it in the human will? The latter cannot be accepted in one form because the human will is either absolutely free or bound by certain limits. If it is absolutely free, no individual would want to acquiesce to the provisions set by other individuals. Nor can they be duly forced into these. If individuals are

bound by certain limits, what are these limits? ... In our understanding, they
consist of the good (husn) and the bad (kubh) created by the ruling [divine]
power in nature. Therefore, law refers to the indispensable relations emanating
from human nature in accordance with the absolute good.[3]

The author of these passages, Namik Kemal (1840–88), was an ardent advocate of constitutional monarchy in the late Ottoman Empire. According to Berkes, he was the first Muslim 'to understand the real essence of liberalism and the meaning of the sovereignty of the people'.[4] In Kemal's view, everyone ought to have the right to participate in government through a constitutional and parliamentary system, because sovereignty belonged to the people. The foundation of the state was constituted by the consent of the people, who possessed inalienable natural rights. Yet by means of a lawful *bi'at*, which can be defined as 'a form of allegiance through which the position of the ruler is legitimised', the right to govern the execution of the government was delegated to the Ottoman dynasty.[5] For this dynasty to remain legitimate, it had to ensure that the state was executing its main purpose, that is, the protection of the natural rights of the people through a constitution and a system of checks and balances. A leading member of the constitutionalist Young Ottoman movement, Kemal believed that the survival of the Ottoman Empire was dependent upon the introduction of a new liberal government.

A prolific writer of influential and highly popular political tracts, plays and poems, in his mid-twenties Namik Kemal became one of the most prominent literati of his time in Istanbul. The originality of his political thought lay in the fact that he sought to reformulate Enlightenment liberalism into an Islamic world view as a hybrid political ideology.[6] Moreover, he was an entrepreneur of emotions, addressing his audience's hearts as much as minds through his enthusiastic poems on liberty, along with his proto-nationalist plays and political tracts. In this emotional sense, Kemal was a romantic liberal. Longing for the introduction of basic natural rights to his motherland, he ardently strove to popularize such liberal ideas as freedom of opinion, freedom of the press and equality, by linking what might prima facie be seen as 'alien' Enlightenment doctrines to Islamic political thought and disclosing 'familiar' elements (or 'analogous structures') in them.

Kemal was a man with a cause. He led with great fervour an intellectual and patriotic campaign against what he held to be predatory Western political and economic encroachments on the late Ottoman world and the cold-blooded rationale of the *Tanzimat* (Reforms). He believed that these reforms were nothing but Western impositions. His liberalism thus bore features emanating from the political milieu in which he lived and wrote: reactionary, proto-nationalist and protectionist, as well as romantic.

In this chapter, I will seek to address three questions about this romantic Ottoman liberal. Who was Namik Kemal? How did he come to formulate his political thought and become one of the most prominent writers of his time? And how did he seek to synthesize the teachings of the Enlightenment and Islam in his writings?

Namik Kemal's liberal ideas were born amid the political, economic and moral tensions of a steadily disintegrating empire. Since the late eighteenth century, the increasing Russian threat in the north, mounting secessionist movements by non-Muslims under the influence of the nationalist ideals of the French Revolution and Western powers' concomitant encroachments had been threatening the territorial integrity and sovereignty of the Ottoman Empire. For security and survival, the Sublime Porte allowed the incorporation of its markets into international trade with free trade treaties in the 1830s. These treaties significantly amplified the privileges of foreigners and stipulated the abolition of all types of monopolies and other mechanisms of economic control, heavily hitting local manufacturers and artisans. Moreover, with the aim of assuring European powers of Ottoman willingness for liberal transformation, an edict was declared in Gülhane Park in 1839. Authored by reform-minded Mustafa Reshid Pasha (1800–48), the edict was a statement of intent granting equality before the law to both Muslims and non-Muslims.

The Gülhane Edict marked the beginning of a continuous administrative and political modernization in the Ottoman Empire, a period known as the *Tanzimat* era. During the *Tanzimat*, a large number of institutions ranging from the first post offices and the consultative assembly of ministers to military schools and universities were established. Consequently, the Ottoman bureaucracy expanded rapidly and political power gradually shifted from the hands of the sultan into those of the bureaucrats. Shifts in power sparked an intra-elite struggle within the Ottoman bureaucracy, partially due to the seeming failure of the *Tanzimat*. Reforms could not prevent the growth of grave financial problems. Domestic rebellions and border disputes continued in the Balkans and Mediterranean islands, and a horrendous civil war erupted in Syria in 1860, which paved the way for further European intervention in Ottoman domestic affairs. These complications engendered a patriotic reaction among certain bureaucrats against the inefficiency of the *Tanzimat* as well as Western encroachments.

Interpersonal rivalries figured largely in this fight as well. When Mustafa Reshid fell from the Grand Vizierate, Reshid's rivals for the office of Grand Vizier, namely Ali and Fuad Pashas, created their own team of bureaucrats and excluded Reshid's protégés. While the latter formed the backbone of the opposition, Namik Kemal would emerge as one of their leaders.

In June 1865, at a picnic party in Istanbul, the excluded civil servants established a secret society called the *Meslek* (the Method). Inspired by the Carbonari movement in Italy, the members of the *Meslek* called themselves the Young Ottomans (Türkistanin Erbab-ı Şebabı) and came to be known in Europe widely as the *Jeunes Turcs*. A witness and the first historian of the society, Ebuzziyya Tevfik (1849–1913) tells us that its major goal was to introduce constitutional government in place of absolute monarchy, but no other source confirms this.[7] As a matter of fact, it is difficult to determine what brought these men together other than their collective opposition to Ali and Fuad Pashas and their pandering to the demands of the Great Powers. They were a group of diverse character where their social backgrounds and dispositions, worldviews, writing styles and political aims were concerned. Namik Kemal shortly became a leading figure of the movement, in the limelight more often than most due largely to his charisma and his writings' popularity.

When the *Meslek* was founded, Namik Kemal was twenty-five years old. He was originally from an aristocratic family. His father was the chief augur of the palace who dealt with supernatural affairs that at times directly influenced the sultan's political and social decisions. Kemal received a formal secular and an informal religious education, mastering French as well as Arabic. In 1863, he entered the Translation Office as a civil servant, which opened the doors for him to a stream of new ideas.

The Translation Office was an institution of special importance for the establishment of lasting synergies between European and Ottoman political thought. Many leading bureaucrats, including Ali and Fuad Pashas, served at the office at the start of their careers. Almost all Young Ottomans also worked as clerks at this bureau and acquainted themselves there with Western political systems and ideas.[8] European writings such as the plays of Molière and Voltaire or the works of Adam Smith and Ricardo were studied or translated into Ottoman Turkish at this office. Their encounter with Western political thought influenced many civil servants of the bureau.

In the internecine struggles of the Sublime Porte, all figures inspired by Western political ideas were modernists of some kind. What distinguished the Young Ottomans from the ruling *Tanzimat* elites were their differences of opinion about the type of government needed and the methods necessary to maintain political and cultural integrity. Ali and Fuad Pashas, who alternately held the positions of Grand Vizier and Minister of Foreign Affairs between 1858 and 1871, saw the survival of the Ottoman Empire in a wholesale political and administrative transformation.[9] They were both admirers of 'Western civilization' and mesmerized by nineteenth-century colonial languages that revolved around the concepts of 'civilisation' and 'humanity'.

In their understanding of the *Tanzimat*, 'civilisationism' (*medeniyetçilik*) was the mainstream ideology, where 'civilisation' referred to giving individuals absolute security and 'their blessing with order and wealth'.[10] Ali and Fuad therefore placed great importance on the protection of individual rights and on the limitation of arbitrary rule through law. Yet the two *Tanzimat* reformists preferred an authoritarian state with an expanded *meşveret* (consultancy) to the sultan rather than a constitutional regime. They favoured the Austrian or Prussian model of enlightened absolutism, and sought to create a similar structure in the Ottoman Empire – a rule of law where the sultan's power would be limited by *meşveret* while the executive power would remain in the hands of a few competent men.

This was where the attacks of Namik Kemal and other Young Ottomans began. Kemal believed that the attitudes of Ali and Fuad Pashas built up 'dissonance and strife' between the high bureaucrats, 'as high as the walls of the Bosphorus, and the people at the lower end. The government perpetually tyrannized, the people permanently remained in desolation.'[11] He instead suggested the sharing of political power between the sultan, the bureaucrats and the people by opening a parliament that would be the voice of the latter.

In 1867, the liberal opposition to the Sublime Porte was reinforced by the support of the Egyptian prince, Mustafa Fazil Pasha, who, in an open letter in *La Liberté* on 24 March, pointed out to the sultan the failure of the *Tanzimat* and demanded a transformation of the empire through a comprehensive constitution. In response, the Porte curtailed liberties in Istanbul. The Press Law was amended to tighten controls, and Kemal was suspended from journalism indefinitely. Upon this, along with other leading Young Ottomans, Kemal fled to France. The group joined forces there with Mustafa Fazil Pasha, who provided generous financial support to the movement to publish their journals *Muhbir* (Informer) and *Hürriyet* (Liberty). Kemal stayed in Europe until 1870, after which he returned to Istanbul and continued his struggle in the capital. Six years later, the model he designed for the Ottoman Empire, namely a constitutional monarchy with a parliament providing representation for all, would be officially promulgated.

Namik Kemal published some of his most significant tracts in *Hürriyet* during his voluntary exile in Europe. What distinguished him from other liberal writers of his time was not only his systematic formulation of a political philosophy but also the emphasis on religion within this philosophy.

The series of essays titled '*Usul-ü Meşveret Hakkında Mektuplar*' ('Letters on a Constitutional Regime') that appeared in *Hürriyet* in 1868 and 1869 were Namik Kemal's first attempts to crystallize his liberal formulation. In this work, Kemal delineated the basic teachings of liberalism, such as the inviolable natural rights of the individual, the separation of powers and a constitutional system of government. He maintained that the main reason for the failure of the *Tanzimat* was the fact that the execution of justice, legislation and administration were all gathered in the hands of the leading bureaucrats. This did limit the powers of the sultan, but it made things worse, worse than the old regime, because the new regime not only failed to protect the basic rights of the people but, by introducing pseudo-liberties, it allowed for further foreign interference and gave rise to existential threats and grave economic and political problems.[12]

Therefore, Kemal suggested, the *Tanzimat* regime had to be replaced by a new system, which would threaten the liberties of the individuals less. In his view, given the realities of the Ottoman Empire, this new system ought to be none other than constitutional monarchy. He argued that the parliamentary and constitutional regime that Napoleon III established in France after decades of political turmoil and instability was the system that the Ottomans could take as a model. Now that constitutional regimes had already proved to be the most efficient and widely accepted regimes in the 'civilized' Western world, they did not need to rediscover America.[13] Kemal was candid enough in his 'Letters' to accept that there had to be an element of imitation in the Ottoman transition to a constitutional regime. Yet he suggested the articles of the French Constitution and the 1839 and 1856 Edicts be fused to respond to the demands of Ottoman society, their ethics and customs.

Just as Ali and Fuad Pashas, Namik Kemal also wrote about fostering harmonious relations between the various religious and ethnic groups (millets) of the empire. His method, however, did not rest on a wholesale transformation. Unlike the secular postulates of Mustafa Fazil Pasha, in Kemal's political philosophy one finds a clear attempt to marry Islamic practice and religious law with Western political thought. While borrowing the ideas of 'national sovereignty' from Rousseau and 'separation of powers' from Montesquieu, Kemal strove to show that these ideas were already present in Islamic political thought, which was why he sought to use Islamic terms such as *meşveret* as counterparts of European political practices. The question was how transition to liberal governance and a harmonious empire could be possible under Shari'a, when about 40 per cent of the subjects of the sultan were non-Muslims.

The answer to this question that we can find in Namik Kemal's writings rests on the inclusive role of liberal institutions and a philosophy of justice. He believed that the representation of non-Muslims in the parliament (i.e. their participation in law-making mechanisms) would allow them to enjoy equal rights with Muslims and get their voices heard. They would be granted a new space to express their discontent, instead of resorting to violent conflict, which would also reduce the risk of further secessionist movements. Rights and liberties guaranteed by the rule of law and a parliament where non-Muslims would be represented would serve as the new social glue for a united Ottoman identity.[14]

According to Kemal, justice did not necessarily exist in what the majority chose or found most useful. Laws were required to limit the natural rights of individuals in order to protect the rights of other individuals. For Kemal, the main question was how the limits of individual rights were to be defined. The individuals themselves could not define or decide this, because, if it was left to the individuals, the limits might not be recognized and anarchy might prevail. He therefore underscored the importance of a source of law other than popular sovereignty. 'That source was the *husn* (good) created by God in nature. Right was determined according to the degree to which human beings conformed to the abstract good.'[15] Individual rights and limits could then be limited through laws conforming to the *husn* (abstract good). And the *husn* would be decided upon not through the *fatwa* (a ruling) of the Sheikh-ul Islam (religious leader), but through *fiqh* (the theory or philosophy of Islamic law) and the Shari'a laws, which had been a product of centuries of experience and which would be adapted to contemporary needs. Kemal thus endeavoured to underscore the importance of a home-grown written code drawing inspiration from the teachings of Islam, which would replace the arbitrary rulings of the Sheikh-ul Islam. Yet he remained ambiguous on how and why non-Muslim elements would be subject to an Islamic constitution. It is uncertain if Kemal was ever aware of this contradiction, or the fact that the Divine Law of the Shari'a was incompatible with the separation of powers.[16] For Kemal, the political principles of Islam were 'entirely' compatible with civilization, progress and the modern understanding of justice that the two entailed.

Where the economy was concerned, given the grave financial situation of the empire and his antipathy to increasing Western encroachments legalized by free trade treaties, Kemal was an overtly anti-imperialist, defensive and protectionist liberal. He opposed the premature incorporation of the Ottoman peasantry into the capitalist world.[17] His liberalism was determined more by a commitment to constitutionalism, separation of powers and an inclusive understanding of justice than a comprehensive defence of freedom in all spheres, including the economic and moral.

Namik Kemal's writings were widely read and used by generations of modernist thinkers in the Islamic world, such as the Persian Jamal ad-Din al-Afghani and the Russian Muslim Ismail Gasprinksy. That being said, perhaps the most direct fruit of his work was the 1876 Constitution and the establishment of the first Ottoman imperial parliament.

Forming an alliance with liberal-minded statesmen such as Midhat Pasha and with the backing of liberals in Europe, the Young Ottomans contributed to the dethronement of Sultan Abdulaziz and his replacement by Abdulhamid II in 1876 on the condition that the new sultan would promulgate a constitution. Having lost their lives in 1868 and 1872 respectively, Fuad and Ali Pashas were no longer in the picture. A constitutional monarchy was declared for the first time in the Ottoman Empire in December 1876. Namik Kemal sat on the committees that drafted the first imperial constitution.

The Ottoman experience with constitutionalism in the 1870s was a short-lived one, however, due to the Russian war of 1877–8 and the parliament's inability to take urgent decisions in times of crisis. After Sultan Abdulhamid II 'temporarily' suspended parliament and the constitution in 1877, Namik Kemal was once again sent into exile where he occupied himself with writing a political history of the Ottomans until his death in 1888.

A new political struggle for constitutional monarchy began thereafter at the hands of a new generation of writers and statesmen, namely the Young Turks. The Young Turks, who keenly read Kemal's work, embraced his proto-nationalism and constitutional liberalism. They staged a revolution and brought back constitutional monarchy in 1908 and intermittently held political power in the next decade. Their understanding of political liberalism differed from that of Kemal due to their secular and positivist propensities. Following the fall of the empire in the aftermath of the First World War, a new generation of Young Turks founded the Republic of Turkey based on the principles of national sovereignty and secularism in 1923.

Kemal's liberalism was central to the history of liberalism in Turkey, though his appeal to Islam in formulating his ideas and his seeming failure to address the political demands of non-Muslims would mark the dichotomous and divisive element between conservative and secular liberals in Turkey for decades to come.

Khayr al-Din Basha

Nouh El Harmouzi

There can be no doubt that the hostile action against property cuts off hopes,
and with the severance of hope comes the severance of activities, until finally
destitution becomes so pervasive that leads to annihilation. ... Among the most
important things the Europeans have gathered from the lofty tree of liberty are
the improvements in communications ... with these societies the circulation
of capital is expanded, profits increases accordingly, and wealth is put into the
hands of the most proficient who can cause it to increase. ... We have seen
that the countries which have progressed to the highest ranks of prosperity are
those having established the roots of liberty and the constitution, synonymous
with political Tanzimat. Their people have reaped its benefits by directing
their efforts to the interests of the world in which they live. One of the benefits
of liberty is complete control over the conduct of commerce. If people lose the
assurance that their property will be protected, they are compelled to hide it.
Then it becomes impossible for them to put it into circulation. In general, if
liberty is lost in the kingdom, then comfort and wealth will disappear, and
poverty and high prices will overwhelm its peoples. Their perceptiveness and
zeal will weaken, as both logic and experience reveal.[1]

Khayr al-Din (1820–90) was prime minister of Tunisia and grand vizier of the
Ottoman Empire. He was the author of Tunisia's 1861 constitution, the first
written constitution of a Muslim-majority country, and of the book entitled *The
Surest Path* (1867). Nevertheless, Khayr al-Din is an often overlooked figure,
despite his influence on Muslim constitutional movements in the Ottoman
Empire. Born in the Caucasus region, probably between 1820 and 1830, in his
youth he was taken as a Mameluke slave to Istanbul. After thorough training in
various fields such as martial arts, court etiquette and Islamic studies, Mamelukes

were freed. However, they were still expected to remain loyal to their master and
serve his household. Khayr al-Din was later resold to an agent of Ahmad Bey of
Tunis. He was given a modern as well as religious education by Ahmad Bey. In
addition to Arabic, he learned French and spent four years in Paris. His world
view was based on an education which was formed both by his Islamic culture
and his Western experience.

From Mameluke slave to Grand Vizier, the life of Khayr al-Din was an
exceptional example of meritocracy. He rose through the ranks of the Tunisian
government and became prime minister and a key promoter of reforms,
including a more transparent and lighter system of taxation, the insertion of
secular subjects in the education offered by the country's key teaching mosques
and acceptance of the need for a ruling council with real powers to advise and
legislate on behalf of the ruler, the Bey. Threatened by Khayr al-Din's attempts
to limit his power and wishing to preserve his authority, the Bey ended up
dismissing Khayr al-Din in 1877.[2]

Khayr al-Din's success in putting Tunisia on firmer financial footing, staving off
colonial advances by the British and French consuls, and his advocacy of limited
liberalization and representation came to the attention of the Ottoman sultan
Abd al-Hamid, who promoted him to Grand Vizier of the Ottoman Empire in
1878. Khayr al-Din's attempt to advance a programme of reforms was short-lived,
however, and he was dismissed in 1879. Remaining in Istanbul, he dedicated the
last years of his life to writing *The Surest Path*. He died in 1890. As an author, Khayr
al-Din was inspired by and often quoted the book of the well-known fourteenth-
century Muslim historian and thinker Ibn Khaldun.[3] Both Khayr al-Din and Ibn
Khaldun wrote their books after renouncing political life. The two books analyse
the problem of the rise and decline of states, and each consists of an introduction,
presenting general principles, and several parts. The difference is that Ibn Khaldun's
book deals with the history of Muslim dynasties, while most of Khayr al-Din's
analyses the history, political structure and military strength of European states.
The importance of the work of Khayr al-Din lies in the introduction to his book.
At the beginning, he explains the two aims of his work:

> First, to persuade and urge those who are fervent and determined among
> statesmen and Oulamas (religious scholars) to adopt, as far as they can, whatever
> is favorable to the welfare of the Islamic community and the development of its
> civilization, such as the expansion of the boundaries of science and learning
> and the preparation of the pathways which lead to wealth and are the basis of
> everything.[4]

His second aim was to warn members of the Muslim community against closing their eyes to what is laudable and in conformity with their own religious law in the practices of believers of other religions, simply because they have the belief engraved on their minds that all acts and institutions of those who are not Muslims should be avoided. Inspired by what he saw during the four years he spent in the strongest and most advanced modern countries, Khayr al-Din wanted to show the roots of civilizations' strength. He argued that, in his time, the surest way to strengthen Muslim states was by borrowing ideas and institutions from Europe. He wanted to convince orthodox Muslims that to do so was not contrary to the Sharia, that is, to Islamic religious law, but in harmony with its spirit.[5]

Khayr al-Din posed the question of the separation and limitation of powers, based on both Western experience and Islamic tradition, and he can be considered the first Middle Eastern constitutionalist. He aimed to depersonalize power and substitute the rule of law for the arbitrary rule of an individual. In his book, he explained that justice is the only rigorous basis for the state, and that in normal situations the only guarantee of justice is the limitation of the power of the rulers.[6] There may be a ruler who acts rightly due to his innate goodness and the knowledge given him by reason, but such men are rare, and there is no assurance that they will continue in the paths they have chosen.

In addition to being inspired by the experience of the European nations of his time, Khayr al-Din also understood the importance of limiting powers from a religious perspective, according to which checks and balances on power are needed for humanity to thrive. According to Khayr al-Din, the power of the ruler should be limited in two ways: first by law, either revealed or natural (Sharia law or Al Qanun al Aqli natural law), and secondly by consultation. There are two classes whom the ruler should consult, the Oulama and the notables or businessmen (*a'yan*). They must be able to speak freely, ensure that he is following the right path and prevent him from doing evil. With the exception of a ruler with innate rectitude, the best state is that in which both types of limitations exist, and stable laws are guarded by those qualified to interpret them. The Islamic community in its original form and during the golden age of Islam was such a state, and as long as it respected these rules, it had been prosperous, strong and highly civilized.[7]

Khayr al-Din believed that the Islamic community could only recover its strength if it learned the lessons of Europe and adopted those that were not contrary to the Sharia. But what exactly were those lessons? As a soldier and statesman, he was concerned with both military and economic strength. But he was convinced that strength was a product of something else: material power depended on education, and education in its turn depended on political institutions. The basis of Europe's strength and prosperity was political institutions based on justice and freedom, in other words, responsible ministries and parliaments. Liberty, Khayr al-Din claimed, needs to be understood in three senses: 'One is called "personal liberty"; this is the individual's complete freedom of action over himself and his property, and the protection of his person, his honour and his wealth. He is equal to others before the law so that no individual need fear encroachment upon his person or any of his other rights.'[8] While Ibn Khaldun viewed injustice as the root cause of the empire's decline, Khayr al-Din pointed to lack of freedom as the source of social, economic and political problems. He asserted that the absence of liberty would lead to poverty and rising prices.

The second meaning of freedom is political. Political liberty reflects 'the demand of subjects to participate in the politics of the kingdom and to discuss the best course of action'.[9] Alongside these liberties, 'there remains to the public something else which is called freedom of the press, that is people cannot be prevented from writing what seems to them to be in the public interest, in books or newspapers …. Or they can present their views to the state or the chambers, even if this includes opposition to the state's policy'.[10]

In short, Khayr al-Din's contention is that welfare and material prosperity are not possible without freedom of the person, of the press and of participation in government. Freedom stimulates men to work by giving them the assurance that they will collect the fruits of their labour. Additionally, economic prosperity is not possible without the free movement of goods and people, and the free economic association to which the Islamic Golden Age and modern Europe owed its material achievements. He also stressed that if Muslim countries attempted to adopt the objective reasons behind European progress, they would not be adopting Christianity. They would simply be adopting the modern equivalent of the early institutions of the Islamic community. He is at pains indeed to make the parallel clear. What are the characteristic institutions of modern Europe? They are responsible ministers, parliaments, freedom of the press. But the modern idea of the responsible minister is not very different from the Islamic idea of the good vizier, who gives counsel without fear or favour, and parliaments and press are equivalent to 'consultation' in Islam. Members of parliament are what the religious scholars and notables were in the Islamic State, 'those who bind and loose'.[11]

In confronting the most sceptical and recalcitrant clerics of his time, Khayr al-Din referred to the need of reinterpreting religious texts in the light of social and economic changes, while never denying the divine origins of those same texts. Khayr al-Din stressed a well-known Islamic doctrine, which emphasized the importance and the necessity of pursuing whatever benefits the majority of people as long as it is not in contradiction with the spirit of religion. He also emphasized the need to contextualize judgements according to time and place. In light of this, a rule which made sense at certain point in time in a specific place may become obsolete and irrelevant as humanity advances. Khayr al-Din was well aware that he needed to argue in favour of his positions from a religious perspective in order to be heard and to deliver a message that would resonate with the ruling elites of his time.

By asserting that the success of European nations was mainly due to strong institutions, and that the decline of previous civilizations was caused by the decay of such institutions, Khayr al-Din argued for the need to reform and replace the Ottoman institutions of his time. He must have been aware that such reforms had to be realized in an incremental way and that they would collide with the interests of a certain elite. Nevertheless, he deemed those reforms necessary for the Ottoman Empire and continued to preach them, even at the high cost of his own dismissal.

Khayr al-Din focused on the objective conditions for the success of liberal reforms, including, among others, education, respect for the rule of law and greater government accountability. Unfortunately, the reforms actually undertaken in the majority of postcolonial North African and Middle Eastern countries overlooked those preconditions. Today, the work of Khayr al-Din on the importance of strong institutions is still relevant. In Tunisia, the long-entrenched authoritarian regime was forced to give way to popular pressure for change. However, this change carries no guarantee that a democratically accountable system will emerge, as the removal of a dictator represents only the beginning of the end of authoritarian governance. Profound reforms are indeed needed, and high expectations for quick change may lead to a great deal of disappointment.

On 2 August 2012, not too far from the town of Borj Ali Raiis in Tunisia, after relentless efforts, Professor Abdeljelil Témimi was able to find the grave of Khayr al-Din. In 1968, the Turkish authorities had agreed to return the remains of the grand vizier to Tunisia with the condition that an honourable mausoleum be built for him as a tribute. Despite the agreement with Turkey, the remains of

Khayr al-Din were placed in a vacant government office before being discreetly buried. In a long article published by Al Maghreb newspapers, Professor Témimi condemned this marginalization of a national Tunisian figure, which he attributed to the oversized ego of former Tunisian president Habib Bourguiba. This story may also indicate a desire to erase the legacy of early liberal reformers in the region, thus making it easy to allege that liberal ideas are inspired by outside forces and have no home-grown roots. Khayr al-Din's life and work may serve as an appropriate refutation of this claim.

Jacob Burckhardt's Dystopic Liberalism

Alan S. Kahan

The great harm was begun in the last century, mainly through Rousseau, with his doctrine of the goodness of human nature. Out of this plebs and educated alike distilled the doctrine of the golden age which was to come quite infallibly, provided people were left alone. The result, as every child knows, was the complete disintegration of the idea of authority in the heads of mortals, whereupon, of course, we periodically fall victim to sheer power. In the meantime the idea of the natural goodness of man has turned, among the intelligent strata of Europe, into the idea of progress, i.e. undisturbed money-making and modern comforts, with philanthropy as a sop to conscience. ... The only conceivable salvation would be for this insane optimism, in great and small, to disappear from people's brains. ... A change will and must come, but only after God knows how much suffering.[1]

Men are no longer willing to leave the most vital matters to society, because they want the impossible and imagine that it can only be secured under compulsion from the state. ... Absolutely everything that people know or feel that society will not undertake is simply heaped onto the daily growing burden of the state. At every turn, needs grow, bearing their theories with them, and not only needs, but debt, the chief, miserable folly of the nineteenth century.

Now power is of its nature evil, whoever wields it.[2]

Our task, in lieu of all wishing, is to free ourselves as much as possible from foolish joys and fears and to apply ourselves above all to the understanding of historical development. ... Out of the jumble and confusion we shall win a spiritual possession; in it we want to find not woe, but wealth.[3]

There are many Jacob Burckhardts. The best known is the Renaissance Burckhardt, thanks to his masterpiece *The Civilisation of the Renaissance in Italy*

(1860). There is Burckhardt the founder of cultural history, one of the great masters of historiography, despite his contempt for such professional discussions. There is Burckhardt the disturbingly accurate prophet of the disasters of the European twentieth century. There is Burckhardt the great friend and great opponent of Nietzsche. The list could be extended almost indefinitely. But all the different Burckhardts on the list would have one thing in common – that there was something in each one to make readers of every political stripe uncomfortable, liberals included. He liked Bismarck no more than he liked Jews – which was not at all.[4] He was equally as contemptuous of the view that laissez-faire could save the world as of the view that the government could do so. Both views were entirely too optimistic about human nature.

For Burckhardt, 'liberal' was more often a term of abuse than of praise. Nevertheless, he was a liberal. His quarrel with the liberals of his day (he was born in 1818 and died in 1897) was that he saw them as complicit in the destruction of the foundations of liberal society. Regardless of who or what was responsible for it, however, the future Burckhardt foresaw was grim. He thought so for solidly liberal reasons. As a liberal, Burckhardt wanted to limit power, especially government power, because of the cruelties and savagery it would otherwise inevitably inflict. Burckhardt's liberalism was a 'liberalism of fear', such as the one described by Judith Shklar.[5] He regarded power as evil, and saw it as becoming ever greater and more concentrated. This was a necessary consequence of Burckhardt's view that human nature was not good, *pace* Rousseau, but rather a mixture of good and evil. Burckhardt would have regarded Shklar herself as an insufficiently fearful liberal because she still believed that a liberal society could be preserved in the modern world. Burckhardt's was a dystopic liberalism, a liberalism constructed with (or despite) the expectation that illiberal forms of social and political organization would triumph in the near and medium term.

Burckhardt feared for nothing less than the end of European civilization, the end of the freedom, diversity and individuality that, in his view, were its hallmark. The sources of his fears are described in the quotations above. First of all, the modern state, no matter who ruled it; second, democracy, in both Tocquevillian senses of that word, namely the broad effects of equality and, in particular, universal suffrage; and third, commercial society, that is, the effects of a globalized capitalism, to name only his most pressing concerns. All three were linked to the optimism that had conquered European culture, which encouraged people to hope for too much from power, and to fear it too little.

The modern state, in Burckhardt's view, was acquiring unheard-of powers, and using them for unheard-of purposes. While the form of the state was increasingly open to question, its power and scope were ever greater. People wanted the government to do things; they had become capable of forcing governments to carry out their wishes, and in order to carry them out the state grew ever more powerful – ultimately at the expense of the people. In short, the state was acquiring, with its unprecedented new power, an unprecedented capacity for evil.

Burckhardt largely identified political democracy with threat rather than with opportunity, at least in the modern context (he thought differently about medieval and Renaissance city republics or the *polis*). Nineteenth-century democracy provoked in him the fear of despotism rather than an anticipation of liberation. With the growth of democracy, and especially of universal suffrage, all limits on the state were doomed to disappear. Not that Burckhardt had some better political alternative in mind. He foresaw an alternative to ever-increasing popular demands and ever-growing state intervention to carry them out, but it was not a happy one: 'As long as some power doesn't shout: Shut up! That power can really only emerge from the depth of evil, and the effect will be hair-raising.' Burckhardt foretold that the end of universal suffrage would be a period of 'sheer, unlimited violence, and it will take precious little account of the right to vote … . Such is the inevitable end of the constitutional state, based on law, once it succumbs to counting hands and the consequences thereof.' For those reading Burckhardt during and after the Great Depression and the First World War, with fascism and communism in mind, the meaning of his dark words about democracy seemed clear.[6]

Burckhardt was also afraid of the consequences of what to many liberals seemed naturally good, namely the rise of a commercial society and global capitalism. For Burckhardt, after the French Revolution 'money' became 'the great measure of things, poverty the greatest vice'. The pursuit of greater material well-being was equally all-absorbing for rich and poor. This all-consuming passion encouraged the masses to make ever-greater demands. Driven purely by materialism, the only remaining universally acknowledged standard left, people were willing, in Burckhardt's view, to sacrifice their desire for freedom, their individuality and their diversity whenever necessary to preserve their wealth. Many liberals envisaged a limited state as merely a means of protecting property. Burckhardt thought that they were pursuing a chimaera. The same materialistic impulse which made them want to restrict the state in order to lower their taxes and maximize their profits worked in the opposite direction among the masses, whose equally strong materialism and optimism led them to strengthen the state so that it could fulfil their desires. And the state itself was liable to take control of all the vast wealth created by society, for the purpose of feeding its own insatiable appetite for power.[7]

Burckhardt's fear of modernity did not lead him to become a conservative, however. He did not believe that conservatism had any future, and he was alive to all the defects of its past. There was no golden age, past, present or future, in Burckhardt's view. Although there were some shining moments in European history, all had their shadow sides. He definitively debunked the notion of fortunate and unfortunate periods in history in his *Historical Reflections*. Nevertheless, the period he liked best is revealing. 'We ought never to forget Renan's words about the period of the July Monarchy [1830–48]: "those eighteen years, the best that France ever experienced, and perhaps humanity!"' Yet even they were 'a mere intermission in the great drama'. In the French July Monarchy, where, by contrast, Tocqueville saw an ultimately unbearable stagnation, Burckhardt saw merely a pause in the process of the destruction of European civilization.[8]

According to Burckhardt, nothing was likely to prevent the decline of Western civilization from continuing. While he found attempts to revive the past fruitless (the existing dynasties were merely the 'managers and messenger boys of mass movements'), he saw no remedy for the dangers Europe faced. Although other liberals, notably other 'aristocratic liberals'[9] such as John Stuart Mill or Tocqueville, shared many or even all of Burckhardt's fears, Burckhardt's degree of pessimism was unique among nineteenth-century liberals. He discounted the effects and even the desirability of all the usual liberal responses to illiberalism. Burckhardt was almost equally dubious and fearful of nationalism and internationalism, so often appealed to by other liberals. Even the greatest liberal panacea of them all, universal education, found no grace in his eyes.[10]

In his youth, Burckhardt, a German-speaking Swiss from Basel, had been briefly a convert to German nationalism. He returned from his university studies in Berlin determined to convince his fellow citizens that they were Germans, but he never believed in a German state and soon lost his enthusiasm for nationalism. While he recognized it as a power, as a power it was to be feared more than loved. Nationalism meant centralization of power in national governments, and struggles for power on an international scale, with the corresponding militarism.

His fear of nationalism did not make Burckhardt into an advocate of a 'United States of Europe', however, much less a world government. He mocked the Enlightenment and the French Revolution's talk about 'humanity' and 'cosmopolitanism'. He recognized the powerful cultural, economic and social forces which united Europe, but was equally cognizant of their weakness in times of crisis: 'in unhealthy situations botched by parliaments one falls back on his descent and lineage as a saving solution of the intolerable, until one finally gets his way, without being better off for it than before'. That it is not hard to apply his words to the Greek crisis of 2015 or Britain's vote to withdraw from the European Union as an indication of the power of his political insight.[11] Perhaps because he was writing before the world wars, Burckhardt thought it more likely that national rather than international solidarities would triumph in Europe. In any event, either was likely to increase the desire for greater power to attain greater ends that filled Burckhardt with ever-greater fear for Europe.[12]

Under the circumstances, Burckhardt thought that education was likely to be counter-productive, at least the kind of education which one could offer the masses. In one of his letters, after noting the huge expenses entailed by the free and compulsory primary education recently introduced in Basel, he wrote: 'And naturally, as a result, everyone dissatisfied with everything ... a scramble for higher positions, which are of course very limited in number.' Universal education was only another form of universal optimism. If he thought little of opportunities for the mass man, he thought even less of opportunities for the mass woman. Burckhardt saw no good purpose for 'the absolutely insane insistence upon scholarship that goes on in girls' schools'. The educational system was heading for a dead end. 'And like many other bankruptcies, the schools will one day go bankrupt, because the whole thing will become impossible. ... It may even by that the present educational system has reached its peak, and is approaching its decline.'[13]

Thus, for Burckhardt, all the usual liberal solutions increased the power of the state or the demands upon it in a mutually reinforcing and vicious circle. Power was the problem, and solutions that merely increased the power of one or another aspect of society were no solution. How could power be limited? Burckhardt rejected all the usual answers to this perennial liberal question. He had no faith that the constitutional state could survive the destructive pressures from above and below with which it was confronted. Only by somehow reducing those pressures could breathing room be found.

'The only conceivable salvation would be for this insane optimism, ... , to disappear from people's brains. But then our present-day Christianity is not equal to the task; it has gone in for and got mixed up with optimism for the last two hundred years. A change will and must come, but after God knows how much suffering.' Too much optimism was the ultimate culprit. Could it be reversed by any means short of catastrophe? No merely political, much less economic, solution would be viable. Only a spiritual remedy might work. Speaking in a deeply pessimistic tone about Germany between the Austro-Prussian War and the Franco-Prussian War, Burckhardt wrote: 'If the German spirit … is capable of opposing that violence with a new art, poetry and religion, then we are saved, but if not, not. I say: religion, because without a supernatural will to counterbalance the whole power and money racket, it can't be done.' As a liberal, Burckhardt argued to the end that power had to be and eventually would be opposed. Where this new force was to come from Burckhardt could not say, and in his later period he held out only the vague hope that 'mankind is as yet not destined for downfall, and Nature is creating as graciously as ever'.[14]

Burckhardt's liberal pessimism might have escaped much notice by posterity had it not led to some remarkably prescient remarks about Europe and, especially, about Germany, chiefly found in his correspondence though often hinted at in his posthumously published university lectures, where his views about the present were deliberately put in slightly obscure terms so as not to frighten the students. For example, Burckhardt predicted at various points that militarism would become the 'model for existence' in Germany, and that 'inevitably the military state will have to turn industrialist'; that liberals would gradually abandon their defence of the Jews, who would soon suffer renewed persecution (justified, alas, in Burckhardt's eyes); that constitutional states would be overthrown by violence in the name of the people; that the dynasties would be replaced as heads of state by republican but far more brutal rulers. To readers during the Second World War and the first decades of the Cold War, these statements seemed to be horribly accurate prophecies and Burckhardt's popularity in the Anglo-Saxon and the Germanophone world spiked sharply in this period. Despite his hostility to democracy and his anti-Semitism, both largely glossed over or overlooked by commentators at this time, his warnings about the direction of European civilization were interpreted as accurate predictions of totalitarianism, and the opponents of fascism and communism saw in Burckhardt a prophet who had understood what was to come far better than any of the theorists of progress. For Friedrich Hayek in 1944, Burckhardt was among those writers who could provide Europe 'the political re-education it needs'. An optimistic and, to some degree, superficial reading of Burckhardt, to be sure, yet one that was common in the mid-twentieth century.[15]

Burckhardt, however, was not a Cold War liberal, fighting the Soviets without any reservations about Western society. It is not simply that his context was different, but that his liberalism was far more dystopic than that of the Cold Warriors. He saw no salvation in laissez-faire, which in his view was just as much a product of unbridled eighteenth-century optimism as socialism. Above all, he did not look forward to his side's eventual victory, since he thought that very few people were really on his side. Nor was he apolitical, which has sometimes been suggested, as shown by his close, indeed prophetic observation of the political events of his time.

Burckhardt's only response to modernity was a spiritual one. The son of the senior Protestant pastor of Basel, destined for a clerical career himself, Burckhardt abandoned the field of theology when he lost his faith and became a historian instead. It was in study, for spiritual rather than professional purposes, that Burckhardt found grace – not for liberal society, doomed to taste the dregs of the cup it had brewed, but for the liberal individual. Burckhardt's hints at a spiritual remedy for optimism, a possible revaluation of all values that would make the world safe again for liberalism, for constitutions, a limited state and a free individual by reining in all forms of extravagant hope show that Burckhardt's pessimism was not absolute. 'Once it is understood that there never were, nor ever will be, any happy, golden ages in a fanciful sense, one will remain free from the foolish overvaluation of some past, from senseless despair of the present or fatuous hope for the future.' Burckhardt's liberalism lay precisely in a search for appropriate limits (including that most untimely of limits, a limit on optimism, a limit on what one should *hope for*), for limits that recognized both the strengths and the weaknesses of human nature. If this was politically excluded in the present, then it needed to be intellectually and spiritually conquered by the individual, through contemplation and the study of history.[16]

The passive intellectual resistance to Nazism within Germany (1933–45) has been called an inner or internal migration. Burckhardt was an early internal migrant, who sought in the search for knowledge an asylum for freedom and individuality. As he told his students, 'If in misfortune there is to be some fortune as well, it can only be a spiritual one, facing backward to the rescue of the culture of earlier times, facing forward to the serene and unwearied representation of the spirit in a time which could otherwise be given up entirely to things mundane.' In the end, Burckhardt's dystopic liberalism had an educational programme, but it was not one for this world, at least not for the foreseeable future. Burckhardt's liberalism was a liberalism for stoics.[17]

Part Three

Liberalism Confronts the Twentieth Century

Max Weber

Joshua Derman

In view of the fundamental fact that the advance of bureaucratization is unstoppable, there is only one possible set of questions to be asked about future forms of political organization: (1) How is it at all possible to salvage any remnants of 'individual' freedom of movement in any sense, given this all-powerful trend towards bureaucratization? It is, after all, a piece of crude self-deception to think that even the most conservative among us could carry on living at all today without these achievements from the age of the 'Rights of Man.' However, let us put this question to one side for now, for there is another which is directly relevant to our present concerns: (2) In view of the growing indispensability and hence increasing power of state officialdom, which is our concern here, how can there be any guarantee that forces exist which can impose limits on the enormous, crushing power of this constantly growing stratum of society and control it effectively? How is democracy even in this restricted sense to be at all possible? Yet this too is not the only question of concern to us here, for there is (3) a third question, the most important of all, which arises from any consideration of what is not performed by bureaucracy as such. It is clear that its effectiveness has strict internal limits, both in the management of public, political affairs and in the private economic sphere. The leading spirit, the 'entrepreneur' in the one case, the 'politician' in the other, is something different from an 'official.' ... The struggle for personal power and the acceptance of fully personal responsibility for one's cause which is the consequence of such power – this is the very element in which the politician and the entrepreneur live and breathe.[1]

Max Weber's concern for individual freedom, the rights of man and representative democracy brought him into contact with key elements of the liberal political tradition. Whether this German scholar and politician manqué was *actually* a liberal – and if so, what kind of liberal – nonetheless remains a topic of debate. Some interpreters have seen him as a 'liberal in despair', who drifted away from traditional liberal ideals in his determination to ensure that individual autonomy might still be possible under modern conditions. Others have preferred to regard him as the heir to an established 'elitist' current within the liberal tradition. Finally, there are those who believe that Weber does not belong among liberals at all, but rather in the company of republican thinkers such as Niccolò Machiavelli, Jean-Jacques Rousseau and Alexis de Tocqueville, who sought to cultivate 'the power of the soul' through politics. What makes this idiosyncratic figure, who was born in 1864 and died in 1920, into such a provocative interlocutor for modern liberals? Consider the three questions he poses in the passage quoted above.

The first question is a philosophical one: How is individual freedom possible under the conditions of modern life? Before we can receive an answer, Weber plunges us into the world of high politics, where the 'present concerns' of his text play out. What forces, he now asks, are available to counteract the increasing powers of the state bureaucracy? More specifically, how is democracy, even in a 'restricted sense', to remain possible in light of the creeping expansion of officialdom? The answer is yielded by a third question, 'the most important of all', even though strictly speaking it is not so much a question as an observation. 'Leading spirits' in politics and the economy are fundamentally different creatures than officials, he tells us. Our failure to appreciate and act on this difference endangers individual freedom and the possibility of modern democracy.

Though Weber's questions are meant to build on each other, they are connected not so much by logical inference as by conceptual leaps, which carry the reader from the domain of universal history into the contemporary political dilemmas of late imperial Germany. These dramatic shifts are characteristic of Weber's intellectual formation and temperament. As the beneficiary of a late nineteenth-century German humanistic education, he was capable of approaching the problems of modernity through the perspectives afforded by an encyclopedic knowledge of world history. He was also an impatient and impetuous thinker. No sooner had he begun one project, or one train of thought, than he felt compelled to set off in a new direction, without necessarily having brought his investigation to a conclusion. The unconventional pattern of his academic career also contributed to his interdisciplinary proclivities. After training as a lawyer, he quickly received a chair in political economy, but taught for only a few years before succumbing to a nervous breakdown that kept him from the lecture hall until the final years of his life. In spite of his illness, or perhaps because it granted him a respite from professional pressures to specialize, he was able to make contributions to an astonishing variety of fields: the methodology of the social sciences, the history of capitalism in classical antiquity and early modern Europe, the economic ethics of world religions and the formulation of a distinctive approach to what he called 'sociology'. In addition, Weber was an engaged political thinker. He dabbled in liberal politics as a young man, and in the aftermath of the First World War he advised the committee that drafted the constitution of the new German republic.

Weber's innovative way of thinking is already apparent in the way he identifies his subject matter: 'The advance of bureaucratization'. Weber did not coin the concept or critique of bureaucracy, which first emerged in the political discourse of late eighteenth-century France, but he did extend the concept of bureaucracy far beyond the explicitly governmental officialdom with which it was conventionally associated. As he understood it, modern bureaucracy was a form of administration based on 'recruitment, salary, pension, promotion, professional training, firmly established areas of responsibility, the keeping of files, hierarchical structures of superiority and subordination' (145–6). This kind of officialdom had become a universal phenomenon in the modern West, manifesting itself not only in the administration of the state and private economic corporations but also in the army, church, university and voluntary associations such as political parties. All these institutions were staffed by trained specialists who kept meticulous records and understood their place in a hierarchical chain of command, obeying detailed and regular rules of procedure.

Weber was both appreciative and critical about the impact of bureaucracy, whose expansion, he believed, had become an ineradicable feature of modern life. Once a corps of highly trained officials had taken charge of an organization, he argued, it was essentially impossible to replace or remove them, unless one were prepared to suffer a calamitous drop in efficiency – a scenario that he presumed few people would be willing to countenance. The high standard of living in Western countries depended in large part on the efficient and rationalized form of administration provided by trained officialdom. The advantages of modern bureaucracy, combined with its unusual degree of institutional tenacity, made its advance essentially 'unstoppable'. But while it might be naive to think that one could live without modern bureaucracy, Weber also warned that it was foolish to assume that officials or technocrats could solve the most fundamental problems of modern life – problems that demanded a fundamental choice between incommensurable values or human goals, rather than merely technical solutions.

The politician or entrepreneur who could put forward a 'cause' and rally others in support was 'something different', as Weber put it, from the administrator who prided himself on scrupulously following the instructions of others. While officialdom might possess the virtues of conscientiousness and impartiality, its effectiveness was marked by 'strict internal limits', especially when it came to matters that demanded visionary leadership.

Broadly speaking, the advance of modern bureaucracy threatened what Weber called the 'individual freedom of movement' [*Bewegungsfreiheit*]. Here it is worth considering his choice of terminology. Weber typically used the phrase 'freedom of movement' to signify what we would consider to be liberal rights, such as the freedom of conscience, association or commercial activity. In 'Parliament and Government in Germany', he expressed concern that the predominance of administrative agencies in determining human life chances – something that he imagined might result from the post-war socialization of the German economy – could jeopardize legal rights that previously had been taken for granted. It would be much more difficult for workers to find recourse against maltreatment or exploitation if their employer was the state rather than a private corporation. 'Private and public bureaucracies would then be merged into a single hierarchy,' he cautioned, 'whereas now they operate alongside and, at least potentially, against one another, thus keeping one another in check' (157–8). But Weber had more than just civil liberties in mind. It was not only the sanctity of personal and property rights that Weber wished to 'salvage' from the advance of modern bureaucratic organizations but also the freedom to follow one's conscience and transform the world. In his sociological handbook *Economy and Society*, he argued that the most fundamental of the rights of man, the one which historically paved the way for all the rest, was the freedom of conscience.[2]

How, then, did Weber think his contemporaries in imperial Germany could 'impose limits' on the state bureaucracy and 'control it effectively'? He believed that only the parliament could effectively monitor and constrain the state bureaucracy, and he devoted much of his wartime essay 'Parliament and Government in Germany' to proposing constitutional reforms that would empower it. Parliament was the site where responsible political leaders would be selected, trained and, if necessary, removed. But where should these leaders come from in the first place? Weber's explanation factored in two developments that he regarded as inexorable in a modern mass democracy. The first was the extension of the suffrage, which he believed would eventually encompass all adult males wherever it was contested. The second was the centralization and professionalization of political parties, which were subject to the same 'all-powerful trend towards bureaucratization' as other modern institutions; without a nationally coordinated organization and cadre of full-time administrators, it would be impossible for them to compete for millions of votes. Based on his observations of contemporary British and American politics, Weber concluded that party leaders were invariably the politicians who were most capable of appealing to a mass electorate and mobilizing the party organization behind them. Parliament remained the forum where party leaders demonstrated their fitness and responsibility; it ensured that 'mere demagogues', politicians whose *only* talent was the ability to command a mass following, would not occupy the leading positions in the state (182). But advancement would come through the support of the masses, not seniority in parliament or connections with party notables. This element of 'Caesarism', a form of authority that 'rests on the trust of the masses rather than on that of parliaments', was, in Weber's view, an unavoidable and even desirable feature of democratic politics (220–1). The only alternative was to let party bigwigs handpick the leading candidates, which would likely result in dull, uninspiring politicians who lacked the ability to set new goals or command a mass following.[3]

A successful democratic system that constrained the bureaucracy and provided for dynamic leadership was thus composed of two elements that stood in a productive tension with one another: highly bureaucratized mass parties led by charismatic political figures, and a parliament endowed with significant powers. Weber coolly observed that this form of democracy exacerbated the difference between politically 'active' and 'passive' citizens, relegating the latter to the role of choosing among predetermined candidates every few years. In such a political system, initiative in national politics came primarily from party leaders, 'for it is not the politically passive "mass" which gives birth to the leader; rather the political leader recruits his following and wins over the mass by "demagogy"' (228). Successful party organizations helped pave the way for the rise of a plebiscitary leader, and having done so, put themselves at the service of promoting his political vision: 'Wherever mass democratic parties have been faced with major tasks they have been obliged to submit more or less unconditionally to leaders who had the trust of the masses' (222). If Germans wanted to be governed by politicians instead of officials, and keep the ever-advancing bureaucracy in its place, they would have to embrace both parliamentarism and plebiscitary democracy, warts and all.

One of the distinctive characteristics of Weber's political thought, as illustrated in 'Parliament and Government in Germany', consists in its nuanced evaluation of the possibilities for freedom under modern conditions. On the one hand, Weber paints a picture of the future of humanity that is darkened with resignation. Unlike many classical liberal thinkers, he does not perceive an invisible hand or providential force guiding humanity towards greater autonomy. Weber admits that he cannot keep himself from 'smiling at the anxiety of our littérateurs lest future social and political developments might bestow on us *too much* "individualism" or "democracy" or the like' (159). Bureaucracy is on the march in all spheres of life, and even the 'free' market of mature capitalism, which combines independent entrepreneurs into ever-greater conglomerations, no longer possesses any affinity with individual 'freedom of movement'. Weber sees liberal freedoms as 'achievements from the age of the "Rights of Man"', whose emergence in early modern Europe depended on a constellation of irreproducible factors: small-scale capitalism, an abundance of natural resources and land for expansion, the scientific revolution, and the novel attitudes towards work and self-determination engendered by the Protestant Reformation.[4] The best that can be done today, Weber seems to suggest, is to 'salvage' some of these freedoms through new institutional arrangements. Yet he also makes the case that some irreversible trends of modernity, such as the expansion of rational bureaucracy, contain within them the solutions to their own pathologies. Individual freedom will not be served by the quixotic enterprise of dismantling bureaucracies, but by checking the expansion of one bureaucracy by means of another. In Weber's telling, the highly bureaucratized political party of modern times presents an ideal vehicle for promoting a visionary leader who introduces new ideas, curbs the power of the state bureaucracy and clears a space in which all active citizens can enjoy greater 'freedom of movement', if only for a while.

One of the most problematic aspects of Weber's political thought, at least from the perspective of many liberals, is his view that the fate of individual freedom depends – to a large and perhaps even predominant extent – on the action of singular leaders who know the 'struggle for personal power and the acceptance of fully *personal responsibility for one's cause* which is the consequence of such power'. Weber's wartime journalism presented parliament as the institution that was best suited for safeguarding civil rights, training potential leaders and removing them if they overstepped their bounds. However, in the aftermath of the First World War and the revolution of 1918–19, he quickly grew disillusioned with the functioning of Germany's new national assembly. Proportional representation, lobbying interests and the continued dominance of notables in party politics had created a *'parliament of closed, philistine minds, in no sense capable of serving as a place where political leaders are selected'*.[5] The best way to enable gifted leaders to rise to the top, he advised the framers of the new constitution, was to ensure that the new president was directly elected by the entire population (rather than by parliament), and endowed with the power to determine office patronage, call referenda, cast a delaying veto and dissolve parliament.[6] Only a 'charismatic' leader, who could emerge from outside parliament and potentially outside the party system as well, could provide the kind of leadership that Germany needed.[7]

Weber disclaimed any intention of wanting an unchecked, authoritarian presidency. 'Let the power of the popularly elected president be subjected to whatever restrictions one will, and let us ensure that he is only permitted to intervene in the machinery of the Reich during temporary, irresoluble crises,' he declared.[8] He never lived to experience the abuse of presidential powers under President Paul von Hindenburg, and the success of Adolf Hitler's racist demagoguery would have appalled him. These questions of historical responsibility aside, Weber's intellectual trajectory between 1917 and 1919 raises concerns about how we are to understand the connection between liberal freedoms and visionary leadership in his political thought. As the balance between parliamentarism and charismatic leadership shifted decisively in favour of the latter, we might wonder whose 'freedom of movement' the cultivation and promotion of 'leading spirits' was supposed to serve. Did Weber think that only a few titanic figures were capable of achieving creative autonomy in the modern world? If so, then the rest of humanity would seem to become 'passive' followers or, at best, the mere beneficiaries of elbow room cleared out for them by great politicians and entrepreneurs.

However, the case can also be made that Weber's journalism gives us only a one-sided picture of his political commitments. Weber was fascinated by the apparent successes of American democracy, which he regarded as a potential model for Germany's political evolution. His positive impressions were reinforced by a three-month trip he made to the United States with his wife Marianne in 1904.[9] There he observed that American democracy was based on a dense web of voluntary associations and clubs that required members to constantly demonstrate their qualifications to one another. These associations, like the Protestant sects on which Weber believed they were based, were 'aristocratic' in the sense that only qualified individuals were allowed to join, but they also depended on the 'free consensus of [their] members', who stood before each other as equals.[10] Though Weber portrayed the mass of citizens in a modern mass democracy as politically 'passive' in 'Parliament and Government in Germany', he may have been exaggerating to make a point in a particular polemical context. American democracy, he argued elsewhere, depended on a vibrant civil society to cultivate leadership qualities and responsibility from the grass roots to the top of the political pyramid.

The questions that Weber raised in 'Parliament and Government in Germany' made a powerful impact on twentieth-century political thought.[11] Together with his sociological writings, they launched a wide literature on bureaucracy in its myriad forms, with the result that Weber's name has become almost inseparable from the concept. His vision of social transformation as effected by singular, visionary individuals who introduce new values and command a mass following – culminating in the writings on 'charisma' that he put forward in the last years of his life – pioneered a way of talking about leadership that has left a permanent mark on our language. Great thinkers are often remembered for their questions as much as their answers. Though the constitutional problems of imperial Germany no longer trouble us, the compatibility of liberal freedoms, bureaucracy, democracy and transformative leadership remain an urgent concern, nearly one hundred years after Weber's death.

Was Keynes a Liberal?

Reinhart Blohmert

*But, above all, individualism, if it can be purged of its defects and its abuses,
is the best safeguard of personal liberty ... and is also the best guard of
the variety of life ... the loss of which is the greatest of all the losses of the
homogeneous or the totalitarian state.*

*Half the copybook wisdom of our statesmen is based on assumptions which
were at the time true, or partly true, but are now less and less true day by
day. We have to invent new wisdom for a new age. And in the meantime we
must, if we are to do any good, appear unorthodox, troublesome, dangerous,
disobedient to them, that begat us.*

*In the economic field this means, first of all, that we must find new policies
and new instruments to adapt and control the working of economic forces, so
that they do not intolerably interfere with contemporary ideas as to what is
fair and proper in the interest of social stability and social justice.*[1]

*In some other respects the foregoing theory is moderately conservative in
its implications. For whilst it indicates the vital importance of establishing
certain central controls in matters which are now left in the main to individual
initiative, there are wide fields of activity which are unaffected. The State
will have to exercise a guiding influence on the propensity to consume partly
through its scheme of taxation, partly by fixing the rate of interest, and partly,
perhaps, in other ways. Furthermore, it seems unlikely that the influence of
banking policy on the rate of interest will be sufficient by itself to determine
an optimum rate of investment. I conceive, therefore, that a somewhat
comprehensive socialisation of investment will prove the only means of
securing an approximation to full employment; though this need not exclude
all manner of compromises and of devices by which public authority will
cooperate with private initiative. But beyond this no obvious case is made out*

for a system of State Socialism which would embrace most of the economic
life of the community. It is not the ownership of the instruments of production
which it is important for the State to assume. If the State is able to aggregate
amount of resources devoted to augmenting the instruments and the basic
rate of reward to those who own them, it will have accomplished all that is
necessary. Moreover, the necessary measures of socialisation can be introduced
gradually and without a break in the general traditions of society.[2]

Keynes' father was the registrar of Cambridge University, and his mother was a mayor of that university town. He was thrown into the midst of the English elite from birth – school at Eton and then university at King's College, Cambridge. Despite his elite upbringing, he had no sympathy for the Conservative Party – his lifestyle and his liking for the modern arts were not conservative. As he himself declared:

> How could I bring myself to be a conservative? … That which is common to the atmosphere, the mentality, the view of life of – well, I will not mention names – promotes neither my self-interest nor the public good. It leads nowhere, it satisfies no ideal; it conforms to no intellectual standard; it is not even safe or calculated to preserve from spoilers that degree of civilization which we have already attained.

Keynes was no less critical of the Labour Party, based as it was on the aspirations and interests of a social class that was not his own. He was sceptical both of the party's social base and even more so of its 'autocratic inner ring' – the radical section of which Keynes designated 'the party of catastrophe'. Alienated from both the conservative and labour camps, the Liberal Party became Keynes' intellectual and political home and what he considered 'the best instrument of future progress – if only it had strong leadership and the right program'.[3] He joined the party as a student and remained faithful to it thereafter.

From the beginning, however, Keynes was sceptical about nineteenth-century liberalism, which he viewed as a mixture of claims, illusions and half-truths. It inherited a conception of individualism that was founded on Locke's and Hume's doctrines of 'toleration' and the 'privatization of religion' and provided the basis for a theory of property rights which enshrined the property holder's right to 'do what he liked with himself and with his own'. Keynes described this idea as 'one of the contributions of the eighteenth century to the air we still breathe'.[4] But he argued that it needed more than the praise of individual rights to legitimize the new doctrine of 'laissez-faire'. That was a feat of pure assertion, by which early-nineteenth-century liberals achieved the 'miraculous union' of 'conservative individualism' derived from Locke, Hume, Johnson and Burke and the 'socialism and democratic egalitarianism' of Rousseau, Paley, Bentham and Godwin. Nevertheless, this 'harmony of opposites' would have been hard to establish had it not been for the economists, who sprang into prominence at just the right time. To the philosophical doctrine that government has no right to interfere, and the divine that it has no need to interfere, there is added a scientific proof that its interference is inexpedient. 'The political philosopher could retire in favour of the business man – for [the] latter could attain the philosopher's *summum bonum* by just pursuing his own private profit'.[5]

In Keynes' view, the latter part of the nineteenth century added one more element to liberalism. Liberal thought acquired a dark side, by way of the idea of existential competition introduced by Darwin.

> Nothing could seem more opposed than the old doctrine and the new – the doctrine which looked on the world as the work of the divine watchmaker and the doctrine which seemed to draw all things out of Chance, Chaos, and Old Father Time. But at this one point the new ideas bolstered up the old. The economists were teaching that wealth, commerce, and machinery were the children of free competition. ... But the Darwinians could go one better than that – free competition had built man ... the company of the economists were there to prove that the least deviation into impiety involved financial ruin.[6]

When liberals' individualistic view on the world was combined with these Darwinian ingredients, it fit the needs of the business world perfectly. As Alfred Marshall, Keynes' teacher and the greatest economist of his time wrote, 'Our hopes of progress were centered' on the achievements of business heroes.[7]

Keynes' studies with Marshall equipped him with the dominant microeconomic view of classic liberal economics. But he began to see that this would not be enough to defend liberal society in the coming age. Keynes fitted liberalism with new insights and with new programmes that left behind the old Darwinistic view and the pure laissez-faire attitudes that no longer functioned and had begun to lose their legitimacy. The rest of this chapter will concentrate on his political shift, and sketch the new frame for economic liberalism that Keynes created. It shows how he came to promote a liberal rationale for strengthening the influence of the state on investment.

As a member of the UK Treasury during the First World War, Keynes had seen gold going to the United States and the value of the dollar increase. The United States, as the main purveyor of arms for the Allied armies, grew into a new economic world power, and American money dominated the markets after the war. Most of the world's gold bullion was (physically) in the United States, and the dollar, not gold any more, was the world currency. When Britain under Churchill tried to bind the pound to gold again in 1925, she was obviously dreaming of days that had gone with the war: Britain was no longer in possession of enough gold to cover all her currency obligations. It was impossible to retain the gold standard in the short term. The British elites did not see that fact, and the 'Consequences of Mr. Churchill', as Keynes called this adventurous step, were that exports of British goods – mainly coal – fell. To raise the value of the pound meant also making export goods expensive. The coal industry suffered heavily under this Treasury dictate, and tried to make coal cheaper by slashing the miners' wages. This led to the longest strike in English history, and prompted Keynes to ask:

> Why should the miners, the weakest economic link, who make their living from their wages in the coal industry, accept that dictate? Why should we allow the financial elite to insist on its wishes? The idea of the old-world party that you can, for example, alter the value of money and then leave the consequential adjustments to be brought about by forces of supply and demand, belongs to the days of fifty or a hundred years ago when trade unions were powerless, and when the economic juggernaut was allowed to crash along the highway of progress without obstruction and even with applause.[8]

Keynes argued that the contemporary elite's response to the post-war crisis rested on assumptions that no longer applied. He called for 'new wisdom for a new age' to replace them, recognizing that this enterprise would be criticized as a dangerous departure from the certainties of orthodox classical economics. This new wisdom, however, would enable economic policy-makers to ensure that economic forces were directed in ways that were consistent with prevailing ideas about society and social justice, rather than frustrating them.

With these arguments, Keynes showed a feeling for the democratic value of fairness and a lot more moral respect for the most vulnerable classes than British elites had shown before. In so doing, he confronted the challenges of the new democratic era of the twentieth century. Not surprisingly, this approach brought Keynes into conflict with some members of the Liberal Party, but he presented it as a way of conserving important features of a liberal society that were threatened by the emergence of powerful and extreme socialist tendencies in modern national and international politics. For example, Keynes saw that the British miners were not only more vulnerable than the bankers of the city but that they also tended to move further to the left as the strike went on. This tendency was risky in the new times of democracy that had come about after the war. During that time, the Soviet experiment blossomed, and a lot of intellectuals moved to the political left. Keynes, who was married to a Russian ballet dancer and knew Russia from his travels and his experiences with Russian negotiators at conferences (like Genoa and Rapallo), remained sceptical and was more inclined to make capitalism friendlier than to run the risk of a revolution during which all the cultural capital of the West might be swept away.

Keynes was well aware of the weakening condition of English industry in the face of an ongoing loss of markets. In the second half of the 1920s he designed an economic programme for the construction of houses for the working classes as part of Liberal Party leader Lloyd George's promotion of employment. This programme was already a break with one of the old liberal dogmas, that states must abstain from economic activities. But aside from this political pragmatism, Keynes did not at this time depart from the theoretical framework of liberal economic dogma: free markets, free trade and free treaties. He thus favoured a practical political programme before he got the theoretical frame for it. He had seen the need before he saw the way out of a theoretical dead end. It was not until the 1930s that Keynes began to radically reconstruct the liberal picture of economics. The Great Depression, which broke out in October 1929 in New York, lasted years and opened his eyes to the role of money as store of value, and the role of effective demand in the economic fabric of capitalism. He saw that the labour market had no tendency to self-rebalancing and that unemployment could last longer than was good for the unemployed and for the political system.

This observation was for him obvious proof that free markets do not deliver full employment automatically, as the Classical School had claimed. Members of this school had taught that if workers were willing to lower their wages, the market would balance again. In the Depression, however, wages had sunk to the bottom, employment did not rise and the economy did not get back into motion. Keynes knew that capital is attracted only by profits, and that entrepreneurs invest only if they expect rising demand. The war had accelerated some changes in industrial production, and the new productivity that resulted led to new markets for mass consumption from upper middle class and wealthy customers to the market for mass products. But demand in the main mass-production markets sank as workers lost their jobs and wages. People had to spend what little money they had on the most urgent necessities of food and drink. Discretionary consumption remained constrained. Demand was low, and the whole economy went from stagnation to decline.

In the classical liberal view, crisis was the moment when industries that were not competitive in the market die, and new, more competitive industries come to the fore. So the liberal view was Darwinian, and liberals saw, in crisis, a cleansing effect, like a process of natural selection. But this sort of sanitation, which might be part of economic development in normal times, wastes a lot of talent and skill in times of depression, when millions of people lose their jobs. It also deprives savers of their money when capital values go to rack and ruin. The loss of cultural norms and human suffering are the consequence; when people are thrown out of their careers and life plans, birth rates go down and the social fabric begins to rot. People begin to look for political leaders who will propagate a new social order or revolutionary programmes, and the capitalist system is on the brink of destruction.

As the crisis of the Great Depression went on, there was no light on the horizon and the position of the classical liberal economists became difficult to maintain. There seemed to be a problem with Say's law stipulating that all products would find customers at the end of the day. Obviously, to Keynes, the classical liberal economic creed had proved to be built on sand. Waiting for the moment when the labour market would rebalance itself turned out to be like waiting for Godot – illusory and also dangerous. 'In the long run', said Keynes, 'we are all dead.'[9]

But all the private actors who might affect the situation were under severe economic constraints. It was capital's greed for profits that fuelled the markets, and capital went therefore into branches of the economy where expectations for purchase were rising: supply grows only when demand is expected. Credit could be as cheap as possible, but factory owners would not want to produce anything as long as they did not expect demand for their products. So there could not be an end to unemployment in the face of this dilemma. On the one side, each dismissed worker would reduce the salary balance sheet of the entrepreneur, but on the other side, each jobless worker would also reduce the aggregate purchasing power of the economy. A microeconomic view could not solve this dilemma; only a politically armed macroeconomic perspective could integrate these seeming paradoxes. There was only one actor who could help find a way out of the dilemma: the state. Only the state was exempt from the economic constraints which applied, necessarily, to capital. At this particular historical moment, the state could help fuel the economy as long as necessary to reduce unemployment.

Keynes brought this 'new' old perspective, which had disappeared from sight since Ricardo and his followers, into the mainstream of economic thought. With it, he erased the dark, Darwinian side of liberal economics. The message was that liberal politics has to guard a measure of fairness in a society, and to bring about a social cushion against brutal hardship. This was the song of a new liberalism, which was no longer based on Darwinian laws of natural selection, but on human culture. A liberalism which had been substantially devoted to limiting state intervention had now, with some caution, to equip the state to intervene at critical moments in order to preserve both a liberal society and a liberal economy from potential threats from the extremes of left and right.

Keynes' 'revolution' was very successful. Keynes was already a famous and influential economist, with links not only inside the economics community but also to politics and even journalism. He had a huge number of followers, not only in Britain but also inside the American Roosevelt administration. From its publication in 1936, his *General Theory* would remain the most influential theory for almost three generations. One of his students was Paul Samuelson, whose basic economics textbook was in print for half a century. Keynes' idea of liberalism is still fundamental to the American meaning of 'liberal' today.[10]

It was not until the 1980s that a counter-revolution took place and the old myth of the automatic balancing of the economy through free markets came to the fore again. Amid the turbulence of the time, Milton Friedman argued for the stability of private markets and had a deep distrust of the state. And the idea of an enlightened politics was given up, and supply-side economics, together with the so-called 'new classical macroeconomics' and public choice theory, once again enlarged the distance between economic theory and real economy: as before Keynes, economics would again be a normative-ideological art that had nothing to say about reality, as the Enron scandal and the world financial crises have demonstrated.

This thinking in alternatives – state or markets – was not what Keynes stood for: his ideals were semi-autonomous institutions, which were, in his view, the best mediator between the welfare of the whole society and individual interests – like the Bank of England.[11] Its aim was to feed the British economy with money and hold the currency stable – but not to make a profit. Keynes even believed that joint stock companies, 'where the owners of capital, i.e. the shareholders, are almost dissociated from the management', might evolve in a direction where 'the direct personal interest of the (management) in the making of profit becomes quite secondary'.[12] And indeed, until the end of the 1970s, the idea of joint stock company leaders had been to satisfy not only shareholders but also stakeholders like communities and workers.[13] A change came with Jensen and Meckling and their 'principal-agent-theory', emphasizing shareholders as proprietors, not only as creditors.[14] Keynes saw managers as professionals, not as agents of the proprietors. His trust was on professionals and professional agencies that stood above the constraint of profit-making. But the world for professionals has become smaller and smaller since the sudden deregulation of financial markets in the UK in 1986 ('big bang') marked the entry of the profit-making principle into the realm of the mediators. With the vanishing of professionals from the stock exchanges and the growing influence of finance on the real economy, the dangers of crisis grew, once again bringing the whole deregulated capitalist system to the brink of the abyss.

John Dewey and Liberal Democracy

James T. Kloppenberg

The strongest point to be made in behalf of even such rudimentary political forms as democracy has already attained, popular voting, majority rule and so on, is that to some extent they involve a consultation and discussion which uncover social needs and troubles. This fact is a great asset on the side of the political ledger. De Tocqueville wrote it down almost a century ago in his survey of the prospects of democracy in the United States. Accusing a democracy of a tendency to prefer mediocrity in its elected rulers, and admitting its exposure to gusts of passion and its openness to folly, he pointed out in effect that popular government is educative as other modes of political regulation are not. It forces a recognition that there are common interests, even though the recognition of what they are is confused; and the need it enforces in discussion and publicity brings about some clarification of what they are. The man who wears the shoe knows best that it pinches and where it pinches, even if the expert shoemaker is the best judge of how the trouble is to be remedied. Popular government has at least created public spirit even if its success in informing that spirit has not been great. … No government by experts in which the masses do not have the chance to inform the experts as to their needs can be anything but an oligarchy managed in the interests of the few. And the enlightenment must proceed in ways which force the administrative specialists to take account of the needs. The world has suffered more from leaders and authorities than from the masses. The essential need, in other words, is the improvement of the methods and conditions of debate, discussion and persuasion. That is the problem of the public.[1]

John Dewey (1859–1952) stands as the premier American theorist of liberalism between Abraham Lincoln and John Rawls. Like Lincoln and Rawls, he believed passionately in democracy and individual liberty. Unlike them, he came to political thought through Hegel's idealism. That experience, in his words, left 'a permanent deposit' that distinguished his version of liberalism from the more individualist strands often, although mistakenly, assumed to characterize all of American political thought.[2] *The Public and Its Problems* brings together Dewey's arguments concerning epistemology, ethics and the transformation of liberalism he considered essential for the twentieth-century urban industrial world.

Dewey's roots extended into the soil of rural New England. Shaped by his mother's devout Congregationalism and his grocer father's engagement in the political life of Burlington, Vermont, Dewey frequently invoked the traditions of Jeffersonian small-town 'ward democracy' and Lincoln's commitment to preserving the experiment in self-rule threatened by the Confederacy's defence of social hierarchy and race-based slavery. Educated at the University of Vermont (BA 1879) and Johns Hopkins (PhD 1884) in the German philosophical tradition, Dewey embarked on a scholarly career initially devoted to reconciling idealism with the new psychology taking shape in the laboratories of pioneers such as William James and G. Stanley Hall. From the collision between those sets of ideas emerged Dewey's mature philosophy, a union of his 'native inclination toward the schematic and formally logical' and 'those incidents of personal experience that compelled me to take account of actual material.'[3]

Dewey's first effort to achieve that union, his *Psychology* (1887), proved unconvincing to most reviewers, and when James's *Principles of Psychology* (1890) was published, Dewey converted wholeheartedly to James's phenomenological and physiological approach. At the same time, Dewey was discovering the writings of T. H. Green, who provided a bridge between Dewey's liberal Protestantism and his developing interest in social reform. Dewey's essays 'The Ethics of Democracy' (1888), 'The Philosophy of Thomas Hill Green' (1889) and 'Christianity and Democracy' (1892) show how Green's idealism and Dewey's social-gospel principles merged in his earliest political writings. Democracy became, for Dewey, the vehicle whereby God worked in the world and the means by which the individual could find the truth that could set him free, 'free negatively, free from sin, free positively, free to live his own life, free to express himself'. Long after Dewey had renounced his Christian faith, his commitments to what Isaiah Berlin later called 'positive liberty' and to the transformative power of democratic participation remained the armature of his ideas.[4]

Dewey left his first teaching job at the University of Michigan in 1894 to become chair of the Department of Philosophy, Psychology and Education at the new University of Chicago. During the next half-century, his intense engagement with those three rapidly changing disciplines generated a series of books that established him as the leading figure in American thought and progressive reform. In Chicago, Dewey immersed himself in social action as well as scholarship. He became a close associate of Jane Addams, the founder of Hull House and a leading figure in the national settlement house movement. Dewey's theory of education, no doubt the most influential (although perhaps the least well understood) of his ideas, developed from the interaction between the experiments in teaching and learning conducted at the lab school and the experiences of Addams and her associates at Hull House.

Beginning with his *Outlines of a Critical Theory of Ethics* (1891) and continuing throughout his career, Dewey attempted to link his conception of inquiry and his theories of education and liberal democracy to his moral philosophy. Like Green, Dewey believed that individuals achieve self-realization by contributing their abilities to the well-being of their communities. He also followed Green in his insistence that government action to promote the greater good involved more than simply dismantling outworn restrictions: measures such as compulsory school attendance, regulation of the workplace, the provision of insurance against sickness, accident and old age, and a graduated income tax all seemed to Dewey steps made necessary by the interdependence of life in the twentieth century. The interlinking of his epistemology, his ethics and his politics was among the signal features of Dewey's liberalism, and his ideas informed the work of a broad range of American scholars working in the natural sciences, the social sciences and government for the first half of the twentieth century.[5]

Following Woodrow Wilson's election to the presidency in 1912, Dewey became a more active participant in debates about public policy. Dewey was among those who had looked to the Republican Party, the party of Lincoln, to spearhead change, but Wilson's record as president forced him to reconsider. Although it had been the party of slaveholders and states-rights ideology, the Democratic Party had also been the party of the less fortunate members of American society. Under the influence of Wilson's friend Louis Brandeis, the controversial 'people's attorney' whom Wilson nominated to the Supreme Court, the president was moving to address the problems caused by industrialization more energetically than his bombastic predecessor Theodore Roosevelt. Dewey applauded the progressive policies increasingly identified with the 'new liberalism', a body of ideas that combined John Stuart Mill's commitment to individual autonomy with Green's and Dewey's ideas about using the state to level the playing field. Championed in the United States by *The New Republic*, to which Dewey became a frequent contributor; in Britain by *The Guardian* and by sociologist L. T. Hobhouse's widely read *Liberalism* (1911), the 'new liberalism' was also the subject of Dewey's *Democracy and Education* (1916), which Dewey described as 'the closest attempt I have made sum up my entire philosophy'. Teachers should aim, Dewey argued, not to drill outworn facts into reluctant pupils' brains; they should help them learn to think. Only students who learned how to solve unanticipated problems with creative intelligence were prepared for the larger tasks of democratic citizenship.[6]

Like his associates on *The New Republic*, Dewey initially resisted the entry of the United States into the First World War, but when Wilson proclaimed the establishment of an international organization devoted to preventing future wars and securing self-government everywhere as the nation's war aim, most progressives signed on. Dewey defended American involvement by arguing that Wilson was embracing the principles of philosophical pragmatism: he had identified a problem, war, hypothesized a solution, the League of Nations, and was taking the steps necessary to test that hypothesis. With the benefit of hindsight, many commentators have accepted the judgement of Randolph Bourne and declared Wilson's crusade a fool's errand. Only recently have historians begun to rethink that judgement, pointing out both the galvanizing effect of Wilson's principles in parts of the world struggling to escape colonialism and the surprisingly widespread support for the League of Nations within the United States itself. Had Wilson prevailed at Versailles, had America joined the League and had a stronger League overseen a less punitive peace, would the history of the 1930s and 1940s have proved less catastrophic?

As Europe was unravelling in the wake of the First World War, Dewey was taking his philosophy on the road. Accepting invitations to lecture in Japan and China, he spent most of the 1919–21 period in East Asia, attempting to persuade audiences that their nations should adopt science and democracy, the two central values of the modern world, as their touchstones. One of Dewey's former students at Columbia, Hu Shih, was trying to import Deweyan liberalism into China; there are clear parallels between Dewey's ideas and the reformist May Fourth Movement, a movement struggling to be reborn in contemporary China. Equally clear are the links between Dewey's ideas and those of another former Columbia student deeply indebted to his work, B. R. Ambedkar, the father of India's constitution. In his *Annihilation of Caste* (1936), Ambedkar identified Dewey as the inspiration for his conception of democracy.[7]

Although influential thinkers outside Europe and the United States found Dewey's and Wilson's ideas congenial, the consequences of the First World War demoralized progressives on both sides of the North Atlantic. Many radicals turned towards the new Soviet Union for an alternative to 'bourgeois' democracy. Others, like Dewey's erstwhile ally Walter Lippmann, renounced their faith in 'the people'. As an adviser to Wilson during and after the war, Lippmann learned how complex political problems are, and how easy it is to manipulate public sentiment through propaganda. In a series of articles in *The New Republic*, and then in his best-selling *Public Opinion* (1922), Lippmann punctured the progressives' rosy assessments of the populace: ordinary citizens, their vision blinkered by stereotypes that simplify and distort complicated phenomena, were incapable of the sophisticated judgements required for democratic decision making. *The Public and Its Problems* was Dewey's response to Lippmann's critique.

Dewey acknowledged the problems facing the public. In an ever more complicated world, only the most highly trained specialists seemed capable of understanding the challenges of governance. Expecting amateurs to choose among alternative proposals, when even understanding the problems exceeded their capacity, seemed naive at best. Although Dewey did not use Max Weber's terminology, he identified a similar tension between two forms of reason, value rationality and instrumental rationality. Whereas Lippmann counselled reliance on experts capable of seeing through the fog of custom and ideology to discern the most efficient technical solutions, basing their judgement on calculations incomprehensible to ordinary citizens, Dewey insisted that experts' recommendations, indispensable as instrumental rationality is in the modern world, had to be weighed by the citizenry. 'The difficulty with democracy', Dewey wrote in a review of *Public Opinion* published in *The New Republic*, is even more fundamental than Lippmann realized. 'Democracy demands a more thoroughgoing education than the education of officials, administrators and directors of industry.'[8] Enlightening those in authority only scratches the surface of what democracy requires.

Dewey stressed educating children to become masters of critical inquiry because he considered that sensibility prerequisite to a robust democracy. Adults lulled into passive listening could be duped, but a nation of active investigators would demand explanations sufficiently clear to enable them to make informed judgements for themselves. Dewey's vision of democracy focused so clearly on education because he conceived of citizenship in terms of the Greek ideal of *paideia*. Rather than reserving this ideal for a few superior individuals, though, he wanted to see it extended to every member of society, and he believed that all individuals were capable of making judgements on the basis of their responsibilities to the common good rather than simply seeking their own personal advantage. In another article in *The New Republic*, Dewey conceded that most Americans associated democracy with political institutions and had trouble recovering its 'moral and ideal meaning'. Democracy 'denotes faith in individuality, in uniquely distinctive qualities in each normal human being; faith in corresponding unique modes of activity that create new ends, with willing acceptance of the modifications of the established order entailed by the release of individual capacities'.[9]

In *The Public and Its Problems*, Dewey sketched the processes that 'have effected uniform standardization, mobility and remote invisible relationships', the processes that Weber and other contemporary sociologists such as Ferdinand Töennies identified with the replacement of the face-to-face relationships of community (*Gemeinschaft*) with the evanescent and instrumental relations characteristic of impersonal society (*Gesellschaft*). Aware of the phenomenon that Weber labelled 'disenchantment' and aware of the need for bureaucracy in an ever more complicated and rule- rather than tradition-bound world, Dewey nevertheless persisted in his belief that a properly constituted democracy, with citizens educated to engage in critical inquiry rather than luxuriate in mindless consumption, could ride herd on government officials. Even though administrators would necessarily exercise increasing power in urban industrial societies requiring extensive government regulation, those wearing the shoes, he insisted, should tell the shoemakers where the shoe pinches, not vice versa. Education must help people understand that their desires are not natural but 'artificial' and 'socially conditioned'. Individuals' myopic focus on their narrow self-interest is not grounded in biological drives but is a product of inadequate socialization and recognition of the debts they owe to society. As they came to understand the value of 'positive liberty' and 'real equality', they could renounce the corrosive individualism that Tocqueville identified as a threat to mutuality and focus their attention instead on 'what may be termed a general will and social consciousness'. Against the claims of Lenin on the one hand and Mussolini on the other, American democracy must continue to resist any temptation to embrace a particular vision of the nation's mission. Instead, the United States should remain devoted to open-ended experimentation in its search for the common good, an ideal no longer conceived as the realization of divine providence or Hegel's *Weltgeist* but instead as the result of democratic deliberation and decision making.[10]

During the 1930s, Dewey became increasingly critical of mainstream American politics. In the most radical of his books, *Liberalism and Social Action* (1935), he suggested that recovering from the global depression might necessitate steps in the direction of democratic socialism, a vague ideal reminiscent of that endorsed by John Stuart Mill in his *Autobiography* (1873). Dewey remained equally critical of the Soviet Union, however, and never indulged in the flirtations with communism that tempted many of his allies on the American left. Dewey stands among the few new liberals to survive the interwar years without abandoning his faith in democracy. Six years after *The Public and Its Problems* appeared, Hitler and Roosevelt assumed power, and their contrasting styles of charismatic leadership confirmed the differing assessments of Dewey and Weber on the future of democracy. Even at the height of the New Deal, many of the most ambitious parts of which were designed by Dewey's students and his allies, American politics remained, as Weber predicted, a struggle for power among party professionals who lacked principles rather than a search for the public interest of the sort Dewey hoped to see.[11] In that sense, Weber proved a better prophet. In the years after Weber's death in 1920, however, Germany showed what Dewey suspected, that charisma may represent an even greater threat than bureaucracy to the survival of liberalism and democracy.

Public Ownership and Totalitarianism: Hu Shih's Reflections

Lei Yi

In the lecture that I delivered in June, 15th year of the Republican Era, I said, 'During the 18th century, liberty, equality and fraternity used to be the new religious creed. Since the mid-19th century, however, this creed has been replaced by socialism.' I spoke a lot about this at the time to elaborate on this notion. As I think of it now, I'd say that a public confession would be necessary, although what I am confessing now was a mistake that I made along with many other intellectuals. At that time, a large number of intellectuals believed that socialism would be a logical sequence for the future.

We shall discuss this publicly again: are we on the road to liberation or the road to serfdom?[1]

Hu Shih (1891–1962) is arguably the most influential among the intellectuals who brought liberalism to China. Growing up with a traditional Chinese education, in his late teens he went to the United States, where he studied agriculture and later literature and philosophy at Cornell and Columbia Universities. At Columbia he met John Dewey, under whose influence he encountered liberalism not only as an intellectual tradition but as an ongoing experiment. Returning to China, Hu Shih became an outspoken proponent of liberalism, constitutional parliamentarianism and individual rights, and he advocated bringing China's intellectual and social development in line with the Western model. While he maintained his liberal commitment throughout his life, he was also constantly modifying it and at times even questioning it when confronted with the (chaotic) condition of China. The development of Hu Shih's thinking can be considered a reflection of how liberalism was received in China.

In 1953, the *Free China Journal*, published in Taiwan, serialized Friedrich A. Hayek's monumental work *The Road to Serfdom*, translated into Chinese by Yin Hai-guang. The following spring, when Hu Shih revisited Taiwan from the United States, he gave a lecture entitled 'Starting the conversation with *The Road to Serfdom*' (from which the above passages are taken) in order to promote the public discussion of Hayek's work. He had a high regard for Hayek's views, proclaiming that 'all planned economies are antithetical to freedom, or illiberal', and that 'although liberal thinkers more or less consider socialism an inevitable trend for the future, Mr. Hayek, a renowned economist, has said that all socialisms are anti-liberal, because the foundational principle of socialism is a planned economy'. In that lecture, Hu Shih renounced his blind belief in socialism (in the economic sense) of the past thirty years and returned to a philosophy of individualism, capitalism and liberalism. How did he come to this point at nearly the end of his life? To answer this question, it is useful to take a brief look at the history of the reception of liberalism in China, and at Hu Shih's influence on the process.

Liberalism was first planted in China through the translations of Yan Fu and the introductions of Liang Qi-chao in the late nineteenth and early twentieth century. After studying at the Royal Naval College in England, Yan Fu, one of the earliest Chinese scholars to study in the West, translated a series of Western classics which included Thomas Huxley's *Evolution and Ethics*, Adam Smith's *The Wealth of Nations*, Herbert Spencer's *Study of Sociology*, John Stuart Mill's *On Liberty* and Montesquieu's *The Spirit of the Laws*. The most consequential part of his influence, however, turned out to be Social Darwinism, which resonated deeply with all intellectuals who were worried about China's survival at the time. Liang Qi-chao, who studied Western thought through the medium of Japanese translations, made important contributions by introducing Hobbes, Spinoza, Rousseau, Bacon and Kant into the Chinese-speaking world. In many ways, they were the trailblazers for the intellectuals of the next generation.

Both Yan Fu and Liang Qi-chao prepared and later witnessed the cultural and intellectual flourishing which was unleashed by the so-called 'May Fourth New Culture Movement' (1915–21) – an anti-traditionalist movement, initiated by Hu Shih, that called for creating a new Chinese culture based on democracy and science. As part of its programme for modernization, it advocated a literary reform that enabled (and, some might argue, revitalized) the use of vernacular language, paving the way to broader education and cultural reform. As Hu Shih became one of the leading figures of the New Culture Movement, liberalism was also widely disseminated among intellectuals. However, thanks to other prominent figures like Li Ta-chao and Chen Du-xiu, Marxism-Leninism was also becoming more and more popular in China. In fact, the communist movement became so energized, and its tone so radicalized, that Hu Shih felt obliged to offer a response, despite being reluctant to enter political debates. As the leading liberal intellectual, he wrote the famous essay 'More Study of Problems, Less Talk of Isms' (1919), proposing that social reforms should be realized by incremental changes aimed at solving individual, practical problems rather than by taking up 'fanciful, good-sounding isms'. However, one should bear in mind that Hu Shih himself was more interested in serious academic pursuits such as the re-examination of the national heritage rather than the study of concrete political problems. Nor was his pragmatic approach free of theoretical commitments. His opponents thus argued that he had likewise not exempted himself from basing his proposals on the ideology of experimentalism.

During the so-called Warlord Era (a period in the Chinese republic when political control was divided among military cliques), the warlords suppressed freedom of the press and battled against any journalist who dared to disclose the truth about them by shutting down publishers, or even assassinating journalists. Hu Shih, along with a few other renowned and like-minded intellectuals, published *Declaration of the Struggle for Freedom*, urging the government to protect freedom of speech. In April 1922, in response to the gloomy atmosphere of the political arena at the time, he wrote *Our Political Proposals*, and persuaded over ten other famous intellectuals to undersign this programmatic essay. Based on the fundamental principles of liberalism, the article argued that government is just a tool developed by the people to serve their interests. Therefore, a 'good government' is a government which 'fully utilizes the political regime to serve all members in a society', and one which 'tolerates individual freedom and treasures the development of personalities'. The concrete sign of a good government, according to Hu Shih, is a 'constitutional government', 'because that is the first step towards healthy political reform'. He demanded a 'transparent government' which discloses its financial operations and the procedures of its test-based official-recruiting programme. 'We firmly believe that transparency is the only weapon against shady politics.'[2]

In 1927, after the Nationalist Party unified most of China, it followed the Soviet model and created a 'Party government' system which did not have a constitution. In the wake of a series of dreadful human rights violations by the party after April 1929, Hu Shih published *Human Rights and Contract Laws, Discourses on*

'Human Rights and Contract Laws, When Can We Have a Constitution, The New Culture Movement and the Nationalist Party and Knowing is Difficult, but Doing is not Easy Either' – a series of essays which sharply criticized the Nationalist Party for its human rights breaches and marked the beginning of the human rights movement. The principal argument underlying these essays is that all human beings have basic rights that are inviolable, and that any curtailing of these rights would have to be *preceded by* legal and transparent processes. Therefore, the government should immediately establish a constitution that guaranteed these basic human rights.

However, the Nationalist Party at the time held the view that the Chinese people didn't yet have the ability to participate in politics – an ability which could only be developed by a gradual process of training. According to Sun Yat-sen, the founding leader of the Nationalist Party, this gradual process should consist of three steps: the first step was called 'stratocracy', which aimed at militarily obliterating all the forces of the opposition; the second step, branded 'political tutelage', aimed at establishing law and order, educating the people and constructing local autonomy. Needless to say, neither of these two steps required a constitution. Only then, at the last step, after the Chinese people were finally well-trained in politics, was a constitutional government to be established.

In response to these views, Hu Shih called on the ruling party to lead by example.

> What the people need is civic life under a constitution, while what the government and the party members need is life under the rule of law. The government officials who 'woke up in advance' should use the constitution to train themselves and limit themselves, only then can they expect to lead the people on the path towards republicanism. Otherwise, the party members will be merely paying lip service to 'political tutelage' without its requirements. Granted, maybe the people are not terribly intelligent, but can they be this easily fooled?

His conclusion was: 'We do not believe that political tutelage is possible without a constitution; a system of political tutelage without a constitution can only be authoritarian to the core. We firmly believe that the sole system which is capable of political tutelage is a constitutional government.'[3] By writing these articles, Hu Shih immensely agitated the Nationalist Party. Afterwards, *Crescent* magazine was shut down and Hu Shih himself was persecuted. He was forced to leave Shanghai, which had a tense political atmosphere at the time, and go to Beijing to become a professor at the Beijing University.

Despite taking citizens' individual rights very seriously, Hu Shih was in favour of public ownership, or at least not against it. In July 1925, he took a train to Europe through the Soviet Union and stayed in the USSR for a period of time. He came to have positive feelings about the revolutionary Soviet Union, and wrote about it to his friends in a series of letters. In response to scepticism that the Soviet utopia had no theoretical grounding, he pointed out that the same thing could also be said about capitalism, nationalism or partisan politics. Addressing the question of whether the Soviet system was a model with universal applicability suitable for adoption in China, he suggested that all political systems both have and do not have universal applicability. The crucial point, he argued, is about 'practice'. If a system can be well-practiced, it has universality; if not, then it does not. In particular, he called into question the view that 'once private property was abolished, humanity would no longer have the incentive to strive forward', or the claim that 'it is impossible to achieve high productivity under socialism'. He argued against these views by suggesting that private ownership and money were not the sole motivators for human progress and social development. He insisted that talented people and social elites, the ones with real nobility and high ideals, were not solely striving for private ownership. Therefore, social progress does not necessarily cease when private ownership is abolished, 'because talented people will always strive forward and accomplish magnificent deeds, regardless of what system they work under, be it private or public ownership'. Hence, in Hu Shih's view, the reason why capitalism had such advanced productivity was due to the effective functioning of its 'organism of production' (rather than private ownership). In comparison, socialism had not yet created such advanced organisms of production, which is why it could not yet catch up with the productivity of the capitalist countries. But this did not mean that it could never catch up. Indeed, Hu Shih had high praise of Lenin and Trotsky for their efforts, commenting that, ultimately, the Soviet Union would have the capacity to make better products than America.[4]

In 1926, Hu Shih published a long and influential article titled 'Our Attitudes Towards Modern Western Civilization'. The main point of the article was exactly what Hu Shih rejected three decades later, after reading *Road to Serfdom*, namely, the claim that private property should no longer be seen as a sacred human right as it was in the eighteenth century. Rather, its disadvantages were being increasingly exposed. In particular, the rise of capitalism had created tremendous suffering for the workers, which could (only) be cured by governmental redistribution and/or labour unionization. Unsurprisingly, influenced by the Soviet example, Hu Shih projected most of his hopes onto the socialist movement. Until the 1940s, despite criticizing the Soviet regime, he was never critical of public ownership.

Hu Shih's view was representative. Generally speaking, modern Chinese liberals were inclined to believe that public ownership was capable of bringing a better and more equal society, but they failed to see the relationship between public ownership and totalitarianism. Their ideal sociopolitical system can be summed up as 'Anglo-American politics, Soviet economy'. This yearning for public ownership may well have originated from the Confucian tradition, and the prevailing sense that 'what the people fear is inequality rather than the scarcity of resources' and 'when the Way (or Dao) prevails, public spirit will permeate every inch of the world', a tradition which sees private ownership as an evil.[5]

It was only in 1954, after reading the Chinese translation of *The Road to Serfdom*, that Hu Shih critically reflected upon his advocacy of public ownership and came to have a sober view of the relationship between public ownership and totalitarianism. What caused his change of mind was not only Hayek's economic theories but also (and perhaps more importantly) the radical changes in mainland China after 1949. A series of massive movements such as the Land Reform, the Suppression of Counterrevolutionaries and the Thought Reform had a tremendous impact on him. His growing disillusionment with the Soviet experiment under Stalin also pushed him to revise and criticize the Soviet model. Nevertheless, the encounter with Hayek played a vital role in providing Hu Shih with a theoretical grounding. It was a deeply felt textual moment that paved the way for Hu Shih's return to liberalism.

Translated from the Chinese by Yang Xiao.

Hannah Arendt: Power, Action and the Foundation of Freedom

Roger Berkowitz

In distinction to strength, which is the gift and the possession of every man in his isolation against all other men, power comes into being only if and when men join themselves together for the purpose of action, and it will disappear when, for whatever reason, they disperse and desert one another. Hence, binding and promising, combining and covenanting are the means by which power is kept in existence; where and when men succeed in keeping intact the power which sprang up between them during the course of any particular act or deed, they are already in the process of foundation, of constituting a stable worldly structure to house, as it were, their combined power of action. There is an element of the world-building capacity of man in the human faculty of making and keeping promises. Just as promises and agreements deal with the future and provide stability in the ocean of future uncertainty where the unpredictable may break in from all sides, so the constituting, founding, and world-building capacities of man concern always not so much ourselves and our own time on earth as our 'successors', and 'posterities'. The grammar of action: that action is the only human faculty that demands a plurality of men; and the syntax of power: that power is the only human attribute which applies solely to the worldly in-between space by which men are mutually related, combine in the act of foundation by virtue of the making and keeping of promises, which, in the realm of politics, may well be the highest human faculty.[1]

The inquiry into the 'nature of human power' is at the very centre of Hannah Arendt's political thinking. It is common sense today that power is dangerous, a sentiment heard in the saying: 'Power corrupts, and absolute power corrupts absolutely.' Against this cautionary view, Arendt argues that power is a necessary and salutary quality of politics, one that should rather be augmented than limited. Arendt argues that there is no legitimate government without power; since power emerges from the action of citizens in concert, power involves citizen participation in public affairs and power is the root of all self-government. To secure liberal freedom, Arendt insists, we must both work to augment power and simultaneously to prevent it from being corrupted, or being held in the hands of a single source. Arendt believes that the American Revolution discovered a new concept of power that serves as the solution to one of the great dilemmas of liberal government, how to found a government that is both powerful and stable while also enabling freedom.

Political freedom in liberal theory is opposed to order. If order demands limits on freedom, freedom depends upon the limitation of power. Plato showed in *The Republic* that too much freedom threatens to fall into anarchy and transform into tyranny. Montesquieu, in *The Spirit of the Laws*, argued that republican freedom was made possible by citizenly virtue that could only be nurtured in orderly small non-commercial republics. Rousseau posed the fundamental question of liberalism, which is how to authorize a legitimate order without restricting individual freedom.

Against Plato, Montesquieu and Rousseau, Arendt argues that liberal freedom is best protected not by limiting governmental power, but by augmenting and decentralizing power so as to create multiple centres of power that limit each other. She saw the genius of the American Revolution in the creation of a federal constitutional republic that enabled power not only to exist but to expand at the same time. Arendt argued that this allowed the United States to at once exert and benefit from political power while also preventing that power from becoming oppressive. The core of Arendt's argument in defence of a diffused liberal power is her insight that the American Revolution succeeds because the Revolution made manifest what she calls 'the new American experience and the new American concept of power' (157–8).

Arendt articulates her argument about the importance of the American concept of power in Chapters Four and Five of *On Revolution*; Chapter Four, 'Foundation I: *Constitutio Libertatis*', is about the 'Constitution of Liberty' in American republicanism, and Chapter Five, 'Foundation II: *Novus Ordo Saeclorum*', argues that the American republic brought about a 'Rebirth of the Order of the Ages'. The passage above is taken from Part III of 'Foundation I: *Constitutio Libertatis*'. The passage summarizes, with brevity and force, Arendt's argument about the constitutional foundations of freedom in the new concept of power that emerges in the American Revolution.

To make sense of what Arendt means by the American concept of power and its importance for free and stable government, we must explicate the connections between three main concepts: power, action and the act of foundation. In doing so, we will gain entry into Arendt's overarching argument about the relation between power and freedom that expresses what she calls the 'spirit of the American Revolution'. In short, Arendt's liberalism imagines a limitation on government not through legal or formal constraints but by empowering competing institutional actors that balance each other and thus prevent the abuse of governmental power.

Arendt presents her insight into the nature of human power by first distinguishing power from strength. Strength is something each individual has on his or her own. I can lift so much weight; I can hold out against torture. I may have the strength of my convictions. But individual strength, Arendt argues, is weak when compared with the power of the many. 'The strength of even the strongest individual can always be overpowered by the many.'[2] Strength is always of one person. On the contrary, 'power', Arendt writes, 'corresponds to the human ability not just to act but to act in concert'.[3] Power is the specifically human capacity for acting together with others.

The example of power that Arendt finds at the root of the American Revolution is the experience of making covenants, mutual promises and constitutions. The colonists had a history of acting in concert to build roads, found communities and govern themselves. It was the 'great good fortune of the American Revolution', Arendt notes, that the colonies, prior to the Revolutionary War, 'were organized in self-governing bodies' (156). When the American Revolution broke out and the authority of the English king was rejected, the American revolutionaries were not transported into anarchy, a world without power and order. This is because the colonists were experienced with organized power in government bodies through constituent assemblies. As Arendt notes in the passage above, 'binding and promising, combining and covenanting are the means by which power is kept in existence'. The American concept of power originates in this practice of self-government.

Arendt lays great emphasis on the importance of the constituent assemblies in America. Particularly relevant is the example of Massachusetts. After the people of Massachusetts rejected a constitution proposed by the democratically elected Massachusetts Assembly in 1778, a special election was held in which every town in the state chose special delegates for the express purpose of proposing a new state constitution.[4] Arendt elevates the Massachusetts example in an expository footnote in which she suggests that the decision to call a special convention was a model for the federal constitutional convention and represents a 'principle with the constituents "that the people should endow the government with a constitution and not vice versa".[5] And while Massachusetts was exceptional, it is an exception that proved a rule that the constituent assemblies in the American colonies were 'the most democratically recruited of all such constituted bodies in the Western World'.[6] Nearly 80 per cent of white men were eligible to vote in Massachusetts, and about half of white males could vote in New Jersey and Virginia. Arendt notes that the great exceptions to the American experience of power were the slaves, that 'slavery carries an obscurity even blacker than the obscurity of poverty' and that the 'indifference' the revolutionaries felt towards slaves is 'difficult for us to understand'. She argues, however, that by ignoring the misery of black slaves, the revolutionaries were able to focus their attention on acting together as equals to build powerful institutions rather than addressing persistent inequalities (61). The American revolutionaries were neither guerrilla warriors nor rebels; they were elected representatives fighting not only for liberty from English rule but, more importantly, for the right to govern themselves. Far from limiting power, they were eager to found and augment it.

The American experience of self-government in townships and local assemblies distinguished the American Revolution from those that followed in Europe. 'What was lacking in the Old World were the townships of the colonies,' Arendt observed. Citing Alexis de Tocqueville, she argues that 'the doctrine of the sovereignty of the people came out of the townships and took possession of the state.'[7] It was this experience of self-government that embodied the new American experience of power. Power, as it was understood in the American Revolution, 'was embodied in all institutions of self-government throughout the country' (158).

Arendt traces the American openness to create new centres of governmental power at least in part to the exemplary arrival of the Pilgrims in the New World and the Mayflower Compact. As the Pilgrims on the Mayflower came together off the coast of Plymouth Rock, they decided 'solemnly and mutually in the Presence of God and one another, [to] covenant and combine ourselves together into a civil Body Politick ...; and by virtue hereof [to] enact, constitute, and frame, such just and equal Laws, Ordinances, Acts, Constitutions, and Offices necessary for the common good' (164). Arendt cites these lines from the Mayflower Compact to illustrate the astounding confidence these original settlers had in 'their own power, granted and confirmed by no one and as yet unsupported by any means of violence, to combine themselves into a "civil Body Politick"' (158). This new body politic was to be held together by no force, but simply by the faith each person had in the loyalty of each to their mutual promises. It was this faith in their power to join together and constitute new powers and new governments that, Arendt argues, was the distinctly new and American experience of power.

It is, of course, true that the power to covenant existed prior to America. But the generative idea of power through mutual promises and compacts is most often fleeting; it may flare into existence, but it quickly is extinguished as the new power centres claim for themselves sovereignty and the right to govern. But this is not what happened after the American Revolution, where the 'new American experience and the new American concept of power' were elevated and incorporated into constitutions and institutions 'designed explicitly to preserve it' (158).

The specific institutions Arendt credits with preserving and strengthening the American experience of power are federalist bodies and the federalist spirit of the American Constitution. In each state, after the Revolutionary War, victory was followed not by anarchy but by constitution-making. The 'miracle that saved the American Revolution' was that after the colonists won the war and liberated themselves from England, they immediately, without pause, set about governing themselves. In most other revolutions, the power of acting together in rebellion dissipates into anarchy or terror after liberation. But in America, the rebellion was followed neither by chaos nor restoration of tyranny, but by a 'fever of constitution-making' that 'prevented the development of a power vacuum' (139). What so impressed Arendt was that in the wake of the liberation, the American colonies immediately began governing themselves, so that 'thirteen clocks had struck as one – so that there existed no gap, no hiatus, hardly a breathing spell between the war of liberation, the fight for independence which was the condition of freedom, and the constitution of the new states' (132–3). Without missing a beat, the colonists made use of their experience in self-government to put new constitutions before the people for popular approval.

The difference between American constitutions and their European descendants is that in America the constitutions were not made and imposed by experts but were constituted by the people themselves. Thus the American constitutions were not simply acts of government designed to limit the government and protect civil liberties. Rather, the constitutions were active examples of a people coming together to constitute themselves. Instead of limiting power, the American constitutions were acts that created new powers, and it was this task, 'the creation of new power', that Arendt saw to be the central activity of the American Revolution (140).

The American experience with and love of power is what inspires the federalist structure of the US Constitution. In the Articles of Confederation, immediately following the Revolution, local and state governments formed a kind of alliance, but 'experience had shown that in this alliance of powers there was a dangerous tendency for the allied powers not to act as checks upon one another but to cancel one another out, that is, to breed impotence' (144). The 1787 Constitution addressed this defect not by creating a unified national government, but by adding to the powers of the various states another power centre, 'a new source of power, which in no way drew its strength from the powers of the states, as it had not been established at their expense' (144). The federal government was given enlarged powers to check the state governments, but the state and local and even non-governmental organizations retained their powers so that they could check the power of the national government.

Drawing on Montesquieu and Madison, Arendt's fundamental conviction that 'power must be opposed to power' is the key to her understanding of the uniqueness and importance of the revolutionary American concept of power. 'In this respect, the great and, in the long run, perhaps the greatest American innovation in politics as such was the consistent abolition of sovereignty within the body politic of the republic, the insight that in the realm of human affairs sovereignty and tyranny are the same.' By establishing a federalist division and multiplication of powers – by seeking to generate more powers rather than limit a sovereign power – the American Revolution institutionalized a concept of power that could found liberal freedoms on the foundation of multiplying power across multiple centres.

Power exists in political communities 'wherever people gather together'. But power is fleeting, and it dissipates as soon action ceases and is replaced by rule and obedience. Thus 'power is what keeps the public realm, the potential space of appearance between acting and speaking men, in existence'.[8] This is what Arendt means when she writes of 'the syntax of power'. Power acquires an order; it has its syntax, in a worldly space of appearance. While strength is a natural quality of an individual seen in isolation, power springs up between men when they act together and vanishes the moment they disperse. Thus, power is possible neither in tyrannies – where citizens are excluded from acting together in public – nor in anarchy – where citizens act in opposition to institutional powers. Without lasting political institutions where plural people can act, power disappears, opening the way for either anarchy or the restoration of an old order.

The emergence of power and its establishment in lasting institutions depends upon action. Action is rooted in plurality since, to act in concert, men must be both equal enough to understand each other and distinct enough to require that they actually act and speak in ways that bring them together. Amid such a plurality, to act means to do something so surprising, unexpected and spontaneous that others take notice and begin talking about your action. When others talk about what you have done, tell stories about your deeds, build monuments to your doings and make your actions part of the common world they share with you, then action comes to instantiate power. We see the connection between action and power in actions like Martin Luther King's Montgomery bus boycott or his 'I Have a Dream' speech. Such actions shock and surprise; they lead to new stories and new common truths. Only such new and surprising actions 'break through the commonly accepted and reach into the extraordinary' and thus make other people take notice and begin to talk and act in response.[9] It is the grammar of action that makes possible the coming together of different people for a common end; it is thus action that gives birth to power.

Arendt understood the tradition of self-government in the New England colonies in America to be one example of action that instituted a uniquely American understanding of power. The revolutionaries in America experienced joy after the victory of their rebellion – the specific joys of compacting, covenanting and promising. Arendt refers to Jefferson's famous letter to John Adams, in which he writes: 'May we meet there again, in Congress, with our antient colleagues, and receive with them the seal of approbation "Well done, good and faithful servants".' And she adds: 'Here, behind the irony, we have the candid admission that life in Congress, the joys of discourse, of legislation, of transacting business, of persuading and being persuaded, were to Jefferson no less conclusively a foretaste of an eternal bliss to come than the delights of contemplation had been for medieval piety' (122). The American experience of freedom, power and joy led to the rise of the uniquely American idea of dispersed, federal and democratic power. It is the American experience of power in acting together by covenanting and legislating that leads to the growth of power at all levels of American public life.

Arendt argues that power and action 'combine in the act of foundation by virtue of the making and keeping of promises, which, in the realm of politics, may well be the highest human faculty'. The 'act of foundation' recalls the title of the chapter, 'Foundation 1: *Constitutio Libertatis*'. In the act, by which a plurality of people join together to act and form a powerful institution that can govern itself for common ends, Arendt finds the foundation of liberty and freedom. As she writes, 'Freedom ... becomes the direct aim of political action, is actually the reason that men live together in political organization at all. Without it, political life as such would be meaningless.'[10] Freedom emerges only in governments based on actions that generate power, and thus only in liberal regimes.

Liberalism, rooted in liberty, is about freedom as it exists within legitimate government. For Arendt, liberal governments must combine action with power. Liberalism is about freedom since the *'raison d'être* of politics is freedom'.[11] And a free and liberal politics must encourage action since 'freedom is primarily experienced in action'.[12] Liberalism, therefore, must seek freedom through the generation of power through action.

Against much of the liberal tradition, Arendt argues that freedom is not in the granting or enjoyment of rights guaranteed by a government or constitution. Rather, freedom is actualized in the act of constituting government itself. 'Men *are* free ... as long as they act, neither before nor after; for to *be* free and to act are the same.'[13] This is the central lesson of Arendt's teaching about the American experience of power: freedom is possible only when a revolution succeeds in founding institutions where people act in concert and thus preserve and augment multiple sources of power.

Reading F. A. Hayek

Edwige Kacenelenbogen

*The argument for liberty is not an argument against organization, which
is one of the most powerful means that human reason can employ, but
an argument against all exclusive, privileged, monopolistic organization,
against the use of coercion to prevent others from trying to do better. Every
organization is based on given knowledge; organization means commitment to
a particular aim and to particular methods, but even organization designed to
increase knowledge will be effective only insofar as the knowledge and beliefs
on which its design rests are true. And if any facts contradict the beliefs on
which the structure of the organization is based, this will become evident only
in its failure and supersession by a different type of organization. Organization
is therefore likely to be beneficial and effective so long as it is voluntary and is
imbedded in a free sphere and will either have to adjust itself to circumstances
not taken into account in its conception or fail. To turn the whole of society
into a single organization built and directed according to a single plan would
be to extinguish the very forces that shaped the individual human minds that
planned it. ... There can be little doubt that man owes some of his greatest
successes in the past to the fact that he has not been able to control social
life. His continued advance may well depend on his deliberately refraining
from exercising controls which are now in his power. In the past, spontaneous
forces of growth, however much restricted, could usually still assert themselves
against the organized coercion of the state. With the technological means of
control now at the disposal of government, it is not certain that such assertion
is still possible; at any rate, it may soon become impossible. We are not far
from the point where the deliberately organized forces of society may destroy
those spontaneous forces which have made advance possible.*[1]

Hayek's life spanned nearly all of the twentieth century, from his birth in 1899 to his death in 1992. His whole intellectual endeavour sprang from what he considered to be an imminent and unprecedented threat to humanity, and to European civilization in particular: the coming to power of the socialist ideal. For Hayek, the dispute between a market order and socialism was nothing less than a matter of survival for mankind: 'To follow socialist morality' was to 'destroy much of present humankind and impoverish much of the rest.'[2] Because he knew that the tide of socialism could be successfully stopped only by an equally powerful set of ideals, from *The Road to Serfdom* (1944), the famous pamphlet that first brought him international recognition, to his monumental three-volume *Law, Legislation and Liberty* (1973, 1976, 1979), Hayek's stated and constant goal was to reassert and re-establish the philosophical foundations for a theory of freedom. Throughout his work, he thus consistently sought to defend the classical liberal ideal of a free society, that 'modest and even humble creed' based both on a low opinion of men's wisdom and capacities (Hayek was a fierce critic of all flattering assumptions about the unlimited powers of human reason), and on a fundamental trust in uncontrolled (or spontaneous) social forces.[3]

Unlike most contemporary political philosophers, Hayek made it very clear that he had an agenda. In this sense, his contribution to liberalism is generally perceived as ideological: his whole oeuvre is openly guided by the intent to consolidate the ideal of a free society against that of socialism, both as a concrete political regime and as a unifying doctrine.[4] The Constitution of Liberty (from which the quote above is extracted) is exemplary in this regard: it is Hayek's classic statement on the ideal of liberty, his ultimate philosophical argument in defence of a free society.

Hayek's theory of freedom has two important facets. The first one is a negative definition of liberty as the absence of coercion. By 'coercion' Hayek means 'such control of the environment or circumstances of a person by another that, in order to avoid greater evil, he is forced to act not according to a coherent plan of his own but to serve the ends of another.'[5] Hayek's argument for liberty is, above all, an argument against the use of coercion. In an explicitly Kantian vein, he considers an individual to be free only if she is not and cannot be a tool in the achievement of the ends of another. Coercion can be prevented only by the existence of a private sphere where the individual is protected from such interference. And such a private sphere can, in turn, be preserved only by the existence of general rules, embodied in a written constitution and upheld by state power. When Hayek writes, at the beginning of the excerpt, that his 'argument for liberty is… an argument against the use of coercion to prevent others from trying to do better', he is making a clear case in favour of unfettered, constitutionally bound competition.

Hence the importance, in Hayek's view, of the law or, more precisely, of the general and abstract nature of the law.[6] Insofar as the rules justifying coercion are framed so as to apply equally to all people in similar circumstances, they merely provide the framework within which the individual must act, but within which decisions remain hers. This, in essence, refers to the principle of 'freedom under the law': individual freedom is guaranteed by the fact that laws are general and abstract rules laid down irrespective of the particular cases or persons to which they will apply.

As evidenced by the first two lines of the excerpt, Hayek acknowledges the importance of the state – or of human organizations in general. In his view, the state should act and rule to create a stable and fair context for individuals to pursue their own ends. Hayek even makes a strong case for the state to act so as to reduce inequality of opportunity ('as far as congenital differences permit' and insofar as doing so does not impede the impersonal system of rules under which we all live and act) to ensure certain minimum standards in physical necessities and to organize a comprehensive system of social insurance.[7]

The second facet of Hayek's liberalism, or second pillar of his theory of freedom, is his faith in 'spontaneous forces of growth', that is, in the autonomous forces of social order. Far from a relation of command and obedience (or a hierarchical structure in which the will of superiors determines what each should do), in Hayek's understanding, social order is a means-connected system with no hierarchy of ultimate ends, that is, a 'self-generating', 'endogenous' or 'spontaneous' order arising out of an unplanned matching of intentions and expectations, 'the product of the actions of many men, but not the result of human design.'[8]

This aspect of Hayek's thought is closely connected to his conception of human knowledge, which, according to him, 'never exists in concentrated or integrated form but solely as the dispersed bits of incomplete and frequently contradictory knowledge which all the separate individuals possess.'[9] Because knowledge depends on the circumstances of the fleeting moment, it belongs to each individual in particular (to each 'man on the spot') and to none in general.[10] Hence the importance of the decentralized mechanisms of decision-making which, over time, build upon the habits and institutions which have proved to be valuable.

In time, facts either confirm or contradict the knowledge and beliefs on which various habits and institutions rest, leading either to their survival or to their demise. Echoing his friend Karl Popper, Hayek argues that the beliefs on which successful institutions rest are 'true' until empirical observation (in this case, the 'failure and supersession by a different type of organization') proves them to be false. Decentralized mechanisms of decision based on incomplete and diffuse knowledge are thus crucial for every possible avenue of evolution to be explored. By contrast, information centralization – a typical trait of ever-expanding governments – is particularly harmful to the creation, preservation and utilization of knowledge.

In short, then, to preserve the sources of the growth of Western civilization, to protect and nurture the mechanism through which 'true' or 'dispersed, incomplete and frequently contradictory' knowledge is produced and shared, that is, to insure human innovation and creativity, Hayek recommends a free-market system under the rule of law, with strong constitutional protections of individual rights. He thereby raises a powerful voice against the doxa of his time, which shared an uncritical faith in central planning as a key element of economic reconstruction. Based on his careful observation of the Nazi regime as well as his analysis of the socialist rationale of the time, he excoriates the 'scientistic' attitude – a mechanical and uncritical application, in social sciences, of habits of thought pertaining exclusively to physical science – which ignores both that 'there are definite limits to what we can expect science to achieve' and that 'deliberate control may have deplorable effects'.[11] It is precisely by refraining from exercising such control that, according to Hayek, men allowed for crucial advances of civilization.

The 'contextual', historically situated and polemical character of his argument (directed against the then widespread and far-reaching collectivism and state planning) is an aspect of Hayek's thought that, by comparison with more recent – and abstract – political theory, is often invoked to his disadvantage. The reason for this is not only that the immediate target of his work (enthusiasm for a centrally planned economy) has faded. As social sciences pretend to more and more 'neutrality' by way of quantitative methods, Hayek's enthusiastic support for a specific ideology – which some broadly labelled 'doctrinarism' – is also assumed to explain some of the pitfalls into which his analysis falls. Hayek's rigidity of tone and relative lack of philosophical circumspection have indeed been considered to weaken the logical basis of his theoretical argument.

Yet it is important to note that, as 'historically situated' and 'ideological' as they may be, Hayek's observations remain of great relevance for the history of liberalism, and social and political thought more broadly. In particular, his main epistemological argument – that, because of its inherent complexity and heterogeneity, the only way a large society can be efficiently coordinated is through the free workings of spontaneous processes – is one of the most insightful in the twentieth-century political philosophy. Looking at the way modern progress and contemporary patterns of innovation involve both competition and open environments (i.e., non-institutional forms of collaboration or open-source communities), one has to recognize how perceptive Hayek was in his description and defence of spontaneous processes and the intrinsic unpredictability of the human world.

Today, it is indeed a rather well-accepted fact that progress through innovation requires both a framework of rules and laws that provide a stable and fair context for individuals to pursue their own ends (the first pillar of Hayek's theory of freedom) and the freedom of sometimes collaborative and connective, sometimes destructive and chaotic forces at work in the natural and social world (spontaneous orders).[12] In short, the idea that top-heavy bureaucracies are textbook innovation sinkholes has become somewhat of a truism nowadays.

On the whole, Hayek's intellectual efforts can be understood as part of a handful of early stage investigations into the subject of complex adaptive (autonomous) systems and spontaneous orders. These investigations gave rise, a few decades later, to an entire and specific scientific domain – and related worldview. Together with his work (though not necessarily directly related), over the past four decades, various theoretical efforts – those of Claude Shannon, Norbert Wiener or Ilya Prigogine, to name only a few – have led to the advent of a new paradigm, to which the foundation of the Santa Fe institute in 1984 famously gave one of its first concrete forms.[13]

Moreover, in our ever more hurried world, where information frequently passes as wisdom and the need for public acknowledgement often overrides caution and confirmation, Hayek's call for epistemological modesty, his claim that the first step in any scientific inquiry should always be a frank and open acknowledgement of the limitations of human thought, together with his observation that intellectuals commonly have an inherent tendency to overestimate their own reasoning skills and the correctness of their own thoughts, are quite topical.[14] Despite the repeated proofs of our deep-rooted irrationality, of the existence of myriad inherent biases or of the disruptive role of emotions, the excesses arising in various scientific fields from a seemingly unshakable belief in pure reason remain hard to curb.

Hayek's liberalism, based both on a negative definition of liberty as the absence of coercion and on a defence of the autonomous forces of social order, is a reflection on the natural boundaries of the human intellect and on the greater efficiency of complex and abstract orders. Though Hayek cannot be said to have developed a fully fledged theory of complexity, many of the ideas that were later to define complexity theory are expounded in his writings.[15] For instance, and most notably, elaborating on the idea – crucial to complexity theory – of an abstract, emergent pattern, Hayek writes: 'The "emergence" of "new" patterns as a result of the increase in the number of elements between which simple relations exist, means that this larger structure as a whole will possess certain general or abstract features which will recur independently of the particular values of the individual data, so long as the general structure…is preserved.'[16] This path-breaking focus on the pattern – or emergent – property (as distinct from the set of rules which gives rise to it) is closely connected to Hayek's assumption that an abstract order does *not* depend on the predictability of individual actions – and thus allows for a great diversity (or freedom) of those actions.[17]

As everyday life becomes increasingly populated by artificial intelligence and we find ourselves relying more and more on studies of organized complexity and 'bottom-up intelligence' (called for by such phenomena as crowd funding, crowd lending and ever more distributed networks), Hayek's efforts perceptibly gain a renewed and forceful significance. This only a doctrinaire mind could deny.

Maruyama Masao and Liberalism in Japan[1]

Reiji Matsumoto

As Carl Schmitt has pointed out, an outstanding characteristic of the modern European State lies in its being ein neutraler Staat. That is to say, the State adopts a neutral position on internal values, such as the problem of what truth and justice are; it leaves the choice and judgment of all values of this sort to special social groups (for instance, to the Church) or to the conscience of the individual. ... Questions of thought, belief, and morality were deemed to be private matters and, as such, were guaranteed their subjective, 'internal' quality; meanwhile, state power was steadily absorbed into an 'external' legal system, which was of a technical nature.

In post-Restoration Japan, however, when the country was being rebuilt as a modern State, there was never any effort to recognize these technical and neutral aspects of national sovereignty. In consequence Japanese nationalism strove consistently to base its control on internal values rather than on authority deriving from external laws.

The 'people's right' approach, represented by early liberals of this kind, was from the beginning connected with theories about 'national rights'; and it was inevitable that it should in due course be submerged by them. Thus in the struggle for liberalism the question of the individual's conscience never became a significant factor in defining his freedom. Whereas in the West national power after the Reformation was based on formal, external sovereignty, the Japanese State never came to the point of drawing a distinction between the external and internal spheres and recognizing that its authority was valid only for the former.

Accordingly, until the day in 1946 when the divinity of the Emperor was formally denied in an Imperial Rescript, there was in principle no basis in

Japan for freedom of belief. Since the nation includes in its 'national polity' all the internal values of truth, morality, and beauty, neither scholarship nor art could exist apart from these national values.[2]

Maruyama Masao (1914–96) was without doubt an eminent liberal. But being liberal in Japan, a country in which liberalism is not deeply rooted in culture, is different from being so in Europe or America. Maruyama never tries to formulate, as John Rawls does, his own theory of liberalism. Rather, he prefers, as an intellectual historian, to analyse and describe the movement of ideas in the past and to show his own thought through dialogue with past thinkers. However, with the major exception of Fukuzawa Yukichi, Maruyama rarely chooses liberal thinkers for examination in his study of Japanese thought. As the reference to Carl Schmitt in the lead quotation suggests, he owes much of his understanding of liberalism to its enemies. In these respects, one might find some similarities or parallels between Maruyama and Isaiah Berlin, who, himself committed to Enlightenment ideas, profoundly investigated the meaning and significance of the anti-Enlightenment and even drew a charming portrait of Joseph de Maistre.

Maruyama is not a simple and complacent liberal. He is keenly aware of the weak points of Western liberalism, which were tragically revealed in the political experiences of humankind in the twentieth century. Among his contemporary liberals in the West, he shows greater sympathy with those who are self-critical of the liberal tradition, like Harold J. Laski or Reinhold Niebuhr. Thus, not only does he criticize the tradition of his own country, he also shows in his own way how to survive the world crisis of the twentieth century as a liberal.

Maruyama's liberal thinking is remarkable for his sharp critique of the illiberal tradition in his own country, which unconsciously curbs the minds of the people, including many self-proclaimed liberals. Liberalism (*jiyūshugi*) and related words conveying its central concerns were introduced into Japanese political vocabulary in the nineteenth century. Classical texts of European liberalism were translated (*On Liberty* in 1873 and the first volume of *Democracy in America* in 1881) and widely read amid the political enthusiasm aroused by the Popular Rights Movement. The first political party in Japan born from the movement was named the Liberal Party (*jiyūtō*), although a national parliament was not in existence at the time.

Under the Constitution of 1889, however, liberalism as a political force was consistently marginalized in Japanese politics. In spite of a certain progress of constitutional democracy and party politics during the Taishō era (1912–26), liberal tendencies declined in the following decades of militarism and hyper-nationalism. The persecution (in 1935) of Minobe Tatsukichi, an authoritative Tokyo Imperial University professor emeritus of constitutional theory and member of the House of Peers, whose liberal interpretation of the Meiji Constitution had once been accepted as a standard by the government, tragically showed the vulnerability of liberalism in pre-war Japan.

Thus, under the military government and the heavy pressure of ultra-nationalism, liberalism was virtually dead in Japan when the Second World War began. No liberals criticized the basic values of the Emperor System, and liberal social theories did not provide a plausible analysis of its political and ideological structure. Only Marxists attempted a thoroughgoing critical analysis of the regime, at the price of suffering ruthless oppression.

The significance of Maruyama Masao and his work in Japanese intellectual history is to be understood against this background of the poor record of liberals and the comparatively strong performance of Marxists in pre-war Japan. Born into a family of liberal journalists and studying at the law faculty of Tokyo Imperial University, he inherited the best of pre-war liberalism. Starting his academic career in the critical years of the 1930s, however, he was heavily influenced by Marxist analysis. His first major scholarly work, written around 1940 and published in book form after the war, was a meticulous analysis of the political thought of the Tokugawa period (1603–1867) which became a reference for all subsequent studies of the subject.[3] Methodologically, it followed in the footsteps of the Marxian critique of ideology in its intent to explain the development of social and political thought in connection with changing social structures, but it also revealed Maruyama's distance from orthodox Marxism in that he neither reduced the meaning of ideology to its social function nor considered any set of ideas a mere reflection of the social and economic interests of the social classes which embraced them. His methodological guides were Max Weber, Karl Mannheim and Franz Borkenau, among others.

Maruyama's reading of Tokugawa political thought was motivated by a covert intention to protest against the dominant ideology of the time. Japano-centrism, Confucianism and National Learning (a movement to revive the study of Japanese history and literature) were ideological weapons against modernity, that is to say, Western democracy and liberalism, in sharp contrast to Maruyama's reinterpretation. He explored the intellectual origins of Japanese modernization in the dissolution of the Neo-Confucian mode of thought, and found in the rise of National Learning the basis for the growth of basic ideas of modern thinking: the emancipation of the natural desires of human beings from moralistic restraints. His treatment of the two heroes of his story (Ogyū Sorai and Motoori Norinaga) was particularly striking. In the conventional reading, the former was notorious for his cult of China and therefore a bête noire for all Japano-centric historians, while the latter was applauded for his rejection of Chinese influence and for his reconstruction of the myth of ancient Japan, and therefore celebrated as a godfather of Japanese nationalism. In striking contrast, Maruyama considered Sorai's thoroughgoing critique of Neo-Confucianism as epoch-making, underlining his clear distinction between ethics and politics, the private and the public. He compared this discovery of politics, as distinct from ethics, to the political science of Machiavelli. As for Norinaga, Maruyama focused on his sharp criticism of Confucian moralism and his encouragement of emancipating natural desires and aesthetic feelings, totally ignoring his chauvinism.

After 1945, the terrible consequences of the war and defeat urged Maruyama to reconsider the whole process of Japanese modernization and to explain why the Japanese people were driven in the end to a catastrophic war. His first substantial post-war writing, 'The Theory and Psychology of Ultra-Nationalism', a short but brilliant essay published in May 1946, was an answer to this question and had an extraordinary resonance among the reading public. The essay concentrates on the ideological structure of ultra-nationalism and brings to light the psychological process through which it controls the minds of the people. In the rapid process of nation-building, the Meiji State not only constructed centralized institutions of government and administration but also invented an ideological device which effectively controlled the people and moulded everybody into a loyal subject of the emperor. As suggested in the lead quotation, Maruyama's central argument is that, in Japan, national sovereignty monopolized both spiritual authority and political power, and that, consequently, government authorities did not limit themselves to externally controlling people's behaviour by law but invaded their inner life and regulated their minds. This is exactly the philosophical premise that liberals should have categorically rejected and challenged.

However, thought control under the Emperor System was different from that of totalitarian states like Nazi Germany or Soviet Russia. No systematic ideologies were imposed, nor were concentration camps built for dissenters. Nevertheless, governmental control of the people was effective and conformity in opinion was easily assured, for the government could rule people through a mental attitude deeply rooted in Japanese culture. Quoting from Fukuzawa Yukichi, Maruyama identifies this attitude as a product of 'the imbalance of power' which prevails in human relations in Japanese society. In the hierarchical structure of society, everybody has superiors and inferiors. In each small unit of superior–inferior relations, everybody suffers from an arbitrary exercise of power from above, and at the same time exercises arbitrary power below, thus compensating for his or her own sufferings. Maruyama calls this 'the transfer of oppression' and finds its extreme pathology in the notorious eruption of violence during the war: drill sergeants' bullying of new soldiers, which was a common practice, and the cruel treatment of POWs. This is an acute analysis of the psychological process which many Japanese people knew well through their sad experiences during the war. But Maruyama asserts that this transfer of oppression is not only a product of war or limited to military life. It is embedded in every corner of society, for the Meiji State inherited 'the imbalance of power' from feudal Japan and systematically incorporated it into the hierarchical structure of national order under the emperor. The painful incidents frequently provoked in wartime were only the intensified pathology of a constitutional disease.

The price of the effective control attained through the transfer of oppression is a complete disappearance of the sense of personal responsibility for the exercise of power, for, in this system everybody rules others in the same way as they are ruled, thus becoming unconscious of ruling others. In other words, not only oppression but responsibility could be transferred to others. The legitimacy of an order to one's inferior consists not in the nature of the order, but in the superior position of those who order, as authorized by the emperor, the ultimate source of all values, moral as well as political. In this hierarchical and bureaucratic structure, in which everybody is the prisoner of his or her position, no one could stand on their own feet – not even the highest officials. Maruyama quotes a speech by Tōjō Hideki, the wartime prime minister, saying, humiliatingly, that he was personally nothing but a pebble by the roadside, which only shone in the aureole of His Majesty. Even the emperor is a prisoner of the mythical tradition of his Imperial Ancestors, far from an absolute king or a totalitarian ruler.

This is the central point of Maruyama's acute analysis of the psychological basis for Japanese militarism, fully developed in his careful study of the documents of the International Military Tribunal for the Far East, 'Thought and Behavior Patterns of Japan's Wartime Leaders'. In striking contrast to the German war criminals judged by the Nuremberg Tribunal, he argues, none of the military leaders of Japan summoned to the Tokyo Tribunal recognized their personal responsibility for what they had done. Unanimously, they said, first, that they had only confirmed faits accomplis, which could not have been changed anyway, and, second, that they had had no competence as government officials to do otherwise. Underneath these high officials' apology was a confession of their inability to control their subordinates. Indeed, in many cases, they were, in fact, mere robots manipulated by their subordinates. The two lines of argument of their self-vindication, submission to faits accomplis and refuge in one's limited authority, were not merely a pretext for clearing themselves of the charge of war crimes, but a natural consequence of the mental attitude cultivated in a social structure in which no one took responsibility. Maruyama calls it 'the system of irresponsibilities' and explains it as frequently found in the degenerative phase of authoritarian and bureaucratic states. However, Maruyama's sharp analysis of the absence of responsible leadership in military Japan touches upon something intrinsic to the nature of Japanese society itself, which occasionally reveals its pathology even in our present state of democracy. Indeed, the reactions of the government to the nuclear plant disaster of Fukushima were so confused and irresponsible that they reminded some people of Maruyama's bitter critique of the system of irresponsibilities.

Intellectual emancipation after the war encouraged Maruyama to find the forgotten potential of liberalism in Japan. Particularly attracted to the spread of political ideas in the early Meiji era, Maruyama drew a bright picture of the intellectual scene at the time. He emphasized the healthy aspect of early Meiji nationalism, which had included abundant liberal elements, in contrast to later ultra-nationalism. The most noteworthy of his writings of this sort is his study of Fukuzawa Yukichi (1835–1901, liberal author and publisher influential during the Meiji Restoration). Fukuzawa became his favourite maître à penser, to whom he never ceased to pay respect. Fukuzawa is to Maruyama what Tocqueville is to Raymond Aron.

Maruyama also wrote several illuminating essays on European liberals, from John Locke to contemporaries like Harold J. Laski and Bertrand Russell. His short but suggestive article on Locke's political theory, entitled 'John Locke and Modern Political Principles', was pioneering. Locke's *Two Treatises of Government* had never previously been translated into Japanese and rarely discussed in pre-war Japan. Why was this classical text of European liberalism neglected? Maruyama quotes a passage from Bertrand Russell's *History of Western Philosophy* discussing Locke's thoroughgoing critique of Robert Filmer. The latter's patriarchalism, Russell says, is so ridiculous that no one would take it seriously in the civilized world of the twentieth century except in Japan, where the governing principle is very similar to Filmer's theory of paternal power. Maruyama, quoting this passage, suggested that with the collapse of the Emperor System, Japanese people could for the first time grasp the full meaning of Locke's political theory. He became a prime mover of Locke studies in Japan, which would later grow remarkably.[4] French intellectuals had a long tradition of public debate, while their Japanese counterparts were specialists who provided their expert knowledge and skill to the state. Only in exceptionally rare periods did they form an intellectual community of free and independent individuals, engaging in public debate on politics and society. The post-war period was one of the rare epochs of this kind, comparable to the early Meiji era, and the focus of public debate at the time was naturally the recent past of the country, the war and defeat. Why did Japan, after successfully building the first modern state in Asia, invade China and enter a catastrophic war? Post-war intellectuals shared a sense of moral responsibility and repentance for having done nothing effective to stop the war. It was this shared moral consciousness, according to Maruyama, that drove many intellectuals to join the movement against rearmament and military alliance with the United States. He later invented the phrase of 'the community of remorse' to label the intellectuals united in that shared conscience.

The Heiwamondai Danwakai ('Peace Problems Discussion Group'), in which Maruyama played a leading role, was an example. Started in 1948 as a learned society for studying peace problems in response to a UNESCO statement on peace, it gathered a wide variety of intellectuals and scholars, from conservative 'old liberals' to academic Marxists. With the progress of the Cold War, and especially after the outbreak of the Korean War, it was inevitably forced to address the hot political issues of the time, the conditions for the peace treaty and rearmament. Critically examining the government's policies on these issues – early independence through a partial peace treaty, rearmament and military alliance with the United States – the group proposed alternative policies consistent with the new constitution: a comprehensive peace treaty, neutralism and pacifism. Naturally, the proposal invited criticism. Maruyama replied, as a leading theoretician of the group, by laying down the theoretical foundations for the proposed policies of pacifism and neutrality.

In response to criticism of his views, Maruyama responded with two essays, 'A Letter to a Liberal' and 'Pitfalls of Realism'. In the first, he criticized the ideological reductionism and essentialist thinking of self-proclaimed liberals in Japan. Identifying himself as a liberal, he argued that ideological preference does not automatically determine the position to take on particular issues. In Japanese politics at the time, Maruyama argued, leftist ideology and radicalism were not a real danger. On the contrary, liberal democracy was undermined by the government's oppressive legislation against leftists. Thus, considering the political situation, Maruyama sided with the opposition. Even in the United States, he said, referring to McCarthyism, the ideals of liberal democracy were threatened from within rather than from the outside.[5]

In response to the 'realist' critique of pacifism and neutralism, Maruyama emphasized the plasticity of reality and its subjective nature. Self-proclaimed realists took one aspect of reality for the objective and unchangeable whole. They received a reality as a fait accompli and had no intention of changing it. In other words, Maruyama found in these Cold War realists the same mental attitude as that of the wartime military leaders whom he had criticized. Maruyama's own approach to reality is fully shown in the draft he wrote for a statement of Heiwamondai Danwakai, 'On Peace for the Third Time'. This is an ambitious tract, aimed at providing pacifism with theoretical foundations based on realism. Clarifying the multiple meanings of the phrase 'confrontation between two worlds', a cliché at the time, Maruyama distinguished three different phases of confrontation: the ideological confrontation of liberal democracy versus communism; political and military confrontation between two enemy camps, the Western versus the Eastern; and finally, superpower confrontation between the United States and the Soviet Union. Examining them in detail, he argued that, in any one of the three phases, confrontation was neither absolute nor unchangeable, and that on both sides there were always attempts to avoid confrontation and to reduce antagonism. Particularly noteworthy is that Maruyama recognized the possibility of splits in both camps. Considering the historical tradition of Chinese civilization, Communist China would not be long controlled from Moscow. Europe would not forever be dependent on the United States. Both blocs were not monolithic in reality, but comprised diverse elements which might eventually dissolve the confrontation between two worlds. Thus, amid the high tensions of the Cold War, Maruyama perceived the world of pluralism and diversity to come and explored conditions for peaceful coexistence in the future. Maruyama's careful study of the 'reality' of the Cold War, which anticipated the multi-polarized world to come, was more farsighted than most 'realist' analyses at the time. It was an exemplary liberal critique of Cold War liberalism.

Maruyama was not, of course, uncritical of communism and Marxism. A thoroughgoing critique of Marxist thinking is shown in 'A Critique of De-Stalinization', the longest chapter in *Thought and Behavior in Modern Japanese Politics*. In the editor's preface to the book, Ivan Morris defined the author as 'an independent member of the left', and never uttered the word 'liberal' to describe him. Today, more than a half-century after its publication, liberals in the West would have little hesitation in describing Maruyama as a liberal.

Liberty and Value Pluralism: Isaiah Berlin's 'Two Concepts of Freedom'

George Crowder

[1] I am normally said to be free to the degree to which no man or body of men interferes with my activity. Political liberty in this [negative] sense is simply the area within which a man can act unobstructed by others. ... [2] The 'positive' sense of the word 'liberty' derives from the wish on the part of the individual to be his own master. ... [3] The freedom which consists in being one's own master, and the freedom which consists in not being prevented from choosing as I do by other men, may, on the face of it, seem concepts at no great logical distance from each other.... Yet the 'positive' and 'negative' notions of freedom historically developed in divergent directions, not always by logically reputable steps, until, in the end, they came into direct conflict with each other ... [4] [T]he 'positive' conception of freedom as self-mastery, with its suggestion of a man divided against himself, has in fact, and as a matter of history, lent itself more easily to this splitting of personality into two: the transcendent, dominant controller, and the empirical bundle of desires and passions to be disciplined and brought to heel ... [5] The world that we encounter in ordinary experience is one in which we are faced with choices between ends equally ultimate, and claims equally absolute, the realisation of some of which must inevitably involve the sacrifice of others. [6] Pluralism, with the measure of 'negative' liberty that it entails, seems to me a truer and more humane ideal than the goals of those who seek in the great disciplined, authoritarian structures the ideal of 'positive' self-mastery by classes, or peoples, or the whole of mankind.[1]

Isaiah Berlin's 'Two Concepts of Liberty' (1958) is one of the classics of the liberal canon. It has been said that what John Rawls did for the idea of justice in *A Theory of Justice*, Berlin did for the idea of liberty (or freedom) in 'Two

Concepts'.[2] Yet the precise meaning of Berlin's essay is widely disputed, along with its merits.[3] Berlin's most obvious purpose is to define and contrast two conceptions of liberty, negative and positive – respectively liberty as non-interference and liberty as self-mastery. The immediate political context is the Cold War, and negative liberty is presented by Berlin as the liberty of the liberal-democratic West in conflict with the positive liberty of the communist world. On the whole, Berlin defends the negative liberty of the liberals and is critical of the positive idea.

But things are not quite as simple as that. In the last section of 'Two Concepts', a theme becomes explicit that underlies the whole argument: the plurality and incommensurability of fundamental human values, and the problems that arise when these come into conflict. Berlin is not the straightforward defender of negative liberty that he is often taken to be. Consequently, his liberalism is more complex than is often supposed. Indeed, his thought raises a question that he does not himself confront systematically: How far, given a world of plural values, can liberalism itself be defended?

Like his political thought, Berlin's personal background is more complex than some readers may expect. On the surface, he appears to be a quintessential figure of the British establishment, but he came from a middle-class Russian-Jewish background – he was born in Riga, which in 1909 was part of the Russian Empire. Berlin himself acknowledges 'three strands in my life': English, Russian and Jewish.[4] This inner diversity provides a biographical context both for his visceral opposition to the Soviet regime – his family fled to Britain in 1921 – and for his sympathy with what he regards as the human need for cultural belonging and national recognition, themes that come together with his Jewish heritage in a rather troubled commitment to Zionism.[5]

Berlin's scholarly interests range over several fields, but his master-question is that of the intellectual origins of twentieth-century totalitarianism, especially in its communist form. Ironically, he finds those origins most immediately in the eighteenth-century European Enlightenment. Berlin accepts the values of the Enlightenment – liberty, equality, toleration, rational inquiry – but worries that the scientism of the Enlightenment, its characteristic faith in the authority of scientific method, has led to a narrow understanding of reason and eventually to a dangerous utopianism. This is the pedigree of Marxism. Behind it lies a more ancient belief in moral 'monism': the idea that every ethical question has a single uniquely correct answer and that all such answers are discoverable and harmonious with one another. The possibility of a single monist formula in ethics suggests a single correct formula for social and political organization. The prospect of such perfection necessarily justifies any sacrifice. Soviet tyranny is merely the latest, scientistic form taken by this old idea.

In 'Two Concepts', Berlin links these background ideas to an account of liberty, or more precisely, to an account of the contemporary contest over the meaning of liberty in the world of the Cold War. Berlin acknowledges that when it comes to the idea of liberty there are 'more than two hundred senses of it recorded by historians of ideas' (168). He proposes to examine only two.

First, the negative conception of liberty is the idea that I am 'free to the degree to which no man or body of men interferes with my activity' (passage [1] of the opening extract). Berlin conceives of the negative idea in terms of 'the area within which a man can act unobstructed by others' (169). The typical obstacle to negative liberty is therefore coercion, 'the deliberate interference of other human beings within the area in which I could otherwise act' (169).

However, although Berlin believes that negative liberty is the central goal of liberalism, he also stresses that liberals should take a balanced view of its value. On the one hand, there must be 'a certain minimum area of personal freedom'; 'a frontier must be drawn between the area of private life and that of public authority' (171). What exactly the minimum should be or where precisely the frontier should be drawn is a matter of dispute, although the basic rule is that the degree of individual liberty in a society should reflect that society's understanding of the fundamental requirements of human dignity as these have been accepted over long periods of history. In this, the maximal demands for liberty of the most advanced liberal thinkers, such as Locke and Mill, Constant and Tocqueville, have perhaps been exceptional, and most human societies will settle for less (171). On the other hand, 'liberty is not the only good of men', and there may be good reasons to qualify it in the name of other values, such as equality or justice (172). Berlin is sometimes taken to treat negative liberty as overriding, in contradiction with his own notion of moral pluralism, but this is clearly not true. A liberal society will, of course, place a certain emphasis on negative liberty, but that will never be absolute.

The second of Berlin's two conceptions of liberty, the positive idea, 'derives from the wish on the part of the individual to be his own master' (passage [2]). I have positive liberty to the extent that I have control over my life. While negative liberty is about not being impeded or interfered with, positive liberty is about possessing power or capacity. Negative liberty places limits on authority while positive liberty locates authority in the right place (212).

As Berlin observes, the positive idea may at first seem to be 'at no great logical distance' from its negative counterpart, but he proceeds to explain how the two ideas have come into conflict (passage [3]). Indeed, the positive idea has developed in a way that not only conflicts with negative liberty but distorts the meaning of freedom altogether.

The sequence of development Berlin describes is not one of logical necessity – 'not always by logically reputable steps' – but rather partly historical and partly associational or psychological. The starting point is the idea that positive self-mastery may be obstructed, not only by coercion from an external source, as with negative liberty, but also by aspects of a person's own psychology: fears, beliefs, emotions, appetites. People can experience a sense of their own self as being divided. These conflicting selves are then experienced as 'higher' and 'lower', or more and less authentic: my rational self is typically thought to be more authentically 'me' than my emotional self. The next step is the thought that others may know my genuinely rational interests better than I do. Perhaps this superior knowledge is possessed by experts or by authorities. If so, it may be that these authorities can justifiably coerce my lower self in the interests of my higher self. Finally, in doing so, they may justly say that they are not only acting for my own good but liberating me because they are placing my true or authentic self back in control of my life. In Rousseau's paradox, I am 'forced to be free'.[6]

For Berlin, this conclusion is a 'monstrous impersonation' (180). This is the pattern that lies behind the claims of the twentieth-century dictatorships to have 'liberated' their people. Positive liberty need not necessarily be twisted in this way, but the fact that this is true historically (while the same is not true of negative liberty) points to a distinctive vulnerability at its heart. This can be traced to the notion of the divided self, 'this splitting of personality into two: the transcendent, dominant controller, and the empirical bundle of desires and passions to be disciplined and brought to heel' (passage [4]). Negative liberty is not so susceptible because its underlying conception of the self is wholly empirical: the individual's actual wishes cannot be second-guessed in the same way.

Having laid out the central problem, Berlin proceeds to elaborate different versions of positive liberty and cognate ideas, in each case bringing out latent conflicts with negative liberty and other difficulties. For example, one turn taken by the positive concept is towards liberty as 'self-abnegation', in which the authentic self is secured either by eliminating or by resisting the pull of the lower self (181). The Stoic 'retreat to the inner citadel' is an example of the former manoeuvre; Kant's rational self-control illustrates the latter. While Berlin allows that these may be reasonable models of freedom at a personal level, he sees them as 'the very antithesis of political freedom' (186). In politics, he thinks, we should not merely adapt ourselves to obstacles, we should try to remove them.

Another subset of positive liberty identifies the authentic self with rationality, which frees us from myths and illusions: 'Knowledge liberates' (190). But in the thought of Hegel, Marx and others, this turns into the idea that we are liberated by knowledge of 'historical necessity', which can tempt us to reconcile ourselves to policies and actions that we should not accept. Moreover, the worship of reason embodied in history can become the worship of reason embodied in the state.

Much of what Berlin has said up to this point addresses the context of the Cold War, in which he associates positive conceptions of liberty with either the authoritarianism of state communism or the quietism of those who fail to oppose it. But the positive idea and its cognates are also relevant, and more attractive, in another contemporary political context, that of the decolonization and emergent nationalism of the developing world in the 1950s.

In a section entitled 'The Search for Status', Berlin considers the relation between liberty and recognition: 'The lack of freedom about which men or groups complain amounts, as often as not, to the lack of proper recognition' (201). People need a sense of individual dignity and group belonging but also a sense that, in both dimensions, their identity is acknowledged and respected by those around them. This is a real human need, Berlin agrees, but is it really liberty? His initial answer is that it is 'akin to, but not itself, freedom' (204). Yet, in the end, he finds it hard to deny an element of liberty in recognition, declaring it first to be 'very close' to liberty (205), and ultimately to be 'a hybrid form of freedom' (206).

Berlin reaches that conclusion in part because he believes that the desire for recognition contains an element of the desire for sovereignty, or collective self-rule. This is definitely a species of liberty, in the positive register. Here again, though, his emphasis is on the potential for conflict between positive and negative liberty. Nineteenth-century liberals like Mill and Constant were right to worry that the collective positive liberty of democracy could crush negative liberty unless individuals were protected by 'frontiers of freedom' that were regarded as 'sacred' (209, 210). Still, it is up to each society to find its own balance. It is understandable that newly independent nations are prepared to trade off some of the negative liberty allowed by their former colonial masters in exchange for a less liberal rule exercised by their fellow-nationals.

At this point it seems that Berlin has withdrawn considerably from what appeared to be his stern attitude to positive liberty earlier on.[7] Although he never condemns the positive idea completely, for much of his discussion he gives the strong impression that, in the political realm at least, negative liberty is the safer and perhaps the more coherent ideal. Indeed, he sometimes hints at the thought that the negative idea is the 'normal' or fundamental form of liberty, and that the positive variations are in one way or another metaphorical extensions or departures from it (169, 204). Nevertheless, there are other passages, especially towards the end of the essay, in which Berlin is more inclined to see the two ideas as moral equals: 'The satisfaction that each of them seeks is an ultimate value which, both historically and morally, has an equal right to be classed among the deepest interests of mankind' (212).

In the final section of the essay, 'The One and the Many', Berlin deepens this theme of the ultimate equality of the two liberties by setting it in the context of his underlying idea of value pluralism.[8] The moral monism on which authoritarianism has thrived must be rejected as not only dangerous but false: as humans 'we are faced with choices between ends equally ultimate, and claims equally absolute, the realisation of some of which must inevitably involve the sacrifice of others' (passage [5]). Each speaks with its own unique voice. Consequently, we must make hard choices between the two liberties, between liberty and other goods, and among basic goods in general, when they conflict.

This raises the question, how *can* we choose among conflicting values if they are incommensurable? In particular, why should we follow Berlin in emphasizing the negative liberty that he identifies with a liberal approach to politics? Other values, such as positive liberty, equality, justice and so forth, would seem to be just as fundamental. Berlin admits that there is no simple answer to this; if there were a single formula, the monists would be correct. In different parts of his work, he offers various suggestions.[9] In 'Two Concepts', he argues that reflection on value pluralism itself provides the answer. If we must choose among conflicting values then we should value the freedom with which to make such choices – that is, the negative freedom of choice that lies at the heart of liberalism. 'Pluralism, with the measure of "negative" liberty that it entails, seems to me a truer and more humane ideal than the goals of those who seek in the great disciplined, authoritarian structures the ideal of "positive" self-mastery by classes, or peoples, or the whole of mankind' (passage [6]).

'Two Concepts' is a relatively brief but complex work that raises many issues. For many years, discussion concentrated on the negative–positive distinction and Berlin's critique of the positive idea. Some recent 'republican' critics have seen the negative–positive dichotomy as too confining since it distracts attention from a third conception of freedom as 'non-domination', or the absence not of actual constraints on people but of the power to constrain them.[10] The core notion of liberty for the republicans is neither non-interference nor self-mastery but liberation from slavery or arbitrary power. Other commentators complain that Berlin is too hard on positive liberty as a political ideal since, as Berlin himself allows, positive liberty can take many forms, not all of them authoritarian. Indeed, different kinds of positive liberty have been promoted by significant liberal thinkers such as John Stuart Mill, T. H. Green, Joseph Raz and Will Kymlicka.

In recent years, however, critical attention to Berlin's account of liberty has been supplemented by a new focus on the theme of value pluralism and its implications for the defence of liberalism. Berlin's conceptual link between pluralism and liberalism in 'Two Concepts' is not satisfactory because the sheer necessity of choosing does not make choosing valuable or give us a reason to expand the freedom to choose. Might pluralism and liberalism be linked in some other way? Opinion is divided. On the one hand, there are those who deny that value pluralists can be liberals, at least in the orthodox sense in which individual liberty is emphasized, as against other public goods, in universal terms.[11] On the other hand, there are 'liberal pluralists' who try to restate the connection between pluralism and liberalism in terms more systematic and persuasive than Berlin's.[12] Overall, the legacy of 'Two Concepts' continues to be disputed, but that is a sign of its continued vitality.

Czesław Miłosz

Michel Maslowski

Only the blind can fail to see the irony of the situation that the human species brought upon itself when it tried to master its own fate and to eliminate error. It bent its knee to History; and History is a cruel god. Today, the commandments that fall from his lips are uttered by a clever chaplain hiding in his empty interior. The eyes of the god are so constructed that they see wherever a man can go; there is no shelter from them.[1.]

My childhood was marked by two sets of events whose significance I see as more than social or political. One was the revolution in Russia, with of all its various consequences. The other was the omen of Americanisation ....
Now there is no doubt that Americanisation has carried off complete victory: Americanisation means the product of forces not only lower than man and not only outstripping him, submerging him, but, what is more important, sensed by man as both lower than and outstripping his will.[2]

In fact, only the individual is real, not the mass movements in which he voluntarily loses himself in order to escape himself. ... Here, now, I am only asking myself what I have learned in America, and what I value in that experience. I can boil it all down to three sets of pros and cons: for the so-called average man, against the arrogance of intellectuals; for the Biblical tradition, against the search for individual or collective nirvana; for science and technology, against dreams of primeval innocence.[3]

That truth is a proof of freedom and that the sign of slavery is the lie. ... That objective truth exists ....[4]

Czesław Miłosz was a poet and essayist, not a political writer or a philosopher. However, he was also a sage, whose poems and essays played an important role both in politics and philosophy. It is nevertheless difficult to classify him. Born in central Lithuania, the territory of which belonged to Poland during the interwar period, he regarded himself as an heir of the vast, multi-ethnic and multi-faith Grand Duchy of Lithuania, which had been united with the Kingdom of Poland for four centuries and whose elites had been subject to Polonization. He was also an heir of the Polish independence tradition, close to the liberalism of the nineteenth century, but an opponent of Polish nationalism, and often identified himself with the Left.

From the very beginning, his poetry was characterized by a premonition of cataclysms ('catastrophism') and the importance Miłosz attached to the dignity of the 'ordinary man'. After the Second World War, he started working for the communist government, and worked for two years as the press attaché at the embassy in Washington. In the face of the Stalinization of Poland, while in Paris in 1951 he 'chose freedom' and decided to go into exile. At that time, he started writing for a Polish-émigré magazine, *Kultura*, which worked towards overcoming hatred and promoting cooperation between the former Polish-Lithuanian Commonwealth nations, that is, Ukraine, Lithuania and Belarus. In Paris, he cooperated with the anti-totalitarian Congress for Cultural Freedom and with *Preuves* magazine. In 1953, he published *The Captive Mind*. The book, which was met with a hostile reception from the French Left, eventually became a worldwide success and remains an academic course book today. As Miłosz stated in the book, he wrote it so that 'eternal slaves might speak through my lips'.[5]

In the essay, Miłosz compared the response to ideological pressure of Eastern European intellectuals and common people with *ketman* – an old Persian technique of concealing one's true feelings. Thanks to *ketman*, it is possible to affirm the meaning of a life of honest work and personal integrity in the face of being forced to participate in cruel decisions or practices one disagrees with. In the Soviet Empire, as in old Persia, this method allowed staying true to oneself despite having to submit to the situation. As Miłosz described it, the Soviet system was one that, through the guise of democratic procedures such as elections (counterfeited) or medical aid (KGB agents disguised as nurses), made people identify themselves with the roles imposed on them to such an extent that even married couples would recite the slogan of the day in bed.

The Captive Mind unveiled the illusions of the 'New Faith' or 'diamat' (dialectical materialism, the Marxist orthodoxy), comparing its effects to those of a drug which deprives people of the will to criticize and to break free. From a sociological perspective, the Soviet system, which was supposed to lead to universal brotherhood, was responsible, in fact, for promoting the success of opportunists and to a war of all against all. In terms of anthropology, Miłosz understood the New Faith as a project of reducing the belief in individual freedom and fate, which was a cornerstone of European culture, to a class history and, therefore, to a collective history. It was an effort to resolve the dualism he diagnosed within human beings which allows us to live our own individual lives and our social roles simultaneously, and the tensions and struggles that result from that. To resolve these tensions, the New Faith reduces man to his affiliations, making him a 'social monkey'. Man is thus deprived of all his creativity, not only because of censorship and ideological pressure but also because creation requires complete solitude.

Miłosz's liberalism may be summarized as his opposition to the New Faith in defence of what he considered core values of European culture and humanity. In the face of the alluring Marxist illusion, Miłosz reminds us of the fundamental values of humanity: freedom in creativity, related to solitude and inner autonomy; a need for hope, which he thought could only come through eschatological or religious perspectives; the faith that a human being cannot be reduced to any kind of social doctrine; a faith in family as 'normalcy', and as the basis of every culture; and the value of cultural affiliation, which provides identity as well as the necessity of 'nationalistic' affirmation – however, without hubris or collective egoism.

In *The Captive Mind*, as well as in many of his poems, Miłosz emphasizes the importance of human dignity, regardless of social status, and in the undertone he establishes an alliance between workers and intellectuals. This is why he was later considered the spiritual father of 'Solidarność' ('Solidarity'), Poland's first independent trade union in the years 1980–1, whose activity precipitated the overturning of communist regimes in Central and Eastern Europe. An excerpt from his poem 'You Who Wronged a Simple Man',[6] selected by the workers themselves, was inscribed on the memorial to the victims of the police strike repressions of 1970. Miłosz's receiving the Nobel Prize in the year 1981, alongside the election of a Polish pope, further strengthened the self-esteem and the sense of dignity of the Polish people. As a result, a society enslaved by an imposed communist system started to regain its identity. A few years later this process resulted in the collapse of the Soviet bloc.

In 1960 Miłosz was appointed professor at Berkeley, where in 1968 revolutionary events took place as part of the anti-Vietnam War and Civil Rights movements and the rise of the American counterculture. Berkeley served Miłosz as a vantage point from which he could observe what he considered the mental transformation and crisis of Western civilization, to which he testifies in numerous poems and essays. In 1969 he published a book-length summary of his observations, entitled *Visions from San Francisco Bay*, from which the second and third passages in the opening extract are taken. According to Miłosz, the crisis started together with European 'nausea' (*nausée*): 'The European spirit hated itself, turned against itself, and derided the institutions it had elaborated, perhaps thus masking a painful sense of its own disgrace'.[7] This crisis of self-disgust was exported to the United States, mostly through the theatre of the absurd, taught in schools, as well as through novels and popular theories.

According to Miłosz, in Berkeley the 'American way of life' is distorted. 'New America' is dominated by a hatred for virtues, which is represented by badly shaved beards and marijuana, a substitute for the alcohol used by the defenders of the system.

> To negate virtue, one must oppose industry with idleness, puritanical repression of urges with instant gratification, tomorrow with today, alcohol with marijuana, moderation in the display of emotion with shameless emotionality, the isolation of the individual with the collective, calculation with carelessness, sobriety with ecstasy, racism with the blending of the races, obedience with political rebellion, stiff dignity with poetry, music and dance ... . The place of honor is given to primitive man ... .[8]

The effect was to strengthen the feeling of alienation associated with the mechanization of life, the number of highways and TV reports featuring all the violence in the world. It gave rise to dreams of living on the Fortunate Islands, of free sex (which is anti-erotic itself) and to a deficit of desire, which leads to feelings of boredom within a space with no particular orientation; hence the search for consolation in drugs. As Miłosz had earlier compared the effects of the communist 'New Faith' to a drug providing a feeling of happiness and cheerfulness, which makes all problems insignificant and allows the individual to accept new rulers without objection, so he now compared the American transformation to the effects of LSD. He perceived the revolt of beatniks and hippies as pointless and destructive.

As Miłosz predicted, the communist revolution finally failed, and Americanization succeeded on a world scale. An individual life follows a circular pattern now, devoid of any sense of meaning. Inherited from the Bible, life as the movement of an arrow headed towards its target (or towards a promise of a target, a belief in a destination) has been fundamental to Western civilization from its dawn. Inherited from Christianity, this tradition later took the secular form of a belief in progress – either technical, moral or social. By contrast, Miłosz compared contemporary civilization to a vast landfill site, where young people are being 'trained in nihilism' at school. In his writings, he stood up against any ideology which would require the individual to surrender to the collectivity and which would allow the intellectuals to decide how to save the world, not taking into account the experience of common, ordinary people. Miłosz also rearticulated the value of morality and the virtues: in science, technology and effort.

Although Miłosz criticized the institution of the church, with its sacralization – especially in Poland – of national deities, it is the crisis of religion or the sense of meaning which worried him most, because it leads straight to nihilism, the crisis of humanity.[9] It was nihilism that gave rise to Marxism-Communism, as well as the consumerism of Americanization and the crisis of religious faith. Without a sense of meaning, there can be no freedom, creativity or dignity. According to Miłosz, the religious crisis is related to a collapse of spatial imagination, and as a poet he tried to address this issue. Religious – or rather anthropological and metaphysical – themes dominated the last period of his work.

This period can be considered an attempt to construct an anthropocentric space. The poet situates himself on the edge, between his political sympathies for the Left and faith, which he tries to express using nontraditional language. He professed a degree of anti-clericalism rooted in his youth, which he spent in the very Catholic and nationalistic city of Vilnius. Fascinated by metaphysics and rejecting dogmatism, he was impressed by the intellectual solidity of the edifice of theology, especially of Thomism. Over time he began to perceive religion mostly as a poet and an unprofessed mystic. He admired the nineteenth-century Polish Catholic and nationalist poet Adam Mickiewicz, a friend of Lamennais, the founder of Liberal Catholicism in France, and the group related to *l'Avenir*, Lamennais' newspaper, which fought for the freedom of teaching, separation of church and state and freedom of conscience. The journal, as well as liberalism itself, was condemned by the Vatican, but this model of linking democratic beliefs with faith survived in Polish memory. The quest for freedom from dogmas which might appeal to modern man inspired Miłosz to read esoteric literature (e.g. Origen, Böhme, Swedenborg, Blake, Solovyov, his uncle the Lithuanian poet Oscar Miłosz, Simone Weil). Later, Miłosz was also to become a correspondent of the poet and Trappist monk, Thomas Merton.

Miłosz wrote a series of essays and poems on religion. Pope John Paul II himself would later reply to *Tract* by Miłosz by publishing his own poem, *Roman Triptych* (2003), which touched on some of the questions posed by the Nobel Prize winner. Among the topics raised by Miłosz are the presence of evil in the world, inconsistencies between the dogmas of the cultural imaginarium which dates back to the Middle Ages and the knowledge of modern man, and what can be called an ontological crisis of civilization (a lack of meaning and a lack of a sense of reality). History, the new god of the twentieth century, turns out to be nothing but a cannibalistic idol. Nevertheless, the presence of God, apart from all speculation, can be noticed within the 'interhuman space' and the 'interhuman church' – which explains the need for rituals: 'A ritual constructs a sacral space among those present in It.'[10] The poet, who highlights the irreducible value of the individual at every opportunity ('faith as the secret of individual freedom and individual destiny'[11]), nevertheless acknowledges the need – or even the necessity – for the existence of an institutional church.

Miłosz's ultimate concern is the reconstruction of a modern spatial imaginarium. He regards it as a task he needs to fulfil: 'There have always been a multitude of preachers calling for inner rebirth, a rebirth of the heart, and … this has been no help against cruelty and injustice. … I am not, however, in the least counting on some effort of the will, but rather on something independent of the will – data which would order our spatial imagination anew.'[12] Today, he claimed, 'faith is undermined by disbelief in faith, and disbelief by disbelief in itself'.[13] This is how he approached the problem of the ontological crisis of modern man, related to nihilism and the lack of desire, and finally the disappearance of the sense of a meaning of life in the modern West. This was apparent in Berkeley in 1968, during processions carrying a gigantic phallus, when nudity was not shocking for anyone. This crisis was noticeable even right after the Second World War, in the feeling of emptiness present among intellectuals, an emptiness that they attempted to fill with the rituals of the New Faith. It is not enough to become a part of the masses or crowds. Only what remains with the individual in the face of death possesses any value. A disinherited man, who consumes with no thought of constraint, both literally and metaphorically, turns natural and divine space into a vast landfill site without any meaning at all. It is necessary to recommence working on meaning – the way the task of bereavement is done – and remind a man of his own dignity.

Throughout his life, Miłosz resisted the ideological tendencies dominating his environment. In Catholic, conservative Vilnius he rejected all signs of nationalism, anti-Semitism, national and religious ritualism, therefore siding with the Left. Later, having finished his diplomatic service and broken with the communist authorities, in *The Captive Mind* and *Native Realm* he described the system as one which was supposed to make the people happy, but neglected the individual, with his need for spirituality, freedom and creativity. As he stated in his *Six Lectures in Verse*, 'The true enemy of man is generalization.'[14] At the same time, the manipulation of reason was offensive to common sense and could in no way provide a response to the inner void of modern man.

Miłosz fought against communism as an ideology which, through physical enslavement and intellectual seduction (a kind of drug which relieved the individual of the option of creatively looking for meaning), deprived human beings of free choice. His further rejection of American consumerism, the rejection of the worship of work and discipline, the virtues upon which the creation of America was based, resulted in his identifying 'Americanization' as an ideology of global scope, a new drug compelling and seducing with the 'authenticity' of liberated instincts. Miłosz's refusal to yield to the Western society of prosperity was, in a sense, his way of disagreeing with the passivity and futility of American and French intellectuals, especially those representing the Parisian Left Bank, who – in the name of 'progress' and the dream of a better tomorrow – neglected man and his need for dignity, a meaningful life and hope. Those needs have to be fulfilled in the metaphysical sense, regardless of particular religions. Miłosz regarded himself as Catholic – but in a very specific sense.

Let us attempt to summarize this Copernican revolution of the imaginarium in the modern world, threatened by the catastrophe of nonsense, as declared by Miłosz. The key to Miłosz's new imaginarium could be the picture he remembered from the war years, when, at the railway station in Kiev, overflowing with crowds of refugees and soldiers, he noticed a family sitting in the corner, calmly feeding their children:

> A peasant family – husband and wife and two children – had settled down by the wall.... The wife was feeding the younger child; the husband ... was pouring tea out of a kettle into a cup for the older boy. They were whispering to each other in Polish. I gazed at them until I felt moved to the point of tears. ... This was a human group, an island in crowd that lacked something proper to humble, ordinary human life ... their isolation, their privacy in the midst of the crowd – that is what moved me.[15]

Human relationships liberated from the hell of war, from individual misfortunes, created a space for freedom. Similarly, a search for new images of space might renew the feeling of meaning and the possibility of faith. The new imaginarium consists in a transformation of vertical space, frozen in place for eternity, into an interrelational, dynamic, horizontal space, and in the evocation of a transcendental plane, most apparent from an eschatological perspective. In fact, the fulfilment of God's promise is always before us, and its final fulfilment is the end of time. Faith constitutes the mystery of freedom and individual vocation. And if clear thought and a vehement will are essential, we cannot forget about desire, which brings about thought, and about the emotions rooted in archetypes and existential experience that revive ancient symbols, without which the human being would not have been able to leave the kingdom of animals.

Miłosz's overcoming of his own solipsism and individualism from a liberal perspective took place as part of this evolution, too. Miłosz understood this during his visit to the Dordogne region of France, from which Homo sapiens had gone out and spread throughout the whole of Europe and the world.

> The country of the Dordogne is ... a prenatal landscape so hospitable that prehistoric man, twenty or thirty thousand years ago, selected the valley of the Vézère for his abode. ... Gradually ... I stopped worrying about the whole mythology of exile ... I was like an ancient Greek. I had simply moved from one city to another. My native Europe ... dwelled inside me.[16]

John Rawls

Chad Van Schoelandt

The political culture of a democratic society is characterized (I assume) by three general facts understood as follows.

The first is that the diversity of reasonable comprehensive religious, philosophical, and moral doctrines found in modern democratic societies is not a mere historical condition that may soon pass away; it is a permanent feature of the public culture of democracy. Under the political and social conditions secured by the basic rights and liberties of free institutions, a diversity of conflicting and irreconcilable – and what's more, reasonable – comprehensive doctrines will come about and persist if such diversity does not already obtain....

A second and related general fact is that a continuing shared understanding on one comprehensive religious, philosophical, or moral doctrine can be maintained only by the oppressive use of state power. If we think of political society as a community united in affirming one and the same comprehensive doctrine, then the oppressive use of state power is necessary for political community. In the society of the Middle Ages, more or less united in affirming the Catholic faith, the Inquisition was not an accident; its suppression of heresy was needed to preserve that shared religious belief. The same holds, I believe, for any reasonable comprehensive philosophical and moral doctrine, whether religious or nonreligious. A society united on a reasonable form of utilitarianism, or on the reasonable liberalisms of Kant or Mill, would likewise require the sanctions of state power to remain so. Call this 'the fact of oppression.'

Finally, a third general fact is that an enduring and secure democratic regime, one not divided into contending doctrinal confessions and hostile social classes, must be willingly and freely supported by at least a substantial majority of its politically active citizens.[1]

Throughout his career, John Rawls (1921–2002) sought a public basis for members of society to resolve fundamental disputes. Importantly, Rawls was not concerned merely to know what the right resolution or answer to the dispute would be. He was interested in the principles and procedures that the members of society could plausibly use themselves to come to form agreements. It was not enough for the society to *be* fair, good or righteous if the members of society could not themselves mutually recognize that fact. This chapter first explains why Rawls thinks it is difficult to get such agreement, particularly within a society respecting basic liberal rights like freedom of thought. Next, the chapter presents Rawls's proposal for how a liberal conception of justice may meet the challenge and provide a public basis of agreement.

Members of any society will face interpersonal disagreements of some sort. Al and Betty, for instance, may disagree about whether or not the tree should be removed from between their houses. These disagreements may remain fairly contained, for those in dispute may be bound by long personal histories, shared religion and common understandings of the relevant moral considerations. The disputants may be able to simply discuss the matter and come to agree on the most important considerations, such as whether it is more important to have shade in the summer or for the garden to have more sun, and thus resolve the dispute. Importantly, many personal disputes can be resolved by appeal to mutually accepted forms of conflict resolution and systems of social rules, such as property rights. Al and Betty may not agree on the relative harms and benefits of the tree, but they may agree about whose property it is on and thus who gets to decide whether the tree stays or goes. There are, of course, many other possibilities for how they may settle the dispute, but the central point remains that Al and Betty may be able to resolve their dispute through shared beliefs, values, practices and the like.

Members of a small-scale, isolated and homogenous society may readily resolve their disputes through appeal to a shared, robust view of the world, or at least through shared institutions for adjudicating their disputes. Modern industrial democracies, however, tend to be characterized by extensive disagreements, with members coming from vastly different cultural and religious backgrounds and holding conflicting moral frameworks. For instance, Al and Betty may disagree about whether trees have intrinsic or only instrumental value, the relative merits of shade and gardens or of the corresponding relaxation and work, the plausibility of various environmental concerns and the responsibilities of individuals for mitigating collective environmental problems, the relevance of subjective factors like pleasure or offence and so on. In such a case, Al and

Betty would not only disagree about the tree but also have starkly different views about what sorts of considerations are even relevant to figuring out what to do with the tree.

Of particular importance is the fact that members of diverse communities will often disagree about the society's fundamental institutions. For instance, the members may disagree about the legitimacy of the society's system of property rights and economic system, the extent to which decisions should be made by majority rule, the way political power is distributed or the liberties extended or denied to various individuals. We should expect members reasoning from diverse moral, religious and philosophical views to come to different evaluations of their social institutions, perhaps leading some to reject those social institutions as illegitimate, lacking authority or unjust. Modern societies are thus faced with a problem of finding a way for members to be reconciled to, rather than alienated from, their most basic social institutions.

One might think that the best way to solve that disagreement is to simply get people to share a religious, moral and philosophic view, particularly the true view. From that shared view, they could agree on the best social institutions, bring them about and form a common allegiance to those institutions. Many philosophers defend particular moral ideals, and derive from these ideas views about the best institutions. If only everyone would be convinced by one of these philosophic views of human flourishing, natural rights, aggregate social utility or the like, then the members of society could unite in support of the relevant social institutions. Such views may support deeply illiberal institutions, such as a theocracy, but they may also support liberal institutions with democratic procedures bounded by protections for rights of conscience, speech, association and other individual liberties. Rawls considers these various cases for liberalism based on deep moral ideal forms of 'comprehensive liberalism'.

As the first paragraph of the opening quote indicates, in Rawls's view, we cannot expect members of society to share a single comprehensive liberal view, or any other comprehensive view for that matter. Deep disagreement and competition between diverse comprehensive religious and moral views are not momentary phenomena we should expect to overcome. Instead, Rawls argues that intelligent, informed and well-meaning individuals, reasoning conscientiously in conditions of freedom of thought and discussion, will tend to disagree about fundamental religious, moral and philosophic issues.

These religious, moral and philosophic disagreements do not necessarily emerge from malice, stupidity or insufficient reflection. They can emerge from various 'burdens of judgement' that good-willed, intelligent people reasoning as best they can will face. For instance, many of the key concepts used in moral reasoning are vague. Happiness, equality, freedom, rule of law, democracy, opportunity and many other moral concepts have unclear boundaries, even if they have some paradigmatic cases of application, so members reasoning from these concepts may come to different moral views. In addition, considerations relevant for selecting a view will often differently weigh conflicting considerations, such as simplicity and explanatory power, or conflicting intuitions. Such conflicts will include conflicting normative values for which there is no obvious balance that all well-meaning and conscientious people must strike. When it comes to the basic institutions of a society, such conflicts will arise because no society can fully realize all values. For any institutions selected, limited resources will allow the realization of some values only by allowing other values to go unsatisfied, but members of the institution may disagree about which values should be promoted at the expense of which other values.

Differences of interpretation of vague concepts along with assigning different weights to the relevant considerations are already sufficient for producing a tremendous diversity of views. We can add to these burdens of judgement the facts that the relevant evidence will often be complex, conflicting and difficult to assess. Experts carefully examining the evidence may come to hold different views even in fairly narrow question, and certainly when it comes to the formation of moral, religious and philosophic views. Furthermore, when it comes to interpreting concepts, weighing considerations and assessing evidence, our personal experience will affect our judgement. Since people will always have different experiences, we should expect them to make these judgements in different ways. These burdens of judgement, perhaps along with others not discussed by Rawls, generate tendencies towards disagreement and, ultimately, a wide diversity of moral, religious and philosophic doctrines. The members of any large-scale society reasoning as well as can be expected, then, will tend to disagree about the nature and requirements of morality, the good life and other issues that people may appeal to in assessing a society's basic institutions.

As our quoted passage makes clear, Rawls believes that the use of oppressive state power could maintain consensus on a comprehensive moral, religious or philosophic doctrine, at least in the context of a large modern society. Since the free reasoning of citizens produces a diversity of views, uniformity of view requires the prevention of such free reasoning. At a minimum, we might expect censorship to prevent members from encountering alternative interpretations of the relevant concepts, conflicting evidence or other considerations that may lead members away from orthodoxy. Even censorship, however, has not been sufficient to prevent scepticism, heresy, protest and resistance to dominant views historically. Societies wishing to maintain uniformity of view have tried many harsh means, including mass propaganda and indoctrination, the torture and execution of heretics, forced confessions and public humiliation of class enemies, inquisitions and purges.

Such oppressive policies can sometimes work to control the views that members of society profess, consider and hold, though dissent often emerges even under such pressure. Oppressive state policies, then, might not be sufficient, but seem to be absolutely necessary for any society to maintain a uniformity of moral, religious and philosophic doctrines. Unfortunately, this applies to liberal philosophic doctrines as much as to illiberal religions and ideologies. So, an attempt to support liberal institutions through a shared embrace of the moral doctrines of, say, John Stuart Mill or Immanuel Kant, would be unstable unless enforced with deeply illiberal, oppressive policies. Liberal institutions depending upon a shared comprehensive moral, religious or philosophical doctrine thus are unstable, either because within the liberal freedoms members of the society will come to hold competing views or because illiberal policies will be adopted to prevent such dissent. If liberal, democratic institutions are to be stable through the free support of their members, it must be through something other than a shared comprehensive view.

Having ruled out comprehensive forms of liberalism, Rawls proposes that a conception of justice for a diverse society should be merely 'political'. There are a number of related features that make a conception merely political, the most obvious of which is that it has a limited scope of application. A merely political conception provides answers only to questions about the basic political institutions of a society and does not apply to other institutions or domains of life. Such a conception may, for instance, require that political institutions be democratic without saying that democracy is good generally, required for churches or the like. In limiting its scope, the political conception maintains agnosticism about the other domains. In contrast, a comprehensive doctrine like utilitarianism answers questions for all domains in the same way, holding that political institutions, religious institutions, families and individual actions should all be chosen so as to maximize the happiness of people collectively.

Part of what enables the conception to have this limited scope is that it is composed of specifically political ideas and values. The central example of this, for Rawls, is the idea of free and equal citizens. Free and equal citizenship regards how members of society stand in relation to political institutions and to each other regarding political issues. For political purposes, citizens are free in that they are seen to have the ability to form, revise and pursue their own conceptions of the good, along with a presumptive claim for doing so. This idea does not require that they have any sort of metaphysical freedom from causation, satisfy or pursue any moral ideals of autonomy, be self-creating and self-sustaining atomistic individuals or other contentious philosophic notions of freedom. A member may see herself as politically free to join or leave her church while also believing that, in other important senses, she is not free because, say, she was called and predestined to be a member, or that she is not morally or spiritually free to leave because apostasy is a moral (though not legal) offence. Equal citizenship and other political values are limited in similar ways.

From these political ideas, Rawls attempts to construct suitable principles of justice. The details of these principles are unimportant here, but we can note that they include principles protecting individual liberties, promoting fair equality of opportunity, and requiring the economic system to be to the benefit of even the least well off in society. These principles, like the political ideas supporting them, have a limited political scope. The principle of liberty, for instance, ensures that members will not be legally punished for their religious expressions, and that their legal rights will not depend upon professed religious belief. Religious associations, however, may make professed belief a condition of membership, and may institute certain punishments for irreligious behaviour such as excommunication for blasphemy. The key here is that, just as the political ideas are narrow in scope and do not compete with other religious or moral understandings of ourselves, the principles are also narrow in their application in a way that minimizes conflict with the moral and religious views members may hold.

These political ideas and principles constitute Rawls's preferred conception of justice, 'justice as fairness'. By building a merely political conception without dependence upon deeper metaphysical or moral views, Rawls hoped to ensure that justice as fairness could be a sort of module within the views of diverse members of society. Were each member to have this module as a part of her complete view of the world, the views of the diverse members would overlap on justice as fairness, making it the focus of what Rawls calls an 'overlapping consensus'. Minimally, this means that each member endorses justice as fairness and it does not excessively conflict with her other commitments, perhaps in the way a member may find her support for her favourite sports team neither conflicts with nor depends upon her Catholicism. More positively, a member may find that justice as fairness coheres with her other commitments, so she has deeper religious, moral or philosophical reasons to endorse justice as fairness. Note, however, that members do not have to have the same deeper reasons for endorsing justice as fairness. In an overlapping consensus, the members may be converging on the conception from very different, even opposing, starting points. Essentially, the wide range of moral arguments for liberalism, including arguments that conflict with each other, provide resources by which diverse members of society can come to endorse justice as fairness for different reasons.

Now we have the pieces for answering Rawls's initial problem regarding how a society can be stable through the free support of citizens despite their inevitable religious, philosophical and moral disagreements. Overlapping consensus on a merely political conception would constitute the free support of citizens without uniformity in their comprehensive doctrines. Justice as fairness could then provide a shared basis for citizens to judge and affirm their common institutions as providing fair terms of cooperation. Unfortunately, even a merely political conception of justice, including justice as fairness, will face yet another problem from disagreement.

At the end of his career, Rawls recognized an important difficulty for his account. As Rawls came to see, reasonable disagreement is not restricted only to matters of religion, morality and philosophy. Reasonable disagreement should be expected to emerge about political values and the conception of justice itself. Thus, while Rawls maintains that justice as fairness is one reasonable conception, he holds that it is unrealistic to believe that the members of a liberal society could be expected to all agree that it is best. We should instead expect members to favour diverse conceptions of justice.

What Rawls came to hope was that there could be overlapping consensus on a set of conceptions that were all recognizably liberal and shared certain key features. In particular, such conceptions would all give some special priority to a list of basic liberties, and assure for all members a claim to adequate resources for exercising those liberties. Many different conceptions may have these features, so perhaps the best we may hope for is that the members of society would hold views that converge on some key features, while continuing to diverge about exact weights and details. Despite holding that disagreement about justice is inevitable, Rawls and his followers do not think it would be particularly extreme. If members of society were split merely between variations of liberalism, sharing in a concern for individual liberties and adequate resources for all to exercise those liberties, then it may be that each member can see the society as sufficiently just to warrant her allegiance. Though a member may think that the society is giving somewhat too little or too much priority to the basic liberties, she could be glad that other members of society share with her an appreciation for the importance of these liberties and that the fundamental policies of the society reflect that importance. Likewise, though she may think the economic structure is not optimal, she may recognize that it enables all members to have means to exercise their liberties and that, as other members would agree, this is a good thing. Each member, then, may recognize the society as adequate for constituting an ongoing system of fair cooperation and likely to be maintained as such by her fellow members. Such recognition, as some recent Rawlsians have emphasized, may ground civic friendship and political community.

In the final analysis, liberalism is presented as something we can all live with. Our disagreements are pervasive and run deep, and perhaps it is beyond hope that we will ever agree on any comprehensive moral basis for the basic structure of society. We may, however, hope that all members can recognize a society allowing each the space to pursue their own views and values as a society providing fair terms of cooperation. It may not be utopia, but it is a community of mutual accountability organized through free endorsement rather than coercive oppression, and that would be a valuable achievement.

Notes

Introduction

1 For some liberals, 'freedom' and 'liberty' are synonyms, whereas others see at least a vague division of function between the two, with freedom having a more positive content, as in 'the freedom to ...' and 'liberty' a more negative one, as in 'liberty from oppression'. But there is no clear pattern to these uses.

2 Andreas Kalyvas and Ira Katznelson, *Liberal Beginnings: Making a Republic for the Moderns* (Cambridge: Cambridge University Press, 2008), 17.

3 Benjamin Constant was among the first to use the word in a political sense, in 1797. By 1810, the first political party to describe itself as 'liberal' had arisen, in Spain. It is worth noting that organized political parties were very new in Europe in 1810, and that liberalism was present at their birth. Liberalism was intimately involved in the creation of modern politics as we know it across the globe. See K. Stephen Vincent, *Benjamin Constant and the Birth of French Liberalism* (New York: Palgrave-Macmillan, 2011), 76–7; Javier Fernandez Sebastian, 'Toleration and Freedom of Expression in the Hispanic World between Enlightenment and Liberalism', *Past & Present* 211 (2011), 161–99.

4 For Mesopotamia, see Henri Frankfort, *Kingship and the Gods* (Chicago: University of Chicago Press, 1948).

5 Kalyvas and Katznelson, *Liberal Beginnings*, 15.

6 Duncan Bell, 'What is Liberalism', *Political Theory* 42, no. 6 (2014), 682–715; Alan S. Kahan, *Liberalism in Nineteenth-Century Europe* (New York: Palgrave-Macmillan, 2003), 1–17.

Chapter 1

1 Montesquieu, *The Spirit of the Laws*, trans. A. M. Cohler, B. C. Miller and H. S. Stone (Cambridge: Cambridge University Press, 1989), Book XI, 155–56. Unspecified references including book, chapter and page numbers are to this edition.

2 Thomas Hobbes, *Leviathan*, ed. Edwin Curley (Hackett Classics, 1994), chapter XXI.

3 Ibid. XIV, 79–80.

4 Ibid. XXI, 143.

5 Montesquieu, *My Thoughts*, trans. and ed. Henry C. Clark (Indianapolis IN: Liberty Fund Inc., 2012), no. 884.

Chapter 2

1 Madame de Staël, *Considerations on the Principal Events of the French Revolution*, ed. Aurelian Craiutu (Indianapolis: Liberty Fund, 2008), 96, 104–5.

2 See Aurelian Craiutu, *A Virtue for Courageous Minds: Moderation in French Political Thought, 1748-1830* (Princeton: Princeton University Press, 2012), 158–97.

3 Staël, *Considerations*, 541.

4 Ibid., 96.

5 On this issue, see Keith Baker, *Inventing the French Revolution* (Cambridge: Cambridge University Press, 1990), 252–305.

6 Staël, *Considerations*, 17.

7 Ibid., 104.

8 Ibid., 633.

9 'Every country, every people, every man are fit for liberty by their different qualities; all attain or will attain it in their own way' (Staël, *Considerations*, 633).

10 Staël, *Considerations*, 753–4.

Chapter 3

1 Benjamin Constant, 'The Liberty of the Ancients Compared to That of the Moderns', in Constant, *Political Writings* (Cambridge: Cambridge University Press, 1988), 310–11.

2 Ibid., 311.

3 Constant, 'The Spirit of Conquest and Usurpation and their Relation to European Civilization', in Constant, *Political Writings*, 77.

4 'Principles of Politics Applicable all Representative Governments', in Constant, *Political Writings*, 177.

5 Ibid., 254.

6 'The Liberty of the Ancients Compared to That of the Moderns', 327.

7 Constant, *Commentary on Filangieri's Work*, ed. Alan S. Kahan (Indianapolis: Liberty Fund, 2015), 316.

8 Isaiah Berlin, *Four Essays on Liberty* (Oxford: Oxford University Press, 1969), 126.

Chapter 4

1 Jeremy Bentham, 'An Introduction to the Principles of Morals and Legislation' [1789], ed. J. H. Burns and H. L. A. Hart, with a new introduction by F. Rosen, in *The Collected Works of Jeremy Bentham* (Oxford: Oxford University Press, 1996), 11–12.

2 Jeremy Bentham, *A Fragment on Government*, ed. Ross Harrison (Cambridge: Cambridge University Press, 1988 [1776]), 97.

3 Ibid., 56.

Chapter 5

1 Alexander Hamilton, John Jay and James Madison, *The Federalist*, ed. George W. Carey and James McClellan (Indianapolis, IN: Liberty Fund, 2001), 181, 194.

2 *The Federalist*, #9, 38.

3 Thomas Jefferson to John Taylor, 28 May 1816, in *Jefferson* (New York: Library of America, 1984), 1392.

4 Jefferson to Samuel Kercheval, 12 July 1816, 1397.

Chapter 6

1 Alexis de Tocqueville, *Democracy in America*, trans. Harvey Mansfield and Delba Winthrop (Chicago: University of Chicago Press, 2000), vol. I part 1, ch. 3, 52, henceforth DA. I cite by volume, part, chapter and/or page numbers.

2 DA, vol. I part 1, ch. 5, 89–90.

3 Letter to Stoffels, 24 July 1836, in A. S. Kahan and O. Zunz, *The Tocqueville Reader. A Life in Letters and Politics* (Oxford: Wiley Blackwell, 2002), 153.

4 DA II 2.1, 482.

5 Pierre Manent, 'Tocqueville: Liberalism Confronts Democracy', in *Intellectual History of Liberalism* (New Jersey: Princeton University Press, 1995), 103.

6 DA, Introduction, 7.

7 Ibid., 6, 400.

8 DA, Introduction, 12, 7. Although conveyed in a stylish, accessible prose these lessons are far from simple. American institutions, Tocqueville insisted, are not to be imitated blindly.

9 The section from which the second passage is drawn stands out for its passionate arguments and personal tone – too revealing, as one reader complained, of Tocqueville's own convictions. Alexis de Tocqueville, *Democracy in America. Historical Critical Edition* (Indianapolis: Liberty Fund, 2009), 142 c.

10 DA II 2.5, 492.

11 'It is at once necessary and desirable that the central power that directs a democratic people be active and powerful', DA II 4.7, 667.

12 Compare DA I 1.8 and I 2.7, 239–42, esp. note 4. and I 2.10. Delba Winthrop, 'Tocqueville on Federalism', *Publius* 6, no. 3 (1976), 93–115.

13 DA II 2.2–8, 482–503.

14 DA 57, 90–1, 489, 498, 515, 667; Aurelian Craiutu, 'Tocqueville's Paradoxical Moderation', *Review of Politics* 67, no. 4 (2005), 620–6.

15 DA I 2.5, 85 and note. In the very chapter praising the effects of American decentralization, Tocqueville includes recommendations for greater oversight of local affairs.

16 DA 48 and 518, 672.

17 DA 64–5, 232–4, 486–8.

18 DA I 2.10. For a fuller discussion of Tocqueville's account of patriotism and the psychology of civic engagement, see E. Atanassow 'Patriotism in Democracy: What We Can Learn From Tocqueville', in Z. Rau and M. Tracz-Tryniecki (eds), *Tocquevillean Ideas: Contemporary European Perspectives* (Lanham, MD: University Press of America, 2014), 39–58.

19 DA I 2.5, 57; II 2.8, 499. R. T. Gannett, 'Tocqueville and Local Government', *Review of Politics* 67, no. 4 (2005), 724, 726–31; J. Koritansky, 'Decentralization and Civic Virtue in Tocqueville's "New Science of Politics"', *Publius* 5, no. 3 (1975), 80–1.

20 Alan S. Kahan, 'Checks and Balances for Democratic Souls: Alexis de Tocqueville on Religion in Democratic Societies', *American Political Thought* 4 (2015), 100–19.

21 Alan S. Kahan, 'Tocqueville and Religion: Beyond the Frontier of Christendom', in E. Atanassow and R. Boyd (eds). *Tocqueville and the Frontiers of Democracy* (Cambridge: Cambridge University Press, 2013), 89–110.

22 'The political world is changing; henceforth one must seek new remedies for new ills' (DA II 4.8, 672).

23 DA, Introduction, 7.

24 DA Introduction, 7. Michael Locke McLendon, 'Tocqueville, Jansenism and the Psychology of Freedom', *American Journal of Political Science* 50, no. 3 (July 2006), 664–75.

Chapter 7

1 Abraham Lincoln, 'Speech on the Dred Scott Decision at Springfield, Illinois', 26 June 1857, in *The Writings of Abraham Lincoln*, ed. Steven B. Smith (New Haven: Yale University Press, 2012), 115.

2 Lincoln, 'To Henry L. Pierce and Others', in *Writings*, 244.

3 See 'Harrison Bergeron', by Kurt Vonnegut, Jr., for a dystopic vision of a United States in which 'nobody was smarter than anybody else. Nobody was better looking than anybody else. Nobody was stronger or quicker than anybody else.'

4 Lincoln, 'Fragment on Slavery', in *Writings*, 58.

5 Aristotle, *Politics*, book 7, chapter 13.

6 Thomas Jefferson, 'Query XVIII: Manners', *Notes on the State of Virginia*, in *The Portable Thomas Jefferson*, ed. Merrill D. Peterson (New York: Viking Penguin, Inc., 1975), 214.

7 Aristotle, *Politics*, book 1, chapter 2.

8 Lincoln, 'Address at Gettysburg, Pennsylvania', 19 November 1863, in *Writings*, 417.

9 Jefferson, 'To Henri Grégoire', 25 February 1809, in *Portable Jefferson*, 517.

10 Jefferson, 'To Roger C. Weightman', 24 June 1826, in *Portable Jefferson*, 585.

11 Declaration of Independence, first paragraph.

12 Lincoln attaches great significance to 'reverence', beginning with his Lyceum address in 1838.

13 Alexis de Tocqueville, *Democracy in America*, trans. Harvey C. Mansfield and Delba Winthrop (Chicago: The University of Chicago Press, 2000), 674.

14 Lincoln, 'Gettysburg', in *Writings*, 417.

Chapter 8

1 John Stuart Mill, *On Liberty* (New York: Bedford/St. Martin's, 2008), Chapter One, 29.

2 Ibid., 27.

3 Mill, 'Autobiography', in *Collected Works of John Stuart Mill*, ed. J. M. Robson and others, 33 vols (Toronto and London: University of Toronto Press, 1963–91), vol. I, 169. Hereafter *CW* followed by volume and page numbers.

4 'De Tocqueville on Democracy in America' (I), *CW* XVIII, 47–90.

5 *CW* IX, 493n.

6 Ibid., 238.

7 John Rawls, *A Theory of Justice* (Cambridge, MA: Harvard University Press, 1999), 118. Fundamental to Rawls' theory of justice, a 'veil of ignorance' is the hypothetical situation in which we allegedly make choices without any knowledge of the particular facts about ourselves.

8 Nicolas Capaldi, *John Stuart Mill* (Cambridge: Cambridge University Press, 2005), 230.

9 'The grand, leading principle towards which every argument unfolded in these pages directly converges, is the absolute and essential importance of human development in the richest diversity.' Wilhelm von Humboldt, *The Sphere and Duties of Government* (Indianapolis: Liberty Fund, 1993). See Capaldi, *John Stuart Mill*, 268–70; Mill, 'Autobiography', *CW* I, 260. See also the introduction to Humboldt's book by John Burrow.

10 *CW* X, 55.

11 It is also a principle one can find in Adam Smith's *Lectures on Jurisprudence*, namely that for Smith each person has a natural right to 'do what he has a mind

when it does not prove detrimental to any other person'. Adam Smith, *Lectures on Jurisprudence*, ed. R. L. Meek, D. D. Raphael and P. G. Stein (Indianapolis, IN: Liberty Fund, 1982), vol. V, 3.

12 'Principles of Political Economy', *CW* III, Book V, Chapter XI.

13 *CW* III, 98; *CW* V, 11, 2.

14 25 October 1865, *CW* XVI, 1108–9.

15 'A Few Words on Non-Intervention', *CW* XXI, 109–24. The essay originally appeared in December 1859 in *Fraser's Magazine*.

Chapter 9

1 Alexander Herzen, 'J. S. Mill and his book On Liberty'. All translations are mine. The selected text, with ellipses removed for ease of reading, is comprised of several excerpts from this essay, which is translated in *My Past and Thoughts: The Memoirs of Alexander Herzen*, trans. Constance Garnett. Revised edition by Humphrey Higgens, with introduction by Isaiah Berlin, 4 vols (London: Chatto & Windus, 1968), vol. 3, 1075–85. A new edition, newly translated and annotated by Robert Harris and Kathleen Parthé, is forthcoming from Harvard University Press.

2 'Omnia mea mecum porto' (Paris, 3 April 1848), and 'Vixerunt!' (Paris, 1 December 1848), in *From the Other Shore*, trans. Moura Budberg (London: Weidenfeld & Nicolson, 1956), 124–25; 79; cf. J.P. Fallmerayer, review of *Von andern Ufer*, in *Gesammelte Werke in 5 Bänden*, ed. G. M. Thomas, v. 2: *Politische und Culturhistorische Aufsätze Türkei. Russland* (Leipzig: Engelmann, 1861), 59.

3 These essays were published as *Vom anderen Ufer* (1849), appearing in Russian as *S togo berega* (1855); other articles were gathered under the title *Briefe aus Italien und Frankreich: 1848–1849* (1850), and as *Pis'ma is Frantsi i Italii* (1855).

4 'To Our Brothers in Russia' (London, 21 February 1853), in *A Herzen Reader*, ed. and trans. Kathleen Parthé, with a critical essay by Robert Harris (Chicago: Northwestern University Press, 2012), 30.

5 Introduction to *From the Other Shore*, 4.

6 'J. S. Mill and his book *On Liberty*' (1859), 1075.

7 Herzen would have been thinking of Milton's landmark text, *Areopagitica: A Speech of Mr. John Milton for the Liberty of Unlicensed Printing to the Parliament of England*, published in 1644.

8 'Robert Owen' (1861), in *My Past and Thoughts*, 3:1217–18, 1226.

9 'J. S. Mill and his book *On Liberty*', 1082.

10 'Farewell' (Paris, 1 March 1849), in *From the Other Shore*, 12.

11 'Vixerunt!' in *From the Other Shore*, 88.

12 'Before the storm' (Rome, 31 December 1847), in *From the Other Shore*, 30.

13 'Letter from Avenue Marigny: III' (Paris, 20 June 1847), in *Letters from France and Italy, 1847–1851*, ed. and trans. Judith E. Zimmerman (Pittsburgh: University of Pittsburgh Press, 1995), 40, 48.

14 'Letter from via del Corso: V' (Rome, December 1847); VI (Rome, 4 February 1848), in *Letters from France and Italy, 1847–1851*, 68, 92.

15 'Ends and Beginnings: Letters to I. S. Turgenev: VII' (29 December 1862), in *My Past and Thoughts*, 4:1734.

16 Letter of Herzen (Rome) to Moscow friends (30 January 1848), in A.I. Gertsen, *Sobranie sochinenii v tridtsati tomakh* [Collected works in thirty volumes] (Moscow: Izdatel'stvo akademii nauk SSSR, 1954–66), 23:57; 'Consolatio' (Paris, 30 March 1849), in *From the Other Shore*, 104.

17 'Again in Paris: III', in *Letters from France and Italy, 1847–1851*, 260.

18 China and Persia were commonly cited as examples of great empires that had collapsed from cultural stagnation.

19 John Gray, *Isaiah Berlin: An Interpretation of his Thought* (Princeton: Princeton Univ. Press, 2013), 31.

20 'Without free speech man is not free.' 'To Our Brothers in Russia', in *A Herzen Reader*, 28.

21 These are the three central demands presented in the opening manifesto of Herzen's journal, *Kolokol* [The Bell]. See 'Vivos voco' (London, 1 July 1857), in *A Herzen Reader*, 55.

22 'The Russian People and Socialism: An Open Letter to Jules Michelet' (Nice, September 1851), in *From the Other Shore*, 188.

23 Or *obshchina*.

24 There is a certain filiation between Herzen's sparse, non-intrusive notion of personal freedom and the concept of 'negative liberty' as defined by Isaiah Berlin in 'Two Concepts of Liberty' [1958], reprinted in I. Berlin, *Four Essays on Liberty* (Oxford: Oxford Univ. Press, 1969).

25 'Consolatio', in *From the Other Shore*, 106.

26 *Du développement des idées révolutionnaires en Russie* (Paris: Franck, 1851), 94–5

27 'The giant awakens', *A Herzen Reader*, 146.

28 See Aileen M. Kelly, *The Discovery of Chance: The Life and Thought of Alexander Herzen* (Cambridge, MA: Harvard University Press, 2016), 524–5

Chapter 10

1 T. H. Green, 'Lecture on Liberal Legislation and Freedom of Contract'. An abridged version of the lecture was published in a temperance newspaper, the *Alliance News*, in late January 1881; it was issued as a pamphlet and later printed in full in Green's

Works; it has often been reprinted. The extract comes from Paul Harris and John Morrow, eds, *T. H. Green, Lectures on the Principles of Political Obligation and Other Writings* (Cambridge: Cambridge University Press, 1987), 199. All other references to Green's works are to this edition.

2   Green, 'On the Different Senses of "Freedom" as Applied to Will and to the Moral Progress of Man', 239.

3   Green, 'Liberal Legislation', 195.

4   Green, 'Freedom', 249.

5   See Peter P. Nicholson, *The Political Philosophy of the British Idealists: Selected Studies* (Cambridge: Cambridge University Press, 1990), 116–22; sections II–V of this book provide the best account of Green's political philosophy.

6   Ibid., 124–5.

7   Green, *Prolegomena to Ethics*, 259.

8   See Avital Simhony and David Weinstein, eds, *The New Liberalism: Reconciling Liberty and Community* (Cambridge: Cambridge University Press, 2001).

9   Green, *Lectures on the Principles of Political Obligation*, 92–6, 132–8; Colin Tyler, *Civil Society, Capitalism and the State* (Exeter: Imprint Academic, 2012), 191–6, 222–3.

10   Green, 'Liberal Legislation', 196.

11   *Lectures on Political Obligation*, 108.

12   Green, *Political Obligation*, 65–106.

13   Green, 'Liberal Legislation', 203.

14   On Green's property theory, see John Morrow, 'Private Property, Liberal Subjects, and the State', in Harris and Morrow, *T. H. Green*, 92–114; Simhony and Weinstein, *The New Liberalism*, 93–101; Tyler, *Civil Society*, 213–30.

15   Green, *Political Obligation*, 171–6.

16   Green, 'Liberal Legislation', 204–9; *Political Obligation*, 176–8.

17   See Simhony and Weinstein, *The New Liberalism, passim*.

Chapter 11

1   The author wishes to thank the editors as well as his colleagues José Antonio Aguilar Rivera, Juan Luis Ossa Santa Cruz and Eduardo Zimmermann for their helpful comments.

2   Domingo Faustino Sarmiento, *Facundo: Civilization and Barbarism*, trans. Kathleen Ross (Berkeley, Los Angeles, London: University of California Press, 2003), 77, 117. This is the edition from which I quote. A previous English translation of this book by Mary Peabody Mann was published under the title *Life in the Argentine Republic in the Days of the Tyrants* (New York: Hurd and Houghton, 1868). The most recent edition

of Mann's translation, with an introduction by Ilan Stavans, was published under the title *Facundo: Or, Civilization and Barbarism* (New York: Penguin Putnam, 1998).

3 Sarmiento, *Facundo*, 239.

4 Janet Burke and Ted Humphrey, 'Sarmiento on Barbarism, Race, and Nation Building', in *Forging People: Race, Ethnicity, and Nationality in Hispanic American and Latino/a Thought*, ed. Jorge J. E. Gracia (Notre Dame: University of Notre Dame Press, 2011), 127–51.

5 Natalio R. Botana, 'Sarmiento and Political Order: Liberty, Power, and Virtue', in *Sarmiento: Author of a Nation*, ed. Tulio Halperín-Donghi, Iván Jaksić, Gwen Kirpatrick and Francine Masiello (Berkeley, Los Angeles, London: University of California Press, 1994), 101.

6 On the transformations of Latin American liberalism in the nineteenth century, see Eduardo Posada-Carbó and Iván Jaksić, 'Shipwrecks and Survivals: Liberalism in Nineteenth-Century Latin America', *Intellectual History Review* 23, no. 4 (2013), 479–98.

7 See Jorge Myers, *Orden y virtud: El discurso republicano en el régimen Rosista* (Buenos Aires: Universidad Nacional de Quilmes, 1995).

Chapter 12

1 Namik Kemal, 'Usul-i Meşveret Hakkında Mektuplar I', *Hürriyet*, 26 September 1869, my translation.

2 Namik Kemal, 'Wa shawirhum fi'l-amr', *Hürriyet*, 11 August 1869, my translation.

3 Namik Kemal, 'Hukuk', *İbret*, 19 June 1872, my translation.

4 Niyazi Berkes, *The Development of Secularism in Turkey* (Montreal: McGill University Press, 1964), 211.

5 Christiane Czygan, 'Reflections on Justice: A Young Ottoman View of the Tanzimat', *Middle Eastern Studies*, 46, no. 6 (2010), 951.

6 Joseph G. Rahme, 'Namik Kemal's Constitutional Ottomanism and Non-Muslims', *Islam and Christian-Muslim Relations* 1, no. 10 (1999), 23.

7 Ebuzziyya Tevfik, *Yeni Osmanlılar Tarihi* (Istanbul: Kervan Yayınları, 1973).

8 Şerif Mardin, *The Genesis of Young Ottoman Thought* (Princeton: Princeton University Press, 1962), 208.

9 Gökhan Çetinsaya, 'Kalemiye'den Mülkiye'ye Tanzimat Zihniyeti', in *Modern Türkiye'de Siyasal Düşünce 1: Tazimatın Birikimi ve Meşrutiyet*, ed. Tanıl Bora and Murat Gültekingil (Istanbul: İletişim Yayınları, 2004), 55.

10 Ibid., 56.

11 Namik Kemal, 'Maarif', *Hürriyet*, 10 August 1869, in Kurdakul, *Namik Kemal*, 184–5, my translation.

12 Namik Kemal, 'Usul-i Meşveret Hakkında Mektuplar VI', *Hürriyet*, 7 November 1869, my translation.

13 'Usul-i Meşveret Hakkında Mektuplar I'.

14 'Usul-i Meşveret Hakkında Mektuplar VI'.

15 Berkes, *The Development*, 212.

16 Czygan, 'Reflections on Justice', 951.

17 Namik Kemal, 'Maarif', *Hürriyet*, 10 August 1869.

Chapter 13

1 Khayr al-Din Al-Tunisi and L. Carl Brown, *The Surest Path; the Political Treatise of a Nineteenth-Century Muslim Statesman* (Harvard Middle Eastern Monograph. Cambridge, MA: Harvard University Press, 1967), 74–7. The *Tanzimat* was a period of reform in the Ottoman Empire, 1838–76.

2 Leon Carl Brown, 'An Appreciation of *the Surest Path*', in *The Surest Path* (Cambridge, MA: Harvard University Press, 1967), 29–30.

3 The *Mouqaddimah*, also known as the *Muqaddimah of Ibn Khaldoun* or Ibn Khaldun's *Prolegomena*, was written by the Arab-Berber historian Ibn Khaldun in 1377. It records an early view of universal history, and remains one of the most important works in Muslim history.

4 Khayr al-Din, *The Surest Path*, 5. Cited by Jeremy Kleidosty, 'What Would Khayr Al-Din Do? The Fusion of Islamic and Western Constitutional Traditions in Khayr Al-Din Al-Tunisi *The Surest Path*', APSA 2012 Annual Meeting Paper. Available at: http://ssrn.com/abstract=2104854, 59.

5 Abdul Azim Islahi, 'Economic Ideas of a Nineteenth Century Tunisian Statesman: Khayr al-Din al-Tunisi', *Islamic Economics Institute*, King Abdulaziz University (2002), 5. Available at: https://mpra.ub.uni-muenchen.de/43519/MPRA Paper No 43519.

6 Brown, 'An Appreciation of *the Surest Path*', 53.

7 Albert Hourani, *Arabic Thought in the Liberal Age, 1798-1939* (Cambridge and New York: Cambridge University Press, 1983), 89. The Islamic Golden Age refers to a period in the history of Islam, traditionally dated from the ninth to the thirteenth century, during which the Islamic world was ruled by various caliphates and science, economic development and cultural works flourished.

8 Khayr al-Din, *The Surest Path*, 76.

9 Ibid., 76.

10 Ibid., 77.

11 Kleidosty, 'What Would Khayr Al-Din Do?', 37.

Chapter 14

1 J. Burckhardt to von Preen, 2 July 1871, in *The Letters of Jacob Burckhardt,* selected, ed. and trans. Alexander Dru (Indianapolis: Liberty Fund, 2001), 143–44.

2 J. Burckhardt, *Reflections on History,* trans. M. D. Hottinger (Indianapolis: Liberty Fund, 1979), 184, 139.

3 J. Burckhardt, *Judgements on History and Historians,* trans. Harry Zohn (Indianapolis: Liberty Fund, 1999), 238–9.

4 On Burckhardt's anti-Semitism, see Lionel Gossman, 'Jacob Burckhardt: Cold War Liberal?', *Journal of Modern History* 74 (2002), 552–3.

5 Judith Shklar, 'The Liberalism of Fear', in *Liberalism and the Moral Life,* ed. Nancy L. Rosenblum (Cambridge, MA: Harvard University Press, 1989).

6 *Selected Letters,* 212–13, 209.

7 *Judgments,* 229; *Reflections on History,* 314.

8 *Selected Letters,* 145; *Judgments,* 231.

9 See Alan S. Kahan, *Aristocratic Liberalism: The Social and Political Thought of Jacob Burckhardt, John Stuart Mill, and Alexis de Tocqueville* (New Brunswick, NJ: Transaction, 2001).

10 *Judgements,* 226.

11 Ibid., 227.

12 Ibid., 183.

13 *Selected Letters,* 216.

14 *Selected Letters,* 144 , 134, 147, 148: *Judgements,* 230.

15 *Selected Letters,* 148, 205, 209, 215; Gossman, 'Jacob Burckhardt', 551, 557.

16 *Judgements,* 3.

17 *Selected Letters,* 129, *Judgements,* 230.

Chapter 15

1 Max Weber, 'Parliament and Government in Germany under a New Political Order' (1918), in *Political Writings,* ed. Peter Lassman and Ronald Speirs (Cambridge: Cambridge University Press, 1994), 159, 161. Subsequent quotations from this text will be followed by parenthetical references. I am very grateful to Peter Baehr and Duncan Kelly for their comments and suggestions on an earlier version of this chapter.

2 Max Weber, *Economy and Society: An Outline of Interpretive Sociology,* ed. Guenther Roth and Claus Wittich (Berkeley: University of California Press, 1978), 1208–10.

3 This is a point that Weber made more explicitly in his later lecture, 'The Profession and Vocation of Politics' (1919), in *Political Writings,* 338–9, 346–7.

4   See Max Weber, 'On the Situation of Constitutional Democracy in Russia' (1906), in *Political Writings*, 69–70.

5   Max Weber, 'The President of the Reich' (1919), in *Political Writings*, 306.

6   Weber, 'The President of the Reich'.

7   See Weber, 'The Profession and Vocation of Politics', 311–12. Though the Weimar Constitution did end up providing for a popularly elected president, it did not endow the office with as much political independence as Weber demanded.

8   Weber, 'The President of the Reich', 307.

9   On their trip, see Lawrence A. Scaff, *Max Weber in America* (Princeton: Princeton University Press, 2011).

10 This description of the Protestant sects, which applies equally to the American voluntary associations in Weber's view, appears in *Economy and Society*, 1204.

11 On Weber's legacy, see Joshua Derman, *Max Weber in Politics and Social Thought: From Charisma to Canonization* (Cambridge: Cambridge University Press, 2012).

Chapter 16

1   John Maynard Keynes, *Collected Writings* (Cambridge: Cambridge University Press, 2012), vol. IX, 305–6. Henceforth cited as *CW* followed by volume and page numbers.

2   Keynes, 'The General Theory of Employment, Interest and Money', *CW* VII, 380, 377–8.

3   *CW* IX, 296–7.

4   'The End of Laissez-Faire' *CW* IX, 272.

5   Ibid., 274–5.

6   Ibid., 276–7.

7   *CW* IX, 286.

8   Ibid., 305.

9   Keynes, 'Tract on Monetary Reform' [1923], *CW* IV, 65.

10 What in Germany is called 'social democratic' politics is closest to this, but the term has a different history.

11 *CW* IX, 289

12 Ibid., 289

13 See, for example, Clarence S. Walton, *Corporate Social Responsibilities* (Belmont, CA: Wadsworth Publishing Company, 1967).

14 Michael C. Jensen and William H. Meckling, 'The Nature of Man', *Journal of Applied Corporate Finance* 7, no. 2 (Summer 1994), 4–19.

Chapter 17

1 John Dewey, *The Public and Its Problems* (1927), in Dewey, *The Later Works, 1925-1953* (hereafter cited as *LW*), ed. Jo Ann Boydston et al. (Carbondale, IL: Southern Illinois University Press, 1984), 2: 364–65. There are two paperback editions of *The Public and Its Problems* (Chicago: Swallow, 1954) and a more recent edition, which contains a fine introduction and bibliography by Melvyn Rodgers (University Park, PA: Pennsylvania State University Press, 2012).

2 On the roots of Dewey's conception of liberal democracy in earlier American thought, see James T. Kloppenberg, *Toward Democracy: The Struggle for Self-Rule in European and American Thought* (New York: Oxford University Press, 2016); and James T. Kloppenberg, *The Virtues of Liberalism* (New York: Oxford University Press, 1998).

3 Dewey, 'From Absolutism to Experimentalism', in *Contemporary American Philosophy*, ed. George P. Adams and William F. Montague (New York: Macmillan, 1930), *LW*, 5: 147–60. On the development of Dewey's philosophy and his relation to a wide range of European and American thinkers, including Hegel, John Stuart Mill, T. H. Green, William James and Max Weber, see James T. Kloppenberg, *Uncertain Victory: Social Democracy and Progressivism in European and American Thought, 1870-1920* (New York: Oxford University Press, 1986).

4 Dewey, 'Christianity and Democracy', in Dewey, *The Early Works* (hereafter cited as *EW*), ed. Jo Ann Boydston et al. (Carbondale, IL: Southern Illinois University Press, 1968), 4: 3–12.

5 On the wide, deep and lasting impact of Dewey's philosophy on American culture, see Andrew Jewett, *Science, Democracy, and the American University* (Cambridge: Cambridge University Press, 2012).

6 Dewey, *Democracy and Education*, in Dewey, *The Middle Works* (hereafter cited as *MW*), ed. Jo Ann Boydston et al. (Carbondale, IL: Southern Illinois University Press, 1980), 9: 92–4. On the transatlantic dimensions of the 'new liberalism', see Kloppenberg, *Uncertain Victory*; and on the British side, Stefan Collini, *L. T. Hobhouse and Political Argument in England, 1880-1914* (Cambridge: Cambridge University Press, 1983); and Peter F. Clarke, *Liberals and Social Democrats* (Cambridge: Cambridge University Press, 1978). Debunking the efforts of these reformers as insufficiently radical has been a transatlantic scholarly preoccupation for decades. Two recent examples are Marc Stears, *Progressives, Pluralists, and the Problems of the State: Ideologies of Reform in the United States and Britain, 1909-1926* (Oxford: Oxford University Press, 2002); and Marc Stears, *Demanding Democracy: American Radicals in Search of a New Politics* (Princeton: Princeton University Press, 2010).

7 On Dewey's correspondence with Hu Shih about *The Public and Its Problems*, see *MW*, 9: 430. On the global impact of Wilson's and Dewey's ideas, see Erez Manela, *The Wilsonian Moment: Self-Determination and the International Origins*

of Anticolonial Nationalism (New York: Oxford University Press, 2007); and
Trygve Throntveit, *Peace Without Victory: Woodrow Wilson and the American
Internationalist Experiment* (Chicago: University of Chicago Press, 2017).

8   Dewey's review of *Public Opinion* appeared in *The New Republic*, 3 May 1922,
286–8; *MW*, 13: 337–44.

9   Dewey, 'Individuality, Equality, and Superiority', *The New Republic*, 13 December
1922, 61–3; *MW*, 13: 295–300.

10 Dewey, *The Public and Its Problems* (New York, 1927), *MW*, 2: 300–3, 328–31,
337–44, 369–70.

11 On the role of Dewey's ideas, advanced by his students and other allies, in shaping
the work of the National Resources Planning Board, which was the source of
the most far-reaching proposals under discussion in the years leading up to
the outbreak of the Second World War and informing Franklin D. Roosevelt's
ambitious plans for a Second Bill of Rights after the war's end, see James T.
Kloppenberg, 'Deliberative Democracy and the Problem of Poverty in America',
in James T. Kloppenberg, *The Virtues of Liberalism*, 100–23; and James T.
Kloppenberg, 'American Democracy and the Welfare State: The Problem of Its
Publics', in *The American Century in Europe*, ed. R. Laurence Moore and Maurizio
Vaudagna (Ithaca, NY: Cornell University Press, 2003), 195–218.

Chapter 18

1   Hu Shih, 'Starting the Conversation with The Road to Serfdom', in *Collected Works
of Hu Shih*, ed. Ou-yang Zhe-sheng (Beijing: Beijing University Press, 1998), vol.
12, 831–6, henceforth *CW*. As no English translation of Hu Shih's Chinese writings
is currently available, this and the following notes refer to the *Collected Works* in
Chinese（胡适：《从〈到奴役之路说起〉》,《胡适文集》第12卷，北京
大学出版社1998年版，第831–836页）. For Hu Shih's English works, see *English
Writings of Hu Shih*, ed. Chih-Ping Chou, 3 vols (Berlin, Heidelberg: Spinger, 2013).

2   Hu Shih, 'Our Political Proposals', *CW*, 3 (1998): 328–31.

3   Hu Shih, 'When Can We Have a Constitution', *CW*, 5 (1998): 534–9.

4   Hu Shih, 'Letters during the Trip to Europe', *CW*, 4 (1998): 41–50.

5   Confucius, *The Book of Rites* (Li Ji), chapter Li Yun (CreateSpace Independent
Publishing Platform; bilingual edition, 2013), 101.

Chapter 19

1   Hannah Arendt, *On Revolution* (New York: Penguin Books, 2006), 166–7.
Unspecified page references are to this work.

2   Hannah Arendt, 'On Violence', in *Crises of The Republic* (New York: Harvest/HBJ, 1972), 143.

3   Ibid., 143.

4   Robert Palmer, *The Age of Democratic Revolution* (Princeton: Princeton University Press, 1959), 223. See *On Revolution*, 299.

5   *On Revolution*, 136, fn. 9, 289–90.

6   Palmer, *The Age of Democratic Revolution*, 190.

7   *On Revolution*, 157 (Tocqueville, *Democracy in America,* vol. I, part 1, ch. 4 paragraph 11).

8   Hannah Arendt, *The Human Condition* (Chicago: The University of Chicago Press, 1958), 200.

9   Ibid., 50.

10 Hannah Arendt, 'What is Freedom?' in *Between Past and Future* (New York: Penguin Group, 2006), 145.

11 Ibid., 149.

12 Ibid., 149.

13 Ibid., 151.

Chapter 20

1   F. A. Hayek, *The Constitution of Liberty* (London: Routledge, [1960] 2006), 33–5.

2   'Was Socialism a Mistake?' in *The Fatal Conceit. The Errors of Socialism* (Chicago: University of Chicago Press, 1988), 7.

3   See F. A. Hayek, 'Freedom, Reason, and Tradition' (Chapter 4) and 'Why I Am Not a Conservative', in *The Constitution of Liberty.*

4   Hayek, *The Constitution of Liberty*, 19. Here and in what follows, I use the term 'ideology' in its most general, unbiased sense, to denote a set of ideas and beliefs which form the basis of a specific discourse or theory on the proper order of society and how it can be achieved. See Robert S. Erikson and Kent L. Tedin, *American Public Opinion: Its Origins, Content, and Impact*, 8th edn (New York: Pearson, 2003), 64.

5   Hayek, *The Constitution of Liberty*, 19.

6   Hayek understands the notion of law in the (Kantian) *Rechtsstaat* tradition. See F. A. Hayek, *The Road to Serfdom* (London: Routledge & Kegan Paul, [1944] 1962), Chapter 6.

7   See Hayek, *The Road to Serfdom*, 120.

8   F. A. Hayek, *Law, Legislation and Liberty*, vol. 1 (Chicago: University of Chicago Press, 1983), 37. Hayek here explicitly recaptures Adam Smith's famous intuition of an 'invisible hand' by which man is led 'to promote an end which was no part of his intentions'. See A. Smith, *An Inquiry into the Nature and Causes of the Wealth of Nations*, ed. E. Cannan (Chicago: University of Chicago Press, 1977), 1: 421.

9   F. A. Hayek, 'The Use of Knowledge in Society', *American Economic Review* XXXV, no. 4 (September 1945): 519.

10 Ibid.

11 Hayek, *The Pretence of Knowledge*, Nobel Prize Lecture, 11 December 1974.

12 Even if they are circumscribed by good rules, markets are not perfect in Hayek's view. There will inevitably be waste and failure in the system, as the latter evolves through a mechanism of trial and error. Many will gain but some will lose, even catastrophically.

13 http://www.santafe.edu/about/mission-and-vision/

14 F. A. Hayek, *The Intellectuals and Socialism* (Menlo Park, CA: Institute for Humane Studies, 1971).

15 See Bruce Caldwell, 'Some Reflections on F. A. Hayek's *The Sensory Order*', *Journal of Bioeconomics* 6 (2004): 1–16.

16 F. Hayek, 'The Theory of Complex Phenomena', in *Studies in Philosophy, Politics and Economics* (Chicago: University of Chicago Press, [1964] 1967), 22–42.

17 Though I can only mention it in passing, it is worth adding that Hayek is recognized today as an early neural network modeller, and that the theory of complex phenomena that informs his account of society also informs his analysis of the human mind (which he describes as decentralized in a complex network). See F. Hayek, *The Sensory Order: An Inquiry into the Foundations of Theoretical Psychology* (Chicago: University of Chicago Press, 1952), and 'Rules, Perception, and Intelligibility', in *Studies in Philosophy, Politics, and Economics* (Chicago: University of Chicago Press, [1962] 1967), 43–65.

Chapter 21

1   In this chapter, Japanese personal names are given in Japanese order: family name first.

2   Masao Maruyama, 'Theory and Psychology of Ultra-Nationalism', in *Thought and Behavior in Modern Japanese Politics*, ed. Ivan Morris (Oxford: Oxford University Press, 1963, expanded edition, 1969), 3–6.

3   Maruyama, *Studies in the Intellectual History of Tokugawa Japan*, trans. Mikiso Hane (Princeton: Princeton University Press/University of Tokyo Press, 1974).

4   Maruyama, 'Les intellectuels dans le Japon moderne', trans. Jacques Joly, in Yves-Marie Allioux, ed., *Cent ans de pensée au Japon*, t.2 (Paris: Éditions Philippe Piquier, 1996). The essay was originally commissioned by Sartre for a special issue of *Les Temps Modernes* (February 1969), but not completed in time because of the turmoil of university life caused by the student revolt.

5   Maruyama, 'Fascism – Some Problems: A Consideration of its Political Dynamics', in *Thought and Behavior in Modern Japanese Politics*, 157–9.

Chapter 22

1   Isaiah Berlin, 'Two Concepts of Liberty', in *Liberty*, ed. Henry Hardy (Oxford: Oxford University Press, 2002), 169, 178, 179, 181, 213–14, 216. The in-text references in this chapter are to this edition.

2   G. A. Cohen, 'Freedom and Money', in *Contemporary Debates in Social Philosophy*, ed. Laurence Thomas (Malden, MA, and Oxford: Blackwell, 2008), 19.

3   See, for example, the contrasting essays by James Tully and George Crowder in Bruce Baum and Robert Nichols, eds, *Isaiah Berlin and the Politics of Freedom: 'Two Concepts of Liberty' 50 Years Later* (New York and London: Routledge, 2013).

4   'Epilogue: The Three Strands in My Life', in *Personal Impressions*, 3rd edition, ed. Henry Hardy (Princeton and Oxford: Princeton University Press, 2014).

5   See Shlomo Avineri, 'A Jew and a Gentleman', in *The One and the Many: Reading Isaiah Berlin*, ed. George Crowder and Henry Hardy (Amherst, NY: Prometheus Press, 2007); and Arie Dubnov, *Isaiah Berlin: The Journey of a Jewish Liberal* (Basingstoke: Palgrave-Macmillan, 2012).

6   Berlin's most substantial discussions of Rousseau can be found in *Freedom and its Betrayal* and *Political Ideas in the Romantic Age*, 2nd edition, ed. Henry Hardy (Princeton and Oxford: Princeton University Press, 2014).

7   Berlin later expressed regret at having seemed to be rejecting positive liberty: see Steven Lukes, 'Isaiah Berlin: In Conversation', *Salmagundi* (Fall 1998): 93; and Isaiah Berlin and Beata Polonowska-Sygulska, *Unfinished Dialogue* (Amherst, NY: Prometheus Press), 120.

8   For other significant treatments of value pluralism by Berlin, see 'The Pursuit of the Ideal', in *The Crooked Timber of Humanity*, 2nd edition, ed. Henry Hardy (Princeton and Oxford: Princeton University Press, 2013); and 'My Intellectual Path', in *The Power of Ideas*, second edition, ed. Henry Hardy (Princeton and Oxford: Princeton University Press, 2013).

9   See, for example, *Liberty*, 42, 27; 'The Pursuit of the Ideal', 17–20.

10   Quentin Skinner, 'A Third Concept of Liberty' (The Isaiah Berlin Lecture), *Proceedings of the British Academy* 117 (2002): 237–68; Philip Pettit, *Republicanism* (Oxford: Oxford University Press, 1997).

11   John Kekes, *Against Liberalism* (Ithaca and London: Cornell University Press, 1997), Chapter 8; John Gray, *Isaiah Berlin*, with a new Introduction by the author (Princeton: Princeton University Press, 2013).

12   George Crowder, *Liberalism and Value Pluralism* (London: Continuum, 2002); William Galston, *Liberal Pluralism: The Implications of Value Pluralism for Political Theory and Practice* (Cambridge: Cambridge University Press, 2002).

Chapter 23

1   Czesław Miłosz, *The Captive Mind*, trans. Jane Zielonko (New York: Vintage International Edition, 1990 [1951]), 220.

2   Czesław Miłosz, *Visions from San Francisco Bay*, trans. Richard Lourie (New York: Farrar, Straus and Giroux, Inc., 1982 [1969]), 181.

3   Ibid., 218.

4   'What I learned from Jeanne Hersch, 2000', in Czesław Miłosz, *Selected and Last Poems* (New York: Harper Collins Publishers, 2011), 248–9.

5   *The Captive Mind*, 250.

6   Trans. Richard Lourie: https://www.poetryfoundation.org/poems-and-poets/ poems/detail/49482.

7   *Visions from San Francisco Bay*, 118–19.

8   Ibid., 154–5.

9   See, for example, his 2002 poem, 'A Theological Treatise': https://muse.jhu.edu/ article/30866.

10 *Visions from San Francisco Bay*, 224.

11 Ibid., 224.

12 Ibid., 221.

13 Ibid., 33.

14 Trans. Czesław Miłosz and Leonard Nathan, ibid., 345.

15 *The Captive Mind*, 248–9.

16 Czesław Miłosz, *Native Realm. A Search for Self-definition*, trans. C. S. Leach (Berkeley, CA: University of California Press, 1981), 293–4.

Chapter 24

1   John Rawls, *Political Liberalism* (New York: Columbia University Press, 2005), 36–8.

Further Reading

Chapter 1

Carrithers, David W., and Patrick Coleman, 'Montesquieu and the Spirit of Modernity', *Studies in Voltaire and the Eighteenth Century* (2002): 09.

Larrère, Catherine, 'Montesquieu and liberalism. The question of pluralism', in *Montesquieu and his Legacy*, ed. R. Kingston (New York: SUNY Press, 2009), 279–301.

Pangle, Thomas L., *Montesquieu's Philosophy of Liberalism* (Chicago: University of Chicago Press, 1973).

Rahe, Paul A., *Soft Despotism, Democracy's Drift. Montesquieu, Rousseau, Tocqueville and the Modern Prospect* (New Haven and London: Yale University Press, 2009).

Shklar, Judith, 'Montesquieu and the New Republicanism', in *Machiavelli and Republicanism* (Cambridge: Cambridge University Press, 1990), 265–79.

Skinner, Quentin, *Liberty before Liberalism* (Cambridge: Cambridge University Press, 1998).

Chapter 2

Blennerhassett, Lady, *Mme de Staël. Her Friends, and Her Influence in Politics and Literature* (London: Chapman and Hall, 1889), 3 vols.

Craiutu, Aurelian, *A Virtue for Courageous Minds: Moderation in French Political Thought, 1748-1830* (Princeton: Princeton University Press, 2012).

Fairweather, Maria, *Madame de Staël* (London: Constable, 2005).

Fontana, Biancamaria, *Germaine de Staël: A Political Portrait* (Princeton: Princeton University Press, 2016).

Gauchet, Marcel, 'Staël', in *A Critical Dictionary of the French Revolution*, ed. François Furet and Mona Ozouf (Cambridge: Belknap Press, 1989), 1003–9.

Herrold, Christopher, *Mistress to an Age: A Life of Madame de Staël* (London: Hamish Hamilton, 1958).

Chapter 3

Dodge, Guy, *Benjamin Constant's Philosophy of Liberalism* (Chapel Hill: University of North Carolina Press, 1980).

Fontana, Biancamaria, *Benjamin Constant and the Post-Revolutionary Mind* (New Haven: Yale University Press, 1991).

Holmes, Stephen, *Benjamin Constant and the Making of Modern Liberalism* (New Haven: Yale University Press, 1984).

Rosenblatt, Helena, ed., *The Cambridge Companion to Constant* (Cambridge: Cambridge University Press, 2009).

Vincent, K. Steven, *Benjamin Constant and the Birth of French Liberalism* (Houndmills: Palgrave Macmillan, 2011).

Chapter 4

Bentham, Jeremy, *A Fragment on Government* [1776], ed. Ross Harrison (Cambridge: Cambridge University Press, 1988).

Bentham, Jeremy, *Of Sexual Irregularities and Other Writings on Sexual Morality*, ed. Philip Schofield, Catherine Pease-Watkin and Michael Quinn (Oxford: Oxford University Press, 2014).

de Champs, Emmanuelle, *Enlightenment and Utility. Bentham in France/Bentham in French* (Cambridge: Cambridge University Press, 2015).

Engelmann, Stephen, *Imagining Interest in Political Thought* (Durham: Duke University Press, 2003).

Rosen, Frederick, *Classical Utilitarianism from Hume to Mill* (London: Routledge, 2003).

Schofield, Philip, *Utility and Democracy: The Political Thought of Jeremy Bentham* (Oxford: Oxford University Press, 2006).

Welch, Cheryl B., '"Anti-Benthamism": utilitarianism and the French liberal tradition', in *French Liberalism from Montesquieu to the Present Day*, ed. Raf Geenens and Helena Rosenblatt (Cambridge: Cambridge University Press, 2012), 134–51.

Chapter 5

Carey, George, *The Federalist: Design for a Constitution* (Champaign, IL: University of Illinois Press, 1994).

Diamond, Martin, *As far as Republican Principles will Admit* (Washington DC: AEI Press, 2011).

Epstein, David, *The Political Theory of The Federalist* (Chicago: University of Chicago Press, 2007).

Zuckert, Michael, 'The Political Science of James Madison', in *History of American Political Thought*, ed. Bryan Paul Frost and Jeffrey Sikkenga (Lanham, MD: Lexington Books, 2003).

Chapter 6

Atanassow, E. and R. Boyd, eds, *Tocqueville and the Frontiers of Democracy* (Cambridge: Cambridge University Press, 2013).

Jaume, Lucien, *Tocqueville: The Aristocratic Sources of Liberty* (Princeton: Princeton University Press, 2013).

Kahan, Alan S., *Tocqueville, Democracy, and Religion: Checks and Balances for Democratic Souls* (Oxford: Oxford University Press, 2015).

Manent, Pierre, *Tocqueville and the Nature of Democracy* (Lanham: Rowman & Littlefield, 1996).

Mansfield, Harvey C., *Tocqueville: A Very Short Introduction* (Oxford: Oxford University Press, 2010).

Welch, Cheryl, ed., *The Cambridge Companion to Tocqueville* (Cambridge: Cambridge University Press, 2006).

Chapter 7

Charnwood, Lord, *Abraham Lincoln: A Biography*, introduction by Peter W. Schramm (Toronto: Madison Books, 1996, originally published by H. Holt & Co., 1916).

Guelzo, Allen, *Abraham Lincoln: Redeemer President* (Eerdmans, 1999).

Jaffa, Harry V., *Crisis of the House Divided: Issues in the Lincoln-Douglas Debates, 50th Anniversary Edition* (Chicago: The University of Chicago Press, 2009).

Morel, Lucas E., ed., *Lincoln & Liberty: Wisdom for the Ages* (Lexington, KY: University Press of Kentucky, 2014).

Schaub, Diana J., 'Lincoln at Gettysburg', *National Affairs*, Spring 2014.

Chapter 8

Capaldi, Nicholas, *John Stuart Mill* (Cambridge: Cambridge University Press, 2005).

Devigne, Robert, *Reforming Liberalism: J.S. Mill's Use of Ancient, Religious, Liberal, and Romantic Moralities* (New Haven and London: Yale University Press, 2006).

Eisenach, Eldon, ed., *Mill and the Moral Character of Liberalism* (University Park: Penn State University Press, 1998).

Kahan, Alan S., *Aristocratic Liberalism: The Social and Political Thought of Jacob Burckhardt, John Stuart Mill, and Alexis de Tocqueville* (Oxford: Oxford University Press, 1992).

Macleod, C., ed., *Blackwell Companion to J.S. Mill* (Oxford: Blackwell, 2017).

Chapter 9

Acton, Edward, *Alexander Herzen and the Role of the Intellectual Revolutionary* (Cambridge: Cambridge University Press, 1979).

Berlin, Isaiah, *Russian Thinkers*, ed. Henry Hardy and Aileen Kelly, 2nd ed. (London: Penguin, 2008).

Herzen, Alexander Ivanovich, *From the Other Shore*, trans. Moura Budberg, (London: Weidenfeld & Nicolson, 1956).

Herzen, Alexander Ivanovich, *Selected Philosophical Works*, trans. Lev Navrozov, (Moscow: Foreign Languages Publishing House, 1956).

Herzen, Alexander Ivanovich, *Letters from France and Italy, 1847–1851*, ed. and trans. Judith E. Zimmerman (Pittsburgh: University of Pittsburgh Press, 1995).

Herzen, Alexander Ivanovich, *A Herzen Reader*, ed. and trans. Kathleen Parthé, with a critical essay by Robert Harris (Chicago: Northwestern University Press, 2012).

Herzen, Alexander Ivanovich, *My Past and Thoughts: The Memoirs of Alexander Herzen*, trans. Constance Garnett, 6 vols. (London: Chatto & Windus, 1924–27). Revised edition by Humphrey Higgens, with introduction by Isaiah Berlin, 4 vols. (London: Chatto & Windus, 1968). Newly translated and annotated by Robert Harris and Kathleen Parthé (Cambridge: Harvard University Press, forthcoming).

Kelly, Aileen M., *The Discovery of Chance: The Life and Thought of Alexander Herzen* (Cambridge, MA: Harvard University Press, 2016).

Malia, Martin Edward, *Alexander Herzen and the Birth of Russian Socialism: 1812–1855* (Cambridge, MA: Harvard University Press, 1961).

Zimmerman, Judith E., *Midpassage: Alexander Herzen and European Revolution: 1847–1852* (Pittsburgh: University of Pittsburgh Press, 1989).

Chapter 10

Dimova-Cookson, Maria, *T. H. Green's Moral and Political Philosophy: A Phenomenological Perspective* (Houndsmill: Palgrave, 2001).

Morrow, John, ed., *T. H. Green* (Aldershot: Ashgate, 2007).

Thomas, Geoffrey, *The Moral Philosophy of T. H. Green* (Oxford: Clarendon Press, 1987).

Chapter 11

Criscenti, Joseph T., ed., *Sarmiento and His Argentina* (Boulder, CO: Rienner Publishers, 1993).

Halperín-Donghi, Tulio, Iván Jaksić, Gwen Kirpatrick and Francine Masiello, eds, *Sarmiento: Author of a Nation* (Berkeley, Los Angeles, and London: University of California Press, 1994).

Sorensen-Goodrich, Diana, *Facundo and the Construction of Argentine Culture* (Austin: the University of Texas Press, 1996).

Chapter 12

Çiçek, Nazan, *The Young Ottomans: Turkish Critiques of the Eastern Question in the Late Nineteenth Century* (London, New York: I.B. Tauris, 2010).

Davison, Roderic H., *Reform in the Ottoman Empire, 1856-1876* (Princeton: Princeton University Press, 1963).

Findley, Carl, *Bureaucratic Reform in the Ottoman Empire* (Princeton: Princeton University Press, 1980).

Hanioğlu, M. Şükrü, *A Brief History of the Late Ottoman Empire* (Princeton: Princeton University Press, 2008).

Mardin, Şerif, *The Genesis of Young Ottoman Thought* (Syracuse: Syracuse University Press, 1962).

Chapter 13

Hourani, Albert, *Arabic Thought in the Liberal Age, 1798-1939* (Cambridge Cambridgeshire; New York: Cambridge University Press, 1983).

Islahi, Abdul Azim, 'Economic Ideas of a Nineteenth Century Tunisian Statesman: Khayr al-Din al-Tunisi', *Islamic Economics Institute*, King Abdulaziz University (2002). Online at https://mpra.ub.uni-muenchen.de/43519/MPRA Paper No 43519.

Kuran, Timur, *Islam and Mammon: The Economic Predicaments of Islamism* (Princeton: Princeton University Press, 2005).

Kuran, Timur, *The Long Divergence: How Islamic Law Held Back the Middle East* (Princeton: Princeton University Press, 2010).

Lewis, Bernard, *What Went Wrong? The Clash Between Islam and Modernity in the Middle East* (New York: Harper Perennial, 2003).

Chapter 14

Gilbert, Felix, *History: Politics or Culture? Reflections on Ranke and Burckhardt* (Princeton, NJ: Princeton University Press, 1990).

Gossman, Lionel, *Basel in the Age of Burckhardt* (Chicago: University of Chicago Press, 2000).

Howard, Thomas A., *Religion and the Rise of Historicism: W. M. L. de Wette, Jacob Burckhardt, and the Theological Origins of Nineteenth-Century Historical Consciousness* (Cambridge: Cambridge University Press, 2000).

Kahan, Alan S., *Aristocratic Liberalism: The Social and Political Thought of Jacob Burckhardt, John Stuart Mill, and Alexis de Tocqueville* (Piscataway, NJ: Transaction, 2001).

Sigurdson, Richard, *Jacob Burckhardt's Social and Political Thought* (Toronto: University of Toronto Press, 2004).

Chapter 15

Beetham, David, *Max Weber and the Theory of Modern Politics* (Cambridge: Polity Press, 1985).

Beetham, David, 'Max Weber and the Liberal Political Tradition', *Archives européennes de sociologie* 30, no. 2 (1989), 311–23.

Ghosh, Peter, *Max Weber and* The Protestant Ethic*: Twin Histories* (Oxford: Oxford University Press, 2014).

Hennis, Wilhelm, *Max Weber: Essays in Reconstruction*, trans. Keith Tribe (London: Allen & Unwin, 1988).

Kim, Sung Ho, *Max Weber's Politics of Civil Society* (Cambridge: Cambridge University Press, 2004).

Mommsen, Wolfgang J., *The Age of Bureaucracy: Perspectives on the Political Sociology of Max Weber* (Oxford: Blackwell, 1974).

Mommsen, Wolfgang J., *Max Weber and German Politics, 1890-1920*, trans. Michael S. Steinberg (Chicago: University of Chicago Press, 1984).

Chapter 16

Clarke, Peter, *The Keynesian Revolution in the Making 1920–1936* (Oxford University Press, 1988).

Galbraith, James K., *The Predator State. How Conservatives Abandoned the Free Market and Why Liberals Should Too* (Free Press, 2008).

Minsky, Hyman P., *John Maynard Keynes* (New York: Columbia University Press, 1975).

Volcker, Paul and Toyoo Gyothen, *Changing Fortunes* (New York: Random House, 1992).

Walton, Clarence S., *Corporate Social Responsibilities* (Belmont, CA: Wadsworth Publishing Company 1967).

Chapter 17

Campbell, James, *Understanding John Dewey* (New York: Open Court, 1991).

Rockefeller, Steven C., *John Dewey: Religious Faith and Democratic Humanism* (New York: Columbia University Press, 1991).

Ryan, Alan, *John Dewey and the High Tide of American Liberalism* (New York: Norton, 1995).

Westbrook, Robert B., *John Dewey and American Democracy* (Ithaca, NY: Cornell University Press, 1991).

Chapter 18

Chou, Min-Chih, *Hu Shih and Intellectual Choice in Modern China* (Ann Arbor: University of Michigan Press, 1984).

Chou, Chih-Ping, ed., *English Writings of Hu Shih* 3 vols (Berlin, Heidelberg: Spinger 2013).

Grieder, J. B., *Hu Shih and the Chinese Renaissance: Liberalism in the Chinese Revolution, 1917-1937* (Cambridge, MA: Harvard University Press, 1970).

Tse-tsung, Chou, *The May Fourth Movement: Intellectual Revolution in Modern China* (Cambridge, MA: Harvard University Press, 1960).

Chapter 19

Arendt, Hannah, *The Human Condition* (Chicago: The University of Chicago Press, 1958).

Berkowitz, Roger, 'Revolutionary Constitutionalism: Some Thoughts on Laurie Ackermann's Dignity Jurisprudence', *Acta Juridica* (2008): 204–18.

Lederman, Shmuel, 'Councils and Revolution: Participatory Democracy in Anarchist Thought and the New Social Movements', *Science & Society* 79, no. 2 (April 2015): 243–63.

Markell, Patchen, The Moment Has Passed: Power After Arendt', in *Radical Future Pasts: Untimely Political Theory*, ed. Rom Coles, Mark Reinhardt and George Shulman (Lexington: University Press of Kentucky, 2014).

Palmer, Robert, *The Age of the Democratic Revolution* (Princeton: Princeton University Press, 1959).

Penta, Joe, 'Hannah Arendt: On Power', *The Journal of Speculative Philosophy*, New Series, 10, no. 3 (1996): 210–29.

Chapter 20

Butler, Eamonn, *Friedrich Hayek: The ideas and influence of the libertarian economist* (Hampshire, Great Britain: Harriman House, 2012).

Caldwell, Bruce, *Hayek's Challenge: An Intellectual Biography of F. A. Hayek* (Chicago: University of Chicago Press, 2003).

Feser, Edward, ed., *The Cambridge Companion to Hayek* (Cambridge: Cambridge University Press, 2006).

Kukathas, Chandran, *Hayek and Modern Liberalism* (Oxford: Oxford University Press, 1989).

Chapter 21

Barshay, Andrew E., 'Imagining Democracy in Postwar Japan, Maruyama Masao as a Political Thinker', in *The Social Sciences in Modern Japan: The Marxian and Modernist Traditions* (Berkley and Los Angeles: University of California Press, 2004).

Kerstein, Rikki, *Democracy in Postwar Japan: Maruyama Masao and the Search for Autonomy* (London: Routledge, 1996)

Sasaki, Fumiko, *Nationalism, Political Realism and Democracy in Japan: The Thought of Masao Maruyama* (London: Routledge, 2014)

Tadashi, Karube, *Maruyama Masao and the Fate of Liberalism in Twentieth-Century Japan*, trans. David Nobel (Tokyo: I-House Press, 2008).

Chapter 22

Cherniss, Joshua, *A Mind in its Time: The Development of Isaiah Berlin's Political Thought* (Oxford: Oxford University Press, 2013).

Crowder, George, *Isaiah Berlin: Liberty and Pluralism* (Cambridge: Polity, 2004).

Crowder, George, and Henry Hardy, eds, *The One and the Many: Reading Isaiah Berlin* (Amherst, NY: Prometheus Press, 2007).

Ignatieff, Michael, *Isaiah Berlin: A Life* (London: Chatto & Windus, 1998).

The Isaiah Berlin Literary Trust, *The Isaiah Berlin Virtual Library*. http://berlin.wolf.ac.uk (accessed 24 January 2016).

Chapter 23

Fiut, Aleksander, *The Eternal Moment. The Poetry of Czesław Miłosz* (Berkeley: University of California Press, 1990).

Hass, Robert, *What Light Can Do: Essays on Art, Imagination and Natural World* (New York: Harper Collins/Ecco, 2011).

Haven, Cynthia L., *An Invisible Rope: Portraits of Czesław Miłosz* (Athens, OH: Ohio University Press / Swallow Press, 2011).

Lapinski, Zdzislaw, ed., *Miłosz like the World: Poet in the Eyes of Polish Literary Critics* (Oxford: Peter Lang AG / Tra, 2014).

Tischner, Lukasz, *Miłosz and the Problem of Evil* (Evanston, IL: Northwestern University Press, 2015).

Chapter 24

D'Agostino, Fred, *Incommensurability and Commensuration: The Common Denominator* (Aldershot: Ashgate, 2003).

Gaus, Gerald, *The Order of Public Reason: A Theory of Freedom and Morality in a Diverse and Bounded World* (New York: Cambridge University Press, 2011).

Lister, Andrew, *Public Reason and Political Community* (New York: Bloomsbury, 2013).

Quong, Jonathan, *Liberalism Without Perfection* (New York: Oxford University Press, 2010).

Vallier, Kevin, *Liberal Politics and Public Faith: Beyond Separation* (New York: Routledge, 2014).

Index

United States
  American Revolution 45, 46,
    153–9
  Articles of Confederation 43, 44, 156
  Constitution 27, 43, 54, 156
  Declaration of Independence 40

utilitarianism 36, 37, 41, 84, 85,
    189, 193

violence 3, 8, 40, 41, 155
Voltaire 101

Weber, Max 123–30, 143

www.ingramcontent.com/pod-product-compliance
Lightning Source LLC
Chambersburg PA
CBHW062019270326
41929CB00014B/2259